SOLDIERS OF MISFORTUNE

SOLDIERS OF MISFORTUNE

Washington's Secret Betrayal of American POWs in the Soviet Union

Jim Sanders
Mark Sauter
R. Cort Kirkwood

National
Press
Books

Washington, D.C.

Library of Congress Cataloging-in-Publication Data

Sanders, James D., 1945-
Soldiers of misfortune:
Washington's secret betrayal of American
POWs in the Soviet Union
James D. Sanders, Mark A. Sauter, R. Cort Kirkwood
320 pp. 15 x 22.5 cm
Includes index.
ISBN 0-915765-83-7 $23.95
1. United States — Relations — Soviet Union.
2. Soviet Union — Relations — United States.
3. Prisoners of war — Soviet Union.
4. Prisoners of war — United States.
5. World War, 1939-1945 — Prisoners and prisons, Soviet.
6. Korean War, 1950-1953 — Prisoners and prisons, Soviet.
7. Vietnamese Conflict, 1961-1975 — Prisoners and prisons, Soviet.
I. Sauter, Mark A.
II. Kirkwood, R. Cort.
III. Title.
E. 183.8S65S26   1992
92-23155 355.1'13--dc20   CIP

PRINTED IN THE UNITED STATES OF AMERICA

Acknowledgments

The following people helped make this book possible:

Bill Paul, former *Wall Street Journal* reporter and now with the International Institute for Prisoners of War. He asked the question. We tried to answer it.

The record keepers: Richard Boylan, Bill Lewis and John Taylor at the National Archives; Dale and Kate in the Still Picture division; and several conscientious Freedom of Information Act officers in the Pentagon, who took seriously their job of releasing government information—even if it embarrassed their bosses. We decided not to include their names, fearing that disclosure of their diligence could hurt their careers.

Defense Intelligence Agency officials like Howard Hill, Joseph Heller and Joseph Schlatter, who apparently cared more about making their bosses happy than really finding out what happened to their brothers in uniform. Luckily, they also didn't work very hard at their disinformation.

The majority of American military officers, men like Walt and Jarvis, who would never knowingly abandon their men.

The Pentagon's former chief spokesman on POW/MIAs, who told co-author Sauter that: "You're the only reporter in America who thinks this [U.S. POWs in the U.S.S.R.] is a story." We often drew inspiration from his disdain.

The few, but persistent, mainstream reporters like Dave Hendrix, Jim Anderson, Larry Jolidon and Doyle McManus, who knew the abandonment of the POWs was indeed a story.

The staff of Seattle's KIRO-TV, its former news director John Lippman and CBS Los Angeles Bureau Chief Jennifer Siebens, for their moral and financial support of co-author Sauter's pursuit of this story. KIRO producer Megan Clark, along with former interns Richard, Laurie, Bill, Colin, Marty, Dan and several others, showed remarkable patience even when forced to share our obsession with finding the truth.

The staff of Tacoma's *Morning News Tribune*, which took up where KIRO left off.

Tony Snow, former editorial page editor of the *Washington Times*, for his support in pursuing the story.

Rep. John Miller (R-Seattle) and Sen. Bob Smith (R-N.H.), who cared more about the POWs than political expediency.

Congressional staffers such as Kris Kolesnik, Tracy Usry, Dan Perrin, Heike Nuhsbaum and Dino Carluccio, who did the tough work while their congressmen and friends in the media got the credit.

The fine government POW/MIA investigators in Moscow—Graham, Saxe and Cannell, who care more about America's missing than their own careers.

The remarkable private researchers and activists who fought for the POWs simply because, as American citizens, they knew it was wrong for our government to abandon its fighting men. The names of these patriots include Wadley, Sampley, Ashworth, Brown, Van Atta and Keeton.

The Ark Project and its Mesinai, Yuzhin and Kazachkov, now taking our research into the real world.

The Ex-POWs of America, especially Clydie Morgan, for helping us track down the pieces of this puzzle.

The staff of ABC's 20/20 and Moscow Bureau, who are carrying on the fight for the truth in Moscow and Washington.

The relatives who never forgot, especially those like Dolores Alfond, Rita Van Wees, Bill Sowles and Lorna Lillard, who fought not just for their own loved ones but for all the missing.

Vicki Shannon of the *Washington Post,* who copy-edited the book and Paul Aron, who gave his editorial advice.

Mel Berger, our agent at the William Morris Agency, who assisted in placing the book with the publisher.

Joel Joseph, Alan Sultan, Shawn Ortiz and Talia Greenberg of National Press Books who had the courage to publish *Soldiers of Misfortune.*

Our wives and families, who have paid the financial and emotional price of a fight for which they were drafted.

Contents

Part IV-The Cold War

Part V-Southeast Asia

Part VI-The Cover-Up

Foreword

by General William C. Westmoreland

General Westmoreland served in the United States Army during World War II and the Korean War. In August 1964, he was made Commander, U.S. Military Assistance Command, Vietnam. General Westmoreland became Chief of Staff of the Army in 1968 until his retirement in 1972.

On Friday, March 18, 1992, an interesting brief ran across the Associated Press wire. It didn't make the newspaper headlines or become a top story on the evening television news, but it was nonetheless an historic four-line item:

"The United States and Russia, 'in a spirit of friendship,' have formed a joint commission to investigate unresolved cases of prisoners of war missing in action dating back to World War II."

A week later, it was announced that Ambassador Malcolm Toon, once the American emissary to the Soviets, was to lead an American delegation to Moscow to begin discussions with General Dmitri Volkogonov, a senior military adviser to Russian President Boris Yelstin.

What's this? The United States and Russia forming a bilateral commission to investigate the disappearance of American prisoners of war going all the way back to World War II, half a century ago? What prisoners? How many? Haven't all the POWs from World War II come home? That's what most people would have asked.

Now Jim Sanders, Mark Sauter and R. Cort Kirkwood, who have worked on the matter for six years, tell a chilling tale. They say the Soviet Union kidnapped 23,500 Americans from German prisoner of war camps in Eastern Europe in the closing days and hours of World War II; Americans that the Soviets kidnapped off the streets of postwar Europe; that the North Koreans shipped American prisoners to the Soviet Union almost from the first days of the indecisive war we fought in Korea; that American airmen shot down on intelligence flights over the Soviet Union were captured and never returned; and that perhaps as many as 300 Americans wound up in Soviet hands during and after the Vietnam War. If true, what a distressing story.

We do know that a few weeks before the U.S.-Soviet Commission on POWs held its inaugural meeting in Moscow, top Russian officials admitted they had kidnapped at least "small numbers" of men from World War II. Who knows what "small numbers" may mean, but in any event, that admission does not discount what the authors present in *Soldiers of Misfortune*. Once the archives of the former Soviet government are laid bare for the world to see, it's very likely the Russian government will admit the truth about Korea and the years beyond as well.

Disturbing as that may sound, there's another story the authors tell that raises questions about the forthrightness of the decision-makers in our government. There's no point reciting the details here; you can read them for yourself and make your own judgment. But I'd like to make a few points from my perspective as a professional soldier who served his country for his entire adult life.

Because of the nature of bureaucracy, both military and civilian, it may be impossible to find out who, for instance, decided not to press the Soviet government to return our men. Was it one man or several? And how much of the decision to keep a lid on the facts can be attributed to bureaucratic inertia?

Whatever the facts, I must say that the elected leaders and military men with whom I served tried, for the most part, to conduct themselves honorably in the wars in which this country has been involved. They always had the best interest of our fighting men at heart. That was true for World War II, it was true for Korea and it was true for Vietnam. In some cases, I did not agree with decisions made, but we live in a self-governing republic in which the military is subordinate to civilian authority.

The United States has traditionally kept the agreements it has signed. As signatories to the Geneva Convention, the United States has obeyed the rules of war, and our military and civilian leaders expect battlefield commanders and fighting men to carry out their orders within the rules all civilized nations observe. That's why Lieutenant William Calley and others were tried and punished for the My Lai Massacre.

Apparently, that wasn't true about the Soviet Union, whose leaders allegedly committed some monstrous crimes. *Soldiers of Misfortune* alleges that Soviets kidnapped American fighting men during Korea, a war that they weren't officially supposed to be fighting, and during and after Vietnam, another war in which they were not involved on the battlefield. Did U.S. government officials know the truth about POWs, and did they withhold that truth from the American people? One can only wonder what the United States could have done about it anyway, the Soviets having denied it.

Whatever mistakes American officials may have made, we can correct them. Unlike so many other people on Earth, Americans are lucky enough to live in a country where citizens can speak their minds, exercise their franchise to vote and have a say in the way our government conducts domestic and international affairs. That *Soldiers of Misfortune* has been published, which wouldn't have been allowed in many other countries, is a tribute to the vitality of American freedom and the republican institutions that serve the people and protect our God-given rights and democratic heritage.

Soldiers of Misfortune is impressively documented. I can't say that I agree with all of the conclusions the authors have drawn, if only because my 40 years in the Army give me a different perspective on how and why officials make the decisions they make. The word "betrayal," for instance, which the authors use in the subtitle, stings the heart and soul, especially for someone like me who took an oath to uphold and defend the Constitution and this nation from their enemies. It's hard for a professional soldier to believe that a comrade-in-arms, either civilian or military, would knowingly be a party to a "betrayal."

One can say this, however: The Russians have admitted they took prisoners, and the United States government, after many years of alleged stonewalling, is finally pressing the Russians for answers about missing Americans from wars in which the Soviet Union was involved on the side of our adversaries.

It is impossible to predict what findings will emerge from the U.S.-Russian POW Commission's deliberations, but it seems fairly obvious that in the six years it took to research this book, the authors may have encouraged our government along the right path, and for that, the families of American POWs and MIAs and the general public owe them their thanks.

April, 1992
Charleston, South Carolina

Preface

"A Cynical Attitude"

"The Department of Defense found these charges [that the U.S. abandoned POWs in the Soviet Union] very surprising. The U.S. Government, including the military, is composed of people whose values and morals derive from the same heritage as their fellow citizens and are sworn to protect and defend the Constitution of the United States. These are not people who abandon their fellow citizens or consider them expendable."

—Public Pentagon statement on U.S. POWs in the Soviet Union, 1992[1]

"The [POW] problem becomes almost a philosophical one. If we are 'at war,' cold, hot or otherwise, casualties and losses must be expected and perhaps we must learn to live with this kind of thing. If we are in for fifty years of peripheral 'fire fights' we may be forced to adopt a rather cynical attitude on this for political reasons."

—Classified Pentagon policy on U.S. POWs, 1955 to present[2]

The hardest telephone call we had to make in researching this book went to a Tulsa therapist named Suzie Ewing. We had discovered documents in the National Archives showing that Ewing's father, World War II MIA Major Wirt Elizabeth Thompson, had been held in Soviet prisons years after the war. On July 16, 1955, the U.S. government asked the Soviet Union for the "prompt release" of Thompson. As far as we could tell, the Soviets never did let him go, but we hoped to learn the final resolution of the Wirt Thompson case from his daughter.

Suzie Ewing was shocked by co-author R. Cort Kirkwood's call. The USG told the Thompson family that Wirt Thompson died in 1944 in the jungles of Burma. Not only didn't the family know what happened to Thompson after the U.S. government asked the Soviets for his release in 1955, Ewing said, but also the Pentagon never even told them that he had been seen alive in Russia. The American government never let the family in on the truth, that Major Wirt Thompson was among the secret army of soldiers of misfortune—U.S. POWs in the Soviet Union.

Starting in 1945, the Soviet Union became the second-largest employer of American servicemen in the world. Over the past five decades, thousands of Americans, all captured and held by the Soviets, have been sent to work building the Soviet economy and servicing the needs of Russian intelligence. *Soldiers of Misfortune* is the story of how those Americans, along with about 31,000 British and Commonwealth soldiers, were seized by the Soviet Union. It is also the bitter tale of how and why their existence was kept secret.

The story begins with what was in reality a secret hostage crisis at the end of World War II. The Red Army "liberated" scores of German POW camps holding thousands of U.S., British and Commonwealth prioners (Commonwealth including Canada, Australia and New Zealand). The Soviets freed more than 20,000 Americans, but may have kept even more hostage.

Soviet dictator Joseph Stalin hoped to use the POWs to force the U.S. and British governments to comply with a secret agreement negotiated at the February 1945 Yalta conference. A classified covenant of the accord required the Allies to return all "Soviet citizens" to the U.S.S.R, even the huge number of former Soviets who did not want to go home.

But the United States and Britain cheated on the hostage exchange, retaining many anti-communist Ukrainians and Byelorussians to help fight the rapidly developing Cold War. Stalin learned of the deceit, and, in return, kept up to 23,500 Americans and 31,000 British and Commonwealth soldiers.

The POWs were shipped east and spread across the Soviet Union's twelve time zones, from Moscow to Siberia, in the vast slave labor system known as the Gulag Archipelago. The World War II Americans were later joined by other U.S. servicemen who had been kidnapped off the streets of Europe, shot down during Cold War reconnaissance flights, transported to Siberia from the battlefields of Korea, and flown from steamy POW camps in Vietnam and Laos to the frigid prisons of Russia.

"Why would the Soviets take American and British prisoners, and why would U.S. government officials keep their knowledge of it a secret?" That's the question we have faced again and again. For the Soviets, the answer is easy. Exploitation of POWs was a long-standing Soviet policy, from the earliest days of the communist revolution, and the Americans were just a tiny part of it: After World War II, the Soviet Union kept an estimated 1.5 million prisoners of war–mostly Germans and Japanese, as well as American, British and French. The prisoners provided labor and technical assistance to the Soviet economy. German POWs, for instance, did everything from help design Soviet airplanes to mine coal. POWs were also used for intelligence purposes and as bargaining chips for foreign aid and diplomatic concessions.

Only now, decades later, is it possible to explain why the U.S. abandoned the prisoners. A full revelation of the POW-hostage crisis in 1945 would have illuminated the dark crevices of the U.S.-Soviet relationship, including the scandalous complicity of the Roosevelt administration with Joseph Stalin, who had been sold to the American public as good old "Uncle Joe," a great and virtuous leader.

Later, during the Korean War, the White House feared that public disclosure of the Soviet Union's massive effort in the war–including the capture of American POWs– could have escalated the war into a deadly superpower confrontation. Similar factors appear to have pertained during the Vietnam War.

Revealing the truth would have invited the disgrace of the incumbent political power structure. And, especially during the 1950s and '60s, it could have increased the risk of war between the superpowers.

So it was politically impossible to get the men back* and because the government would not admit to a problem that could not be resolved, it covered up the hostage crisis and lost Americans in the gulag.

By the time the Soviets were willing to reveal the truth, the American prisoners had been forgotten—by their own government. Even as detente led to major U.S. assistance for the U.S.S.R., there was no significant attempt to use the new superpower relationship to recover the secret prisoners. And when the lost prisoners did become an issue in recent years, the Bush administration treated it not as the "highest national priority"–the phrase used by Bush officials and many other administrations since World War II–but rather as a nuisance to be covered up.

---

* Reports of female POWs held in the Soviet Union are extremely rare and unsubstantiated. Thus, this book, more because of the facts than for convenience, refers to the POWs collectively as men.

As this book goes to press in July 1992, the Russian government has just admitted hiding the truth about American prisoners in the Soviet Union. In a series of dramatic revelations leading up to his June summit with President Bush, Russian President Boris Yeltsin revealed that the Soviet Union had lied about the POW issue, secretly imprisoning U.S. servicemen from World War II to Vietnam.

Within days of Yeltsin's announcements, the White House claimed that it had never known about U.S. POWs in the Soviet Union. This book proves that the Bush administration, along with every administration since 1945, has been deceiving the American people.

It took us years of research to uncover this story. We searched hundreds of thousands of documents and contacted scores of people across the U.S., Russia, Taiwan, Canada, Britain, Australia and New Zealand. We learned that the American government had consciously adopted a "cynical attitude" toward its lost soldiers, hiding their true fate behind highly classified reports and dishonest press releases. In turn, the bureaucracy cynically manipulated the Congress, the media and the American people.

This story will anger many prominent historians, journalists, politicians and military officers: men and women who could and should have exposed the truth long ago. Their dereliction has condemned the POWs and buried the truth about postwar American history. But even as many in those professions suppressed the facts, others fought to reveal the truth. Collectively, their sacrifices allowed us to tell this story.

In the end, it is the sacrifices of the lost POWs that help make this a country where the truth–however delayed– can still be told. Stripped of their constitutional guarantees, abandoned by their leaders, enslaved by Stalinism, but no longer forgotten, the POWs stand as the true heroes of this work.

–The Authors, July 1992

Part I

World War II

Chapter 1

The Changing of the Guards

"Not much changed except the changing of the guards."
–POW Robert J. Miller, "liberated" by
the Soviets from Stalag 3A in April 1945

In the twilight before dawn on April 22, 1945, American POW John L. Connolly rose from the cold of his tent at Stalag 3A and wandered outside to use the latrine.

On his way to the reeking hole, the staff sergeant noticed something unusual–the German guards had abandoned their posts. Connolly was pleased but not totally surprised. After all, everyone in the POW camp, Americans, British and their German captors, had heard the relentless artillery and tank fire of the approaching Red Army.

The war in Europe was grinding to its close as Russian troops moved in from the east and American and British troops from the west. Stalag 3A, near the town of Luckenwalde 50 miles south of Berlin, would soon come under Soviet control. The starving POWs would be liberated, they believed, and then sent home.

But this would be no liberation. Rather, it was the beginning of the largest and most secret hostage crisis in American history. The prisoners at Stalag 3A and other POW camps around the world were to become political bargaining chips in a geopolitical poker game–a game in which the United States would ultimately fold its hand.

On that chilly spring morning in 1945, the Allied POWs saw only the dawn of a day of freedom. When he realized the Germans had fled, 22-year-old Connolly dashed back to the tent to rouse his buddies, Carmen Gomez and Joseph Friedl. All three were from Sioux City, Iowa.

The Germans were gone, "the Russians were coming. Now was the time to head for home. I suggested we get out and head for our lines," Connolly recalled.[1]

Connolly and Gomez went through the fence and headed west toward the American forces. Friedl decided to wait for the Russians, a decision he would live to regret.

The two Iowa boys moved cautiously through the still dangerous German countryside, Connolly slowed by his frozen feet and both men easily tired after losing fifty pounds each on Nazi prison rations of maggot-infested potatoes and rutabagas.

Scrounging for food in abandoned homes, the two Americans avoided bands of surrendering German soldiers and sidestepped a battle between Russian troops and Hitler youths. Finally, after about five days of travel, they reached Magdeburg, a town on the Elbe River, which then separated the U.S. and Soviet forces.

But when the men tried to cross a bridge to the tantalizingly close American line, Red Army troops stopped them at gun point. "The Russians herded us into a bombed-out building. . . . When there were several hundred of us [Americans], they began to march back into Germany."

Wisely refusing to march away from their own lines, Connolly and about a dozen others ducked out of the column as it passed through town. Hours later, they ran across a team of American scout cars under the command of a brigadier general. "The Soviets are taking a column of American POWs back east," Connolly told the general. Flying into a rage, the American officer sped off to catch the column. But the POWs had vanished.

Meantime, the Russians had captured more escapees from Stalag 3A, including American Orpha Ziegler. The Soviets divided these men into three groups and began marching them to a collection point near the Elbe.

Along the way, a British intelligence officer slipped into the ranks and spread the word of an escape plan to be initiated when the column reached three parallel alleys just ahead.

When each of the groups was opposite an alley, everyone ran down the alleys that led to the Elbe River. "The guards fired shots into the air but no one was . . . hit," recalled Ziegler. At the end of each alley, a barge took the men to safety on the American side of the river.

Other stragglers captured by the Russians were not so lucky. Technical Sergeant D.C. Wimberly found himself in the town of Luckenwalde, near Stalag 3A, on the day after the April 22 liberation. The 90-pound Wimberly, wearing a handmade American flag on his uniform, looked up the street to see female military police of the Red Army approaching.

With short-cropped hair worn under khaki caps, long dark cloaks and cavalry sabers, the women made quite a sight as they rode through the town on huge muscled steeds.

The Russians appeared to be herding a column of German POWs back to the Soviet Union. But as the tail end of the column went by, Wimberly recalls, a few of the men saw the flag on his uniform and began calling out.

"Hey! You American? We're American. I'm from Philadelphia . . . Boston . . . Chicago. Help me!" But Wimberly could do nothing but watch.

While the Americans Wimberly saw were trudging east, back at Stalag 3A Soviet troops were replacing the very fences torn down during the Red Army liberation just days before. Lieutenant Colonel Michael J. Calpin and seven friends had dug under the wire fence to escape to the Elbe, but they were stopped by Russian military police, who marched the Americans back to camp. As Luckenwalde alumnus Major Lynn Hunsaker observed, "The Russians kept us prisoners, same as the Germans."

Until early May, the Soviets did allow some U.S. forces in, even while refusing to let the American and British POWs out. American trucks brought in food and medicine, and on May 4 they even took out 1,369 U.S. and British POWs. But that changed the next day.

On May 5, 50 U.S. trucks and 50 ambulances arrived at Luckenwalde to evacuate more POWs. But, as American POW Edward L. Williams recalled, the Soviets had other ideas.

"I was beside the [American] colonel in charge of the truck convoy when he argued with the Russian officer," who refused to allow the trucks to be loaded. The U.S. colonel spoke Russian and translated over his shoulder that the "Russian was not about to release us because we had not been screened for our political beliefs and he could not turn such prisoners loose on the world."

The American officer insisted, urging his Soviet counterpart to release the sick and injured because the Red Army did not have facilities to care for them. The Russian finally gave in on that point. "We loaded up sick Americans and some British into the ambulances like cord wood as high as five and six deep," Williams remembered. "I mean that a man was grabbed by his shoulders and the seat of his pants and loaded horizontally into the ambulance on top of those already in."

POW Richard Egan took his chances with the sick and wounded, fearful he might never get home if American forces failed to return. "After we loaded the more seriously wounded, the truck driver of the last truck said he had more room if anybody wanted to take a chance on trying to get out. . . . As we left, they [the Russians] tried to get us off the truck, and so we left under fire."

Amid the confusion, a lieutenant in the convoy told Hunsaker and the remaining POWs that the crowded ambulances and the trucks that were still empty would stop three miles up the road and wait until one hour after dark, giving them another chance to escape. That invitation lured thousands of American, British and Commonwealth POWs out of the prison, but as declassified U.S. government documents reveal, the Soviets moved in to stop the escape. "[H]earing the unofficial evacuation going on . . . [the Soviets] sent armed guards, forbade the evacuation, threatened to open fire and stopped it. All the ex-POWs were taken back to the camp."[2]

The next day at 2 p.m., another American convoy approached the camp, stopping about two miles away. A jeep driver went into the POW compound and gave wire cutters to a barracks chief, along with directions to 60 waiting U.S. trucks.

The Russians spotted the convoy just before it finished loading. Placing armed guards at the head and tail of the convoy, the Soviet commander ordered the Americans to stay put. But the U.S. colonel in charge faced down the Russian, beginning to draw his Colt .45 and ordering the trucks to move out.

Soviet guards dove into the roadside ditches as the convoy roared to life. The Soviet officer ordered his men to open fire, but the riflemen, perhaps less willing than their officers to kill Allied troops, raised their rifles and fired over the trucks.

"The last I saw," Williams recalled, "the Russian officer was raising hell with the riflemen." Thirteen trucks filled with POWs escaped. "We sped off at top speed," said John Culler. His group of ten trucks made it to the Elbe River town of Magdeburg, "where at a barrier, an American reporter obtained a pass [from the Russians] for them to cross the Elbe."[3] At another point along the river, three more trucks driven by black GIs smashed through Russian barriers to freedom.[4]

The rest of the U.S. trucks drove off empty as the Russians marched the prisoners back to camp at gun point.[5] Soviet officials "put guards around the camp at 50-yard intervals armed with tommy guns, and a cordon around the area two miles from the camp."[6] They announced that the escapes would cease and anyone leaving the camp would be "liable for up to six months' civil internment."[7]

Tightening the Noose

By May 8, security at the Luckenwalde camp was as strict as it had been under the Germans, but Allied prisoners continued trying to escape. "Things got so sticky they [the Soviets] started to shoot and a couple of our guys got clocked," wrote Australian prisoner Norman Dodgson.[8] The two men killed were identified as a Canadian and an American who had early on joined the Royal Canadian Air Force to fight the Nazis.

"I remember the reason that we left instead of waiting at 3A," POW Raymond Twardzik said of his escape. He learned from some Russians that he and his colleagues would be sent to Odessa, on the Black Sea in the southern Soviet Union, to be exchanged for Soviet POWs. "I looked at the map and reasoned that was the wrong direction for me."

As New Zealand POW Bill Dashwood wrote years later, "We became aware that we were being held by the Russians as hostages over the return of Russian POWs to their native country." Soviet officials told the men "the war is over. The repatriation of POWs is no longer a matter between army commanders. It is now a matter between governments. There must be diplomatic negotiations."

What Dashwood and his fellow POWs didn't know was that in late May those negotiations would begin in Halle, Germany. The Soviet objective was to force the return of anti-communist Russians captured by the Allies while fighting for Hitler. Unless the British and Americans gave back the anti-communist Russians, the Soviets would not return the Allied prisoners.

"Apparently we were to be held as hostages," Dodgson had learned, "with the exchange rate of three Russian officers for each British, or the same for six Russian privates. Three Russians for a sergeant or a private for a private."[9]

Rather than end up "digging salt in Siberia," Dodgson and a friend decided, "we were through the wire, made the Elbe and got across" to the American forces on the west bank.[10] It was more than a month before the main camp was exchanged. "The boys were madder than hell. Everybody turned in lengthy reports to no avail. POWs come under the diplomatic side."[11]

"Even today," Dodgson concluded three months after he escaped from the Red Army, "there is cause to believe the Russians are still holding some of our [POWs]. My crew have never been traced and except for myself and the bombardier the other five have simply vanished."[12]

On May 20, 180 Americans and 1,800 British and Commonwealth troops from the camp were exchanged for Russians, but soon after that the hostage swap broke down. The Allies did not return all the anti-communist Russians, and, discovering this, Joseph Stalin refused to return all the American and British POWs.

Changing History

Yet the official Pentagon history of the prison gives no hint of that secret history. It reads as follows:

The PW remained in Stalag 3A until 22 April, when the camp was liberated by the Russians. Stalag 3A was turned over to the Americans on 6 May at which time Lt. Col. Walter M. Oakes and Col. Herte of the American PW took over the camp.[13]

In reality, Stalag 3A was never "turned over to the Americans," nor did Oakes or Herte ever assume control of the camp. In other words, the "official history" is historical fiction.

To this day, the truth about Luckenwalde remains hazy, obscured by disinformation and secrecy. For example, the roster of American and British POWs held by the Soviets at the camp was smuggled out by war correspondent Edward Beattie on May 3. The roster has been lost to history, either by design or by accident.

It is clear that some Americans from the facility were released months and even years after the war ended. Former 3A POW Charles E. Brocker remembered a meeting in December 1945 with several other 3A POWs who had been shipped to the Soviet Union and only recently exchanged. And Joe Friedl, who had decided to wait for the Russian "liberators" rather than escape with his buddies Connolly and Gomez on April 22, was taken to the Soviet Union and not returned until 1946.[14]

Many other Americans from Stalag 3A, men like Sergeant Edward Lawrence Reitz, never returned home at all. The Soviets packed Reitz off to the Soviet Union, where he was reported alive as late as 1956.[15]

The Red Army "liberated" at least 9,579 American and British POWs at the Luckenwalde prison complex, but only 5,343 returned home in organized exchanges and escapes. Another 700 or so straggled back on their own.[16]

The remaining 3,000 men never returned, apparently exchanging Nazi captivity for lifelong Soviet imprisonment. As 3A alumnus Robert J. Miller grimly remembered of his "liberation" by the Soviets, "not much changed except the changing of the guards."

Chapter 2

Prelude to Yalta

"The Russians have already threatened not to turn over to us American prisoners of war whom they get possession of in the German internment camps."
   –Secretary of War Henry Stimson, fall 1944

The tragedy that would overcome so many American POWs in the spring of 1945 was set into motion almost a year earlier. By the summer of 1944, the Allies had stormed Normandy and the end of the war was in sight. It was then that British Prime Minister Winston Churchill began to focus on what he believed was the preeminent threat to peace and stability in Western Europe, the rapidly advancing Soviet army. He ordered the creation of Section Nine in British intelligence to combat this threat.

British intelligence agent Kim Philby soon became the commander of all British anti-Soviet operations. Unknown to his superiors, Philby was a Soviet spy, and his Russian handler focused almost exclusively on Section Nine's operations. Stalin therefore learned of the British plan to use anti-communist Ukrainian and Byelorussian forces in what would be the upcoming Cold War. To get those men out of British hands, the Soviet leader demanded that all "Soviet citizens" under Allied control be returned, by force if necessary.

Within the month, the British Foreign Office had seemingly capitulated to Stalin's demands, declaring that "all Soviet nationals held as prisoners of war in the Middle East would be turned over to the authorities of the Soviet government, irrespective of the question whether or not they desire to be repatriated."[1]

Back in Washington, the U.S. Joint Chiefs of Staff (JCS) controlled the repatriation issue. Chaired by FDR's personal chief of staff, Admiral William D. Leahy, the JCS was often used by the president to bypass the Departments of War and State. It had been transformed by President Franklin D. Roosevelt "from an interdepartmental consulting group into a potential source and instrument of national strategy, lifted above the departmental level and joined in a special link to the President alone."[2] The JCS recommended that the U.S. go along with the British and "return all [Soviet] nationals whether they volunteer or not."[3]

The State Department, however, expressed reservations about forcible repatriation, since German reprisals against American and British POWs would be the likely result of such a policy.[4] The reservation was withdrawn when State learned that the British had already agreed to forcible repatriation.[5]

By October 1944, Stalin had clearly outlined his intent to hold hostage American, British and Commonwealth POWs the Red Army liberated from German captivity. Secretary of War Henry Stimson noted that "the Russians have already threatened not to turn over to us American prisoners of war whom they get possession of in the German internment camps."[6] The British received the same message when Churchill and Anthony Eden traveled to Moscow in October 1944.

The POW issue was to become a high-stakes diplomatic poker game, and the Soviets had already begun to collect their bargaining chips in the form of Allied prisoners. In July 1944, Canadian Alex Masterton was on the run in German-occupied Poland. He had survived the battle of Dunkirk and four years in a Nazi POW camp, but the tough 19-year-old of the Argyl and Sutherland Highlanders was to face the greatest danger from his nation's official ally, the Red Army.[7]

Following two months on the run after escaping from POW camp Stalag 20B, Masterton and two friends arrived in the Soviet city of Odessa, only to be tossed into jail by Soviet officials. After escaping with the help of friendly female cooks, they sought refuge on an American ship, but Soviet police dogs soon rooted out the Canadians, and they were placed back in prison.

Luckily for Masterton and his friends, the captain of the American vessel passed word of their fate to an incoming British ship. Three days later, the British captain arrived at the jail and successfully demanded the release of the Canadians.

Rumanian Roulette

Left behind in the same prison were about 20 Americans from two B-17 crews that crash-landed in the Soviet Union after bombing raids over the Axis oil fields near Ploesti, Rumania. The crewmen told Masterton they were being held without the knowledge of the American government. He kept the name and address of one of the airmen, who was from Michigan. After the war, Masterton unsuccessfully attempted to find him and now believes that he never returned.

On the voyage home, Masterton reported the imprisoned Americans to the British counsel in Istanbul, but when he got back to England, British intelligence told him never to reveal his experiences in the Soviet Union.

The young Canadian was the earliest known escapee from the Soviet Union in the World War II hostage crisis. The information he brought out about American bomber crews being imprisoned confirmed that Stalin's threat to hold liberated POWs hostage to his demands was not an idle one.

The First Forced Repatriation

On November 8, the State Department bowed to Stalin's threats, advising the U.S.S.R. in writing that all Soviet nationals would be repatriated, even from American soil, by force if necessary. Twenty-one days later, that policy decision was implemented when 1,179 Russians who had fought against Stalin in the German Army were loaded onto a Soviet ship in Seattle. Seventy-four did not want to return to the Soviet Union, and two of them either were murdered or committed suicide. Their bodies were found by the Coast Guard after they washed up on an island near the Columbia River.[8] This was the only forced repatriation by the United States before the early 1945 Yalta conference.

The JCS did note that "some of these Russians have kicked at returning and have gone to the extent of attempting suicide," but concluded that it was too late for second thoughts about forcible repatriation.[9]

In November 1944, Harold Macmillan, British resident minister at Allied Force Headquarters, gave the order that "All Soviet citizens, irrespective of the situation in which they are found or of their past history, should be turned over as soon as possible to the Soviet authorities for the latter to dispose of as they wish."[10] Both the United States and Britain had now made a commitment to Stalin to use whatever means necessary to return all Soviet citizens.

Churchill's anti-communist program continued unabated, however, and Stalin pressed for a more formal agreement. In December 1944, the Soviet government initiated negotiations with the American ambassador to

Moscow, W. Averell Harriman,[11] to formulate a written forced repatriation agreement at the upcoming Yalta conference. Since there were already parallel military level negotiations, the JCS recommended that the military and government negotiations be coordinated.[12]

In a letter dated January 2, 1945, Leahy recognized that a quid pro quo existed in the forced repatriation negotiations when he wrote: "regarding arrangements to be made for the disposition of claimants to Soviet citizenship held in the United States as German prisoners of war.... [A]lso bearing on this matter is the request made by the Soviet Government to the American Ambassador in Moscow for negotiations there on a governmental level regarding the same subject, in connection with arrangements for the disposition of American personnel liberated by the Soviet forces."[13]

Soviet Foreign Minister V.M. Molotov had confronted British Foreign Secretary Anthony Eden during a meeting in Moscow in October 1944 with a proposal for the same conditional agreement, to return all British POWs only if an agreement was reached to return all Soviet citizens.[14]

The Dissenters

Some American officials opposed caving in to Soviet demands. Stimson and Attorney General Francis Biddle attacked the forced repatriation of Russians from the United States on the grounds that it violated American standards of due process.

Stimson took the argument one step further. "[I]t may be claimed by thoughtless people that the doctrine of asylum does not apply to our commanders in a foreign land, where they are temporarily military governors," he wrote. Stimson rejected that position, believing that anti-communist Russians captured in Europe should be "under the shelter of the American flag," and he argued that both American tradition and the Geneva Convention required the United States to protect them.[15]

The Geneva Convention mandated that POWs be considered to be citizens of the country whose uniform they were wearing when captured. Soviet citizens fighting against Stalin in the uniform of Germany should have been treated as German soldiers, not Soviet citizens. International law, however, had little impact in the Roosevelt administration. It was never brought up in the internal debate controlled by the JCS.

The SWNCC

The State-War-Navy-Coordinating Committee (SWNCC), which coordinated three departments in matters regarding policies impacting both political and military affairs after the war, and the Joint Logistics Committee met on January 29, 1945, to discuss the latest version of the repatriation agreement that had been sent from the Moscow Embassy. Assistant Secretary of War John McCloy asked "what treatment would be accorded liberated personnel who are not prisoners of war, who claim U.S.S.R. citizenship but do not wish to be repatriated to the U.S.S.R.?" He noted that "repatriation of such persons is, in Secretary Stimson's opinion, contrary to the traditional United States policy of affording asylum to such persons."[16]

It may have been contrary to traditional U.S. policy, but this was a new era. The SWNCC agreed that "such persons would be subject to repatriation under this paragraph [Paragraph Eight] but the point is not a military one and is for the State and Justice Departments."[17]

The State Department representative, James Dunn, did not agree. He believed that "since the implementation of the agreement would be primarily a military matter, it would be preferable to have the agreement between the highest military authorities . . . and not between the governments, so that there would be no possibility that the agreement might be considered a treaty."[18] The planners altered the preamble to reflect that recommendation and forwarded it to the JCS, where Dunn's advice was ignored.

On February 3, the secretary of state sent an urgent telegram to Harriman's team of negotiators in Moscow on behalf of the War and Justice departments as well as State. They unanimously agreed that a "clear distinction should be preserved between former U.S. or Soviet military personnel" who were held by the Germans, and Soviet citizens captured while fighting for the Germans.[19]

This "urgent" advice was ignored. Stalin had demanded a tightly written forced repatriation agreement between the governments, and his demands would be met, at least on paper. Russians captured in German uniform would be repatriated to the Soviet Union.

The retention of certain anti-communist Russians, however, was rapidly becoming a key element in a British plan to combat Stalin in the immediate postwar era. With the successful invasion of Europe at Normandy, Germany's fate was sealed, and in August Churchill began to focus on what he now considered to be the primary threat, the Soviet Union. One month later, he met with Roosevelt in Quebec and personally confronted the dramatic swing toward Stalin the Roosevelt administration was taking.[20]

The Morgenthau Plan

Churchill believed the "Soviet Union had become a mortal danger to the free world," and at Quebec, as the infamous Morgenthau Plan unfolded, it became apparent that Britain could not count on the United States to combat that "mortal danger" as long as FDR and his inner circle reigned. Named after Treasury Secretary Henry Morgenthau Jr., the plan called for Germany to be dismembered, its industrial base dismantled and its skilled population transformed into farm workers.

The Morgenthau Plan would effectively destroy what remained of Germany, but Churchill could not allow that to happen. The British needed Germany's manpower and military expertise for the rapidly approaching postwar confrontation with Stalin.

The British leader secretly parted company with FDR, while publicly supporting him when necessity demanded, and initiated a covert anti-Soviet operation that would eventually result in support for guerrilla warfare in the Baltic, Byelorussia and the Ukraine. The Cold War warriors would be recruited from German military formations that had a high concentration of these nationalities. Moreover, Churchill would keep 700,000 German soldiers under arms as a hedge against a Soviet thrust west after American forces were withdrawn to the war in the Pacific.

Still, the British had their backs against the wall, with a "growing conviction that the Americans and the Russians intend that we shall emerge from this war a third-rate power. Indeed, they no longer take any pains to conceal their intentions," wrote Sir Harold Griggs, the British secretary of state for war, in December 1944, two months before Yalta.[21]

Soviet Agents

FDR's closest adviser, Harry Hopkins, was considered by Soviet intelligence to be their most important American agent. Other Soviet agents, such as Harry Dexter White and Alger Hiss, were strategically placed within the Roosevelt administration, as were a number of other spies, sympathizers and fellow travelers. British fears of a Stalin-Roosevelt collaboration against them were well-founded. They therefore created a new classification, "'Guard,' to prevent the Americans from learning anything about messages of far-reaching importance or controversial matters which must never become known to the United States."[22]

Churchill's decision to initiate a covert anti-Soviet operation would eventually seal the fate of 50,000 American, British and Commonwealth POW hostages who were never returned, but it was a tactic that the strategic reality of postwar Europe demanded in view of Stalin's European ambitions. That Churchill would agree to a forced repatriation agreement he already knew would have to be violated, and therefore place thousands of American and British POWs at risk, indicates the lengths to which he felt he must go to counter the rapidly shifting balance of power toward Stalin.

Chapter 3

The Yalta Agreement

*"In an alliance the allies should not deceive each other.
Perhaps it is naive? Experienced diplomatists may say,
'Why should I not deceive my ally? But I as a naive man
think it is best not to deceive my ally even if he is a fool.
Possibly our alliance is so firm just because it is not so
easy to deceive each other?"*
                                   –Joseph Stalin, February 1945

By the time American, British and Soviet negotiators
were ready for the Yalta conference, Britain's preparation
for a secret war against Stalin and FDR's increasingly
pro-Stalinist tilt had shaken the foundation of the Big
Three's wartime alliance against Germany. It was against
this backdrop that an ailing Roosevelt, a beleaguered
Churchill and an imperialistic Stalin landed in the Crimea
for the conference that would decide the fate of not only
two million Soviet citizens in the West, but also more than
100,000 American and British POWs who would come
under Stalin's control.

The violent resistance, deaths and suicides caused by the implementation of the earlier informal agreement to forcibly repatriate Soviet citizens from American soil forewarned the Roosevelt administration of the bloody consequences of the written agreement being negotiated in Moscow.

On January 3, 1945, Secretary of State E.R. Stettinius telegrammed Ambassador Harriman that the department was "extremely anxious" that the negotiations differentiate between "Americans found in German prisoner of war" camps and "Soviet nationals found among German prisoners of war taken by the American forces." There could be "no connection" between the two, he wrote, but his advice on this score was simply ignored along with the rest of his objections. When the telegram landed in Moscow, diplomat George F. Kennan's written instruction was to file it, nothing more.[1] The secretary of state's opinion on this subject was not sought or valued.

From an organizational point of view, American policy was in complete disarray. Only FDR and his select group knew what the program was, and they were not communicating with the administration's nonbelievers, who advocated treating the party holding U.S. hostages, Stalin, as an adversary.

Two weeks before Yalta, the Soviets demanded that the definition of Soviet citizens in the agreement be "those civilians forcibly removed from Russia for labor purposes, those Russians who were fighting with the German Army, and actual Soviet soldiers who were prisoners of war."[2]

The first point, about civilians "forcibly removed" from the U.S.S.R., was a euphemism for "all" civilians. Stalin even tried to broaden these terms by including language in the formal Yalta Agreement requiring continued forcible repatriation from the continental United States.[3] The language was removed from the agreement but the Soviets were quietly advised that even this exception would be lifted once Germany surrendered. The secretary of war and attorney general had created so much trouble for FDR within the traditional executive branch over forcible repatriation's violation of U.S. law and international treaty that such language simply could not be included in the agreement.[4] Roosevelt also certainly had fresh memories of the media's attacks on him after the Morgenthau Plan was exposed in September 1944.

The War Department recognized that the Soviet proposal presented "serious political questions. It contemplates an ultimate agreement on the governmental level, and final action will have to be taken by the State Department."[5] State Department personnel, however, would be shut out of the decision-making process, except for the U.S. ambassador to Moscow, who reported directly to Roosevelt.[6] The military negotiations, which were limited to the actual mechanics of the exchange, were coordinated with the government-level negotiations.[7] In the final analysis, it was FDR's aides, not State or Justice, that had the final say at Yalta on any issue not directly related to the simple mechanics of the exchange.

Less than two weeks before the Yalta conference, the State-War-Navy Coordinating Committee (SWNCC) went over the proposed agreement one last time in order to prepare a final report for the Joint Chiefs of Staff and Ambassador Harriman to use "as a basis for discussion."[8] Once again, the bureaucrats warned in writing that Paragraph Eight of the proposed language would require the forcible repatriation of Soviet citizens "who do not wish to be repatriated." They concluded, however, that forcible repatriation "is not a military consideration and is for the State and Justice Departments."[9]

On the Table

On February 9, two days before the signing of the Yalta Agreement, the American, British and Soviet negotiators met at Vorontzov villa, British conference headquarters.

The record of the conversation reveals that two important points were still on the table. The Soviet Union wanted language inserted requiring their specific approval before any American or British planes entered Soviet air space to pick up liberated prisoners of war. The Soviet language was agreed to. The practical result of this change was a ban on the use of air transport to repatriate POWs.

The lone exception, based solely on Soviet priorities, was Stalag Luft 1 at Barth, Germany. Former Soviet General A.A. Vlasov and one of his Russian-staffed, anti-Stalinist divisions, which Stalin badly wanted, were forcibly returned to Soviet control in exchange for the 10,000 American, British and Commonwealth POWs who were flown out of Barth over a three-day period by American bombers.[10]

The British negotiators also wanted to exchange notes with the Soviet Union "concerning nationals of other countries [Belgium, Holland and Poland] in British uniform who were liberated by the Russian armies."[11]

During the negotiations, "citizen" was the word used in conjunction with both American and Soviet personnel. But in the final draft of the agreement a seminal change was made. For the United States, "citizen" was changed to "subject," someone who owes his allegiance to a country. The Soviets retained the word "citizen," which can be interpreted to mean someone who owes allegiance to the nation of his birth, in this case the U.S.S.R. Even if someone born in the Soviet Union had later willingly switched his nationality to another country, under the Yalta Agreement he would still be considered a "citizen" of the U.S.S.R.[12]

The agreement was signed by General John Deane on February 11, 1945. Kennan forwarded the correct version of the agreement to the secretary of state.[13]

Shortly after the agreement was signed, the Soviet Union began to test its key elements. The Soviet ambassador to the United States, Andrei Gromyko, wrote to the acting secretary of state, Joseph Grew, advising him that he expected the U.S. to return all Soviet citizens "promptly to the country of their birth, which would be in congruence with the spirit of the agreement signed in Crimea on February 11."[14]

The Secret Cable

A second, secret plan or codicil was agreed to at Yalta by FDR, Churchill and Stalin. Although it has been hidden behind a bureaucratic wall of "national security" for five decades, its existence began to be exposed seven weeks after Yalta.

In a March 31 top-secret cable to the American Embassy in Moscow, Stettinius said the Yalta Agreement "requires the following action by the United States":

> a. The return to the Soviet Union of all Soviet military personnel held as prisoner of war by the Germans and liberated while in prisoner of war status from German prisoner of war camps.
>
> b. The return to the Soviet Union of Soviet citizens "not physically within the territorial limits of the United States" who are Soviet citizens.
>
> c. The return to the Soviet Union of Soviet citizens captured in German uniform, other than those who demand that they be retained as German prisoners of war and thus come under the Geneva Convention.[15]

Stettinius's use of quotation marks around the phrase "not physically within the territorial limits of the United States" indicates that he was quoting from an agreement other than the one signed by General Deane, because that language is not in Deane's version of the Yalta Agreement;

nor can the intent of the second and third paragraphs be traced to the agreement Deane signed.

Paragraph C had been Stalin's central focus since October 1944, when he promised both the United States and Britain that he would not return all their "liberated" POWs unless all anti-communist Soviet citizens were returned to his control. Although the point was clearly recognized by the various governmental deliberating bodies in the months leading up to Yalta, it is not addressed in Deane's version of the agreement.

A binding agreement to return Soviets citizens was reached, however, that the United States and Britain would adhere to until 1947–except when Stalin demanded certain Byelorussian and Ukrainian SS troops deemed essential by the West for the coming Cold War.

The JCS ensured that this secret agreement would be administered by the executive branch when it advised the "Theater Commanders that, if their Soviet colleagues raise any question as to the interpretation of the agreement they should reply that such questions should be taken up on a Government basis with Washington."[16]

The wording of this secret agreement would once again surface in late May 1945, when the British, American and Soviet governments formally reaffirmed the language of sections A and C. Section B was altered to mandate the forcible return of all Soviet civilians, including from the United States, even though the State Department's legal section opinion was that it was unconstitutional to do so.

On the evening of February 8, 1945, at a dinner with Roosevelt and Stalin where alcohol flowed freely and many toasts were offered, the Soviet dictator gave the following salute to his British "ally" Churchill:

> In an alliance the allies should not deceive each other. Perhaps it is naive? Experienced diplomatists may say, "Why should I not deceive my ally?" But I as a naive man think it is best not to deceive my ally

even if he is a fool. Possibly our alliance is so firm just because it is not so easy to deceive each other?[17]

This cryptic toast appears to have been a reference to Churchill's secret maneuvering on the repatriation issue. But true to his word, Stalin never tried to deceive the allies on the issue of repatriation. He clearly stated that he would not return all American, British and Commonwealth POWs unless his demands were met. As Anthony Eden's personal papers state, Stalin "pressed hard for the repatriation of all Soviet citizens" at Yalta. It was in fact the most important issue faced at the conference.[18]

As long as FDR was alive, the United States had every intention of fully implementing the accords. Churchill, however, had other plans. He had ordered British intelligence to revive "anti-Soviet operations,"[19] and after the conference that program continued unabated. "With Nazi Germany finished, the British intended to turn attention back to secret warfare against communism,"[20] in order to offset what they viewed as an alliance between Stalin and FDR that would destroy Britain as a military power and give the Soviet Union control of Europe.

Churchill hid his decision from Roosevelt and even created internal means of withholding such information from the United States.[21] Kim Philby, a Soviet mole in British intelligence, later admitted that "virtually all of my Soviet contact concerned the future of Section IX,"[22] under which the anti-Soviet program was planned and implemented. Stalin, thanks to Philby and numerous other Soviet spies within British intelligence and other government offices, knew well before the Yalta meeting that all Soviet citizens would not be returned by Britain.

The Soviets also had five agents with access to the White House and sixteen in, or close to, American intelligence.[23] Stalin was therefore aware of the powerful elements within the U.S. military and intelligence that, given the opportunity, would join the British anti-Soviet program or develop one of their own. He would shortly give them a graphic example of what would happen to American, British and Commonwealth POWs in Soviet hands if his demands were not met.

Chapter 4

From Yalta to Odessa

"No arguments will induce the Soviets to live up to our interpretation of the [POW] agreement except retaliatory measures which affect their interests. . ."
–U.S. Ambassador to Moscow W. Averell Harriman,
March 14, 1945

By the time the Yalta Agreement was signed in February 1945, more than 3,000 Americans were behind Russian lines in what is now Poland.

To deal with the POWs, Stalin placed the head of the Soviet secret police, Lavrenti Beria, in command of the Soviet repatriation effort, and Colonel-General Filip Golikov of the NKVD, the Soviet intelligence group, was assigned by Beria to head the Soviet Repatriation Commission. These officers, the same men who had carried out Stalin's brutal orders during the purges of the 1930s, now controlled the fate of American prisoners.

At first, Beria's lieutenants had no organized program for dealing with liberated POWs. The "Russians marched us out of the camp and to a place where some main roads crossed. There they told us we were on our own," recalled an American prisoner liberated from Stalag 3C.[1]

Many Americans were robbed by passing Soviet troops. One group was marched at gun point to a Soviet hospital and forced to give blood before being allowed to continue.[2]

"About 4:00 p.m., 3 February 1945, three American officers: . . . arrived in Lublin, Poland, and reported to the [Soviet] military authorities for repatriation to American control. No effort was made to identify these officers and they are being held in a room under guard like enemy aliens instead of Allied Officers," reported one Army document.[3]

The Yalta Agreement, at least from the Western perspective, was supposed to ensure that the Allied POWs were quickly moved from German camps to the Soviet port of Odessa for shipment home. But the Soviets soon proved they would not comply with the spirit or letter of the treaty.

Five days after the Yalta Agreement was signed, Ambassador Harriman in Moscow wrote V.M. Molotov, people's commissar for foreign affairs, outlining seven key points authorized by the agreement that the U.S. government wished to implement immediately, including those granting permission for: a U.S. team to go to Lublin to contact American POWs; the team to contact prisoners outside Lublin; the team to travel on U.S. aircraft and use them to evacuate U.S. prisoners; a U.S. team to set up in Poltava; the Poltava team to stockpile supplies and airlift them to concentrations of prisoners; and evacuation of American POWs from Poltava to Cairo. The seventh point was for information on all liberated Americans in the area.[4]

This should have been a routine request. It wasn't. Only the first point, allowing a U.S. team in Lublin, was ever approved.

The Soviets strictly regulated repatriation, calling off shipments at the last minute and insisting always upon clearance from Moscow for every prisoner released.

American POWs at Odessa were guarded by Russian soldiers carrying loaded rifles with fixed bayonets, and Russian security was more stringent there than German security had been in the various prison camps. A number of American officers who went to Poland at various times to coordinate the hunt for liberated POWs were ordered out very quickly at Russian insistence.[5]

When Harriman pursued the issue with Molotov and A.Y. Vyshinski from the People's Commissariat for Foreign Affairs, the Soviets falsely claimed to have already shipped all former POWs to Odessa by rail, including those who had been hospitalized.[6] Therefore, according to the Soviets, there was no reason to honor the U.S. request.

But reports continued to flow in with the names of Americans still under Soviet control in Poland. Five officers who reported in at the Moscow Embassy on February 19 turned over a list of 58 Americans they had seen in Poland. Nine never returned.[7]

Three days later, 19 additional names arrived in Moscow. Four were not repatriated, including three last seen in Wegheim, Poland. That same day, Sergeant George Lukashewitz arrived in Moscow with the names of 16 enlisted men liberated by the Russians at Stalag 3C and "now making their way toward Warsaw."[8] Three of those men never made it to Odessa.

Amid this chaos, Lieutenant Colonels James D. Wilmeth and Curtis B. Kingsbury, and Tech 5 Paul Kisil, who made up the only American contact team allowed in Poland by the Soviets, arrived in Lublin, Poland, on February 27, 1945.

Shortly after landing, they met with the Soviet commandant of Lublin, Colonel Bogdanov, and with four members of the Soviet Repatriation Authority. "The Soviet attitude was quite cold and unfriendly. The authorities told

Colonel Wilmeth that the situation was being handled adequately, his help was not needed, and implied that his presence, also, was unnecessary."[9] They also told Wilmeth that the headquarters of the Soviet Repatriation Group in Poland had moved to Praga the day before his arrival. Wilmeth suggested that Praga was where the American contact team should locate, but was told that permission must come from Moscow.[10]

Written Permission

While waiting for that permission, he asked to visit American ex-POWs, but he was told that he could not because he "had no permit to show that he had a right to be in Lublin."[11] Wilmeth, a small man with a large personality, then pointed out that "his having been brought by Soviet plane should be sufficient permission."[12] It wasn't. He needed a written permit, and it would have to come from Praga.

Wilmeth ended the meeting with a request to visit nearby POWs that night.[13] There were 90 Americans in town. The American officers were from Oflag 64 and the enlisted personnel from Stalag 3C, overrun January 31, 1945.[14]

On February 28, Wilmeth had a second meeting with the Soviet repatriation authorities. They reported that four collecting points were in operation: Lublin, Praga, Cracow and Lodz.[15]

They also noted that 2,422 Americans had arrived at Odessa by February 26, 1945. Five-hundred-twenty had been shipped from Lublin on February 23, and 280 from Lodz on February 26, for a total of 3,361 en route to or at Odessa.

The Soviet officials claimed, however, that they didn't know the total number of Americans liberated from prison camps by Red forces.[16]

On the day the Soviets made that statement, Stalag 2B was overrun by the Red Army. Of the 7,087 Americans at

2B, the State Department estimated 2,000 were liberated by the Soviets.[17] That meant about 5,300 Americans were then behind Soviet lines.

Unable to reach most of those men, since he was restricted to the area right around the city of Lublin, Wilmeth grew increasingly frustrated. He requested permission to have direct communication with the Moscow Embassy and visit all POW collecting points, including Odessa.

As he told the chief negotiator, the Yalta Agreement gave Wilmeth, as the American representative in Poland, the "right to receive immediate information about released Americans, and to have immediate access to the camps where they were located."

The American colonel even offered to lend his copy of the agreement to the negotiator, who refused, ending the meeting on a less than cordial note.[18]

Wilmeth's demands for travel rights were based on immediate concerns. Anna Louise Strong, a war correspondent who had managed to get to Warsaw and return overland to Moscow, reported to the embassy that on February 25, "the Red Army published a bulletin saying that POW collection camps were being established at Wrzesnia, Lodz, Praga, and Lublin." The bulletin also "forbade POWs to avoid these places and ordered them to report to the nearest Soviet Commandant to ask to be sent to one of these camps."[19] POWs who failed to obey would be subject to immediate incarceration.

Concerned about the situation, General John Deane, a senior U.S. official in Moscow, telegrammed Wilmeth on March 12, advising him not to leave Lublin because Deane was coming there.[20] The Soviets, however, were determined to see that this did not happen.

The chief Soviet negotiator arrived in Lublin the same evening and advised Wilmeth that, effective the next day, "Lublin would cease to be a collecting point, therefore, there was no need for Col. Wilmeth's party to remain in

Lublin." He also told Wilmeth that "the party had no right to remain in Lublin as its permit had expired." Wilmeth demanded that the Russians put their orders in writing. They refused, and Wilmeth stayed in Lublin.

Meantime, the U.S. government, through the efforts of Ambassador Harriman, and even FDR, had been attempting to obtain permission for Deane to "make a trip to the front areas where our freed prisoners of war were located ... to Lublin, Praga, Lodz, Resnya and other places where [they] might be concentrated."[21]

Deane met with a Soviet general in Moscow on March 6 in a further attempt to get the Soviet government to honor the Yalta Agreement and allow American officers to visit liberated American POWs in Soviet-controlled territory.

When the Soviet said that Lieutenant General K.D. Golubev was in charge of such matters, Deane noted that Golubev had been less than helpful. At a meeting the previous week, Golubev had said that Deane could visit the requested repatriation locations, but later said the American general could not go. Golubev had also promised to set up immediately certain repatriation points. The next day, Deane received a letter saying they were not being established.[22]

Harriman continued to push on the diplomatic front. On March 7 he met with V.G. Dekanozov, assistant people's commissar for foreign affairs. Harriman indicated that early planning for the evacuation of American POWs had gone well, but since February 26, the date of the last meeting, "the situation had greatly deteriorated."[23]

Dekanozov retorted that "only yesterday he had talked to General Golubev on the subject" of American ex-POWs in Poland. "According to the most recent information, there were now 1350 prisoners of war in Odessa. These were now being placed on a British ship for evacuation." He also said: "The Soviet Commission dealing with the evacuation of prisoners of war had figured that there were approximately 2100 liberated American prisoners of war in Poland."[24]

Dekanozov rejected an earlier Harriman letter estimating that 3,000 American prisoners of war were still in Poland. But Harriman responded that more recent information showed "there were a total of over 4000 American prisoners of war [in Poland or the Ukraine] of which some 1200 had been evacuated to Odessa."[25] In other words, the American implied that Russia had almost 2,000 more prisoners than it was admitting.

The meeting ended with Harriman requesting that a "quick decision with respect to General Deane's trip to Poland" be made. "Mr. Dekanozov stated that he would endeavor to give a reply tomorrow."[26]

The next day Edward Page, second secretary of the U.S. Moscow Embassy, contacted S.K. Tsarapkin of the People's Commissariat for Foreign Affairs, requesting a decision on Deane's trip to Poland. Tsarapkin claimed Deane would "have to make certain arrangements with the Poles in connection with, for example, visas and other formalities."[27]

The American Embassy, having anticipated that stalling tactic, had already contacted the Polish representatives in Moscow, who assured them that General Deane needed no visa.

Despite that, the Russians still refused to authorize the trip. But Page said "he [Tsarapkin] promised me an answer tomorrow on the question." Page also informed Tsarapkin that the "Ambassador not only desired General Deane to proceed to Poland" to look for Americans, but he also wanted "to go to Sagan where 300 wounded officers were reported to be located, and to any other places in Poland where American prisoners were said to be concentrated."[28]

Tsarapkin responded that "according to Soviet information there were no more American prisoners in Poland.

1350 had already reached Odessa and 900 were en route thereto at the present time."[29]

Page disputed those Russian figures and attempted to break the deadlock by telling Tsarapkin "that in view of this conflict the most advisable course would appear to be to send General Deane and a Soviet officer to investigate conditions on the spot."[30]

The final Soviet decision came on March 11, after weeks of bickering. The Soviets contacted Harriman, "disapproving General Deane's trip to Poland on the grounds that as there were no longer any American ex-prisoners of war in Poland."[31] That, of course, was untrue.

Harriman's Protest

And when it became apparent that the diplomatic efforts of the Moscow Embassy had failed, Harriman contacted Roosevelt by telegram and attempted to obtain his personal intervention to resolve the crisis:

> As I have continued reports of the presence of American ex-prisoners of war including a substantial number hospitalized at various points . . . and more coming in and out every day, I wrote a strong letter to Molotov protesting and insisting that the Soviet Government grant the 'small courtesy' to the United States Government of allowing General Deane to make a survey of the situation in Poland and visit our prisoners, particularly our sick and wounded who we knew still remained in Poland.
>
> Today I am informed by General Deane that the permission for our contact team to remain at Lublin has been withdrawn and that a plane scheduled to leave today from Poltava for Lublin with a load of supplies had been canceled.
>
> This team at Lublin has been the only means by which we have been able to give help to our ex-

prisoners in Poland and has been working day and night with those who have found their way to Lublin. I am therefore protesting to Molotov today that our contact team should be allowed to remain in Lublin.

General Deane and I feel strongly that we should make an issue of the matter of having our much needed contact officers in Poland which is clearly within our rights under the Prisoner of War Agreement signed at Yalta, not only in order to take care of those who are still in Poland but also because of the probability that there will be substantial numbers liberated by the Red Army in the future.[32]

On March 14, Harriman followed up with a telegram to the secretary of state: "no arguments will induce the Soviets to live up to our interpretation of the agreement except retaliatory measures which affect their interests."[33]

He recommended that the State and War departments "come to an agreement on what retaliatory measures we can immediately apply in the event an unfavorable answer is received by the President from Marshal Stalin."[34]

Among Harriman's ideas were:

1. That General Eisenhower issue orders to restrict the movements of Soviet contact officers in France to several camps or points of concentration of their citizens far removed from the point of liberation, comparable to Lwow and Odessa; 2. That Lend Lease refuse to consider requests of the Soviet Government additional to our Fourth Protocol Commitments for such items as sugar, industrial equipment or other items that are not immediately essential for the Red Army and the Russian war effort. 3. That consideration be given to allowing our prisoners of war now en route to Naples to give stories to the newspapers of the hardships they have

been subjected to between point of liberation and arrival at Odessa and that in answer to questions of correspondents the War Department explain the provisions of our agreement and the Soviet Government's failure to carry out the agreement according to any reasonable interpretation.

While the State Department and White House were debating their response, Wilmeth fought to hold on at Lublin, even though he had been ordered to leave. On March 12, he was given additional information on shipments of Americans from various collecting points. Fifty-seven more had been shipped from Lodz, 715 from Praga and 139 from Lublin. Fifteen remained at these locations.[35]

Soviet Diversion

Wilmeth also learned that the Soviets were attempting to divert all POWs away from Lublin. Very few were getting through the "cordon of both Soviet and Polish guards." They were told that no American officers were in town and they would have to go to one of the four Soviet collecting points.

On March 16, a U.S. plane arrived from Poltava with a letter from Deane advising Wilmeth that he still intended to come to Lublin. Apparently Deane held out some hope that FDR would actually approve retaliatory measures and force the Soviets to abide by the Yalta Agreement.

However, Soviet troops on the plane said Colonel Wilmeth must return with the aircraft to Poltava the next day–that General Deane had sent the plane for this purpose. Wilmeth refused to leave, "stating he had orders to await General Deane in Lublin, and this he would do, unless he received word from General Deane, or a written order from Soviet authorities to depart earlier."[36]

Apparently Wilmeth developed information while at Lublin confirming that thousands of POWs were still at large in Poland: On March 19, three liberated British POWs arrived in Moscow from Wilmeth's headquarters in Lublin with "a report which suggests that there are thousands of our liberated prisoners still in Poland."[37] He had been forced to send the message by courier because the Soviets would not forward his messages from Lublin.

Finally, on March 22, the U.S. government gave in, and Deane sent Wilmeth orders to return to Moscow by plane.[38] But no airplane had arrived for Wilmeth and his party by March 26, so the Soviets pressed him to leave by train. He demanded that the order be put in writing, but the Soviets refused. He was then told that if he "refused to leave by train, there would be a 'big scandal' and that Colonel Wilmeth probably would not get to Moscow," a less than veiled threat that he might join the American POWs in Siberia.[39] The next day, an American plane arrived and Colonel Wilmeth and company returned to Poltava.

The First Battle of the Cold War

The United States had declared defeat in its attempt to recover all U.S. POWs from Poland.

FDR, the commander in chief, had been asked to authorize pressure to force the Soviets to comply with the Yalta. But the president's response confirmed what Stalin most likely already knew from his White House spies, that Roosevelt was too tired, too sick and too pro-Soviet to force the issue.

"NO repeat NO retaliatory action will be taken by U.S. forces at this time for Soviet refusal to meet our desires with regard to American contact teams and aid for American personnel liberated by Russian forces," the president directed.[40]

Upon returning to Moscow, Colonel Wilmeth issued a report covering the "Soviet attitude toward the evacuation of American prisoners of war." He wrote that "liberated

American prisoners of war have been forced to eat, sleep, and march with captured German prisoners."[41] Their treatment was "such as to cause many Americans to go into hiding in the homes of private citizens all over Poland, to wait until [they receive] some assurance that they can be safely evacuated from the country."[42] Of the eighteen messages given to the Soviets for transmission to Moscow, he reported, only three were received, and they "were so garbled the meaning was not clear."

The Red Army refused to let Wilmeth move supplies to Lublin or "visit two wounded American ex-prisoners of war, [only] 26 kilometers from Lublin." The Soviets said there were no airfields at Cracow and Lodz, thereby denying the contact team access to those cities, even though the cities did have excellent airfields.

The Soviets asserted that no American ex-POWs were at Lodz. But "every time an ESCOM plane went there the crew saw several such prisoners," Wilmeth wrote. They claimed that Wrenznia was not and had not been a collecting point for former POWs. But POWs passing through Lublin "in many instances reported collection and shipments from Wrzesnia."[43]

On several occasions, American personnel at Poltava were able to "recover some escaping U.S. POWs whom they would have been able and willing to repatriate in U.S. aircraft. The Russians, however, refused to permit this and demanded that the escapees be surrendered to them for transport to Odessa."[44]

Wilmeth later admitted knowing, even from his obstructed view of events, that 600 American POWs were kept by the Soviets. This fact, however, is not in his final report.[45]

The last reference to ex-POWs under Soviet control in Poland or Odessa was made in a Department of State "top secret" telegram dispatched from AFHQ headquarters at Caserta, Italy, on April 13, 1945.[46] After a "minimum of processing," Soviet nationals were flown to Bari, Italy, "to await shipment to Russia," by boat.[47] "A shipment of 884 Americans who arrived there [Odessa] April second are now being held up under Russians at Bari."

But only 248 Americans were repatriated through Odessa after April 2.[48] Soviet field repatriation officials admitted that 4,275 American ex-POWs were en route to Odessa as of March 12. The additional 884 noted in the Bari message brings the total to 5,159.

According to those figures and at least two State Department records, a minimum of 5,200 Americans were behind Soviet lines in Poland, but only 2,858 were returned by the Soviets.[49]

Colonel Wilmeth thought he had discovered why Soviet troops treated Allied personnel in such a manner. Americans coming through Lublin told him that the "Red Army front line had been using the battle-cry 'on to England.' Everyone in and behind the Red Army front lines was talking about the war between the U.S.S.R., and England and America . . . ."

In reality, Stalin's war with the West had already begun. The diplomatic maneuvering in Poland, along with the taking of U.S. POWs, reflected the first skirmishes of the Cold War.

Chapter 5

The Hostage Swap at Odessa

The first reluctant returnee called off the boat by the NKVD was a Russian colonel. "He saluted and gave his name, rank and serial number—and Bam! They bashed his face in with a rifle butt." "Russian colonels don't surrender," Soviet guards told the dazed officer, whereupon he was hustled down the gangplank and shot in the head.
—The Odessa POW exchange, spring 1945

Colonel Wilmeth and his team, trapped in Lublin under the dead weight of Soviet bureaucracy and hobbled by the weakness of the FDR administration, could only guess at the full extent of what was happening to U.S. POWs in the Polish countryside.

In February 1945, the American government received an ominous intelligence report about Poland that would soon become terribly familiar: "Information has been received by the British that in the absence of proper identification of their nationalities British and American nationals may possibly have been sent [to] Russian concentration camps."[1]

Over the next four months, American and British POWs who escaped from Soviet control in Germany, Austria and Poland would repeat this message, sometimes adding that they were being transported to the Soviet Union in box-cars, mixed with German POWs.

On February 14, Sergeant H. Brooks penned a message from U.S. and British officers and sergeants held in Poland:

> At the moment we are with the Russian Army in Nowy Sacz for over 3 weeks and no responsible parties have been notified of our presence and whereabouts. We have no freedom, and have been told that we are internees. Kindly send immediately an officer you'll hasten our departure.[2]

Sergeant H. Brooks's departure was apparently never hastened, for his name is not on the Odessa roster of all POWs repatriated from Poland.

The same day Brooks signed his plea for help, General John Deane, head of the U.S. Military Mission to Moscow, sent a message to the Pentagon naming 32 American ex-POWs who were in Lodz, Poland, under the care of the Polish Red Cross. Two of these named individuals never returned.

But some Americans did return with the truth.

In February, four U.S. POWs escaped from the Nazis in northern Germany. The group headed east toward Soviet lines, escaping again after being recaptured by the Germans and thrown into a small town jail.

Eventually, the Americans made it to Soviet lines, where they were initially ordered to join the Russians and fight the Germans. Three days later, they were given a horse and set off to the east. Russians searched them for watches at each checkpoint, and they were even used to move Jewish bodies.[3] Finally, they were put on a train to Moscow, where Edmund D'Arcy, sick with blood poisoning, was separated from his three comrades, whom he would never see again.

Upon arriving in Moscow, D'Arcy was held in isolation and forbidden contact with the American Embassy.[4] The Soviets, who mistook him for an officer because of a cap he was wearing, had female interrogators fluent in English grill D'Arcy and other Americans held there about the Norton bomb sight, the bazooka and other American weapons systems.

Finally, he was allowed to contact the U.S. Embassy in Moscow,[5] then placed on a train to Kiev. From Kiev he was sent to Odessa, where a U.S. Army Air Force lieutenant colonel was in charge of Americans awaiting transportation home. Since D'Arcy spoke Russian, the colonel asked him to stay near the Soviet officials and, without letting them know that he understood Russian, to find out what they were saying.[6]

The British ship Tamora docked at Odessa in March, 1945, carrying a load of Russians who did not want to return home. As D'Arcy watched the Red Army unload the Ukrainian and Soviet POWs, he learned the truth about forcible repatriation and its link to the POW swap.[7]

The first reluctant returnee called off the boat by the NKVD, Soviet intelligence, was a Russian colonel. "He saluted and gave his name, rank and serial number–and Bam! They bashed his face in with a rifle butt."

"Russian colonels don't surrender," Soviet guards told the dazed officer, whereupon he was hustled down the gangplank and shot in the head.

The next victim was the former consort of a German general. She too was unceremoniously shot at the end of the gangplank. In all, D'Arcy remembers up to 50 people being executed. "They took them down to the end of the dock and eliminated them," he recalled.

The rest of the Russians were loaded into boxcars. "They are taking us to Siberia," they told D'Arcy, who was standing nearby. "What are you going to do there?" D'arcy asked them. Their reply: "They are going to work us to death."

"So then I asked the Russian major why they were going to Siberia. 'They've learned so much in Germany we are going to give them the opportunity to build a modern town, then maybe they'll be happy here.' "

After the Russians were unloaded, the Tamora was cleaned, then loaded the next day with American and British POWs. D'Arcy was the last man to get on board, where he was kept isolated from the other passengers throughout the trip.[8]

The American and British governments now had firsthand knowledge of the bloody consequences of the recently signed Yalta Agreement.

Chapter 6

The Halle Negotiations

"There is every indication that the Russians intend to make a big show of repatriation of our men, although I am of the opinion that we may find a reluctance to return them all, for an appreciable time to come, since those men constitute a valuable bargaining point."
—Major General Raymond W. Barker,
chief U.S. negotiator at the May 1945
Halle POW conference with the Soviet Union

By mid-April 1945, the American and Soviet armies were rapidly converging on the Elbe River in central Germany. The U.S. rolled in from the west and Red Army from the east, crushing between them what remained of the German war machine.

As the Soviets moved farther west into Germany, finally crossing the Oder River, the movement of "liberated" American POWs to Odessa had stopped.

About 100,000 American and British prisoners of war in central Germany were about to be overrun by the Soviet Army. Their enormous numbers and close proximity to

American lines mandated a new approach to swapping POWs, and by late April, the two sides considered opening negotiations to deal with the changing circumstances.

Stalin was in a much stronger position, now that he had acquired at least 100,000 pawns for his game of hostage politics. His agents also had direct access to all of Western Europe, where the British would be hiding their anti-communist assets.

Adding to the intrigue was the recent death of Roosevelt. Harry Truman was an unknown quantity and, now that pro-Stalinist White House leftists and spies had lost their source of power, anti-communists within the American government were beginning to stir.

It was against that backdrop that Andrei Vyshinski called American Minister-Counselor George F. Kennan to his Moscow office on April 30. Vyshinski was the brutal Stalinist who ran the Soviet Union's "show trials" used in the 1930s to liquidate Stalin's many real and imagined enemies, and now he would take a leadership role in another historic violation of human rights.

"Now that our forces are linked up in Germany, Vyshinski says we should effect repatriation of our respective liberated prisoners of war directly across our line of contact in Germany instead of by sea,"[1] Kennan reported.

He warned Washington that the Soviet Union was pushing to recover all of its defectors and that if the

> proposal is accepted, I think it likely that the Russians will do their best to interpret our acceptance in such a way as to oblige us to hand over at once all the Russians we find, regardless of their status, before we have had a chance to do any sifting among those found to have been fighting with the Germans.[2]

Shifting to Sifting

Two days later the State Department accepted Kennan's concerns, supporting "sifting" to "screen out those who may be found fighting with the German armed forces."

In effect, U.S. diplomats were recommending that the Yalta Agreement to return "all" Soviets be secretly abrogated, a major policy swing toward Churchill's Cold War plan.

The sifting proposal accepted, U.S. policy shifted toward the English plan of retaining Ukrainians and Byelorussians for anti-Soviet covert operations behind the Iron Curtain, operations later overseen by Kennan.[3]

Under the Yalta accords, however, sifting was a gross violation of a signed international agreement. "All" Russians fighting for the Germans were supposed to be returned to the Soviet Union, by force if necessary. Like the British before them, U.S. officials were now attempting to secretly back out of this agreement. The Soviet response was to keep Allied prisoners as hostages.

Within the week, the Supreme Headquarters Allied Expeditionary Force (SHAEF) advised the Moscow Embassy that "thousands of United States and British Prisoners of War held in close confinement under unsatisfactory conditions" were in POW camps behind Soviet lines. The message concluded that "unless this evacuation can be effected promptly, there may well ensue most undesirable consequences."[4]

SHAEF was not guessing at what those undesirable consequences would be. American and British officers, along with Office of Strategic Services (OSS) personnel, had scouted those camps. They knew that the compounds had been locked down, with armed guards posted and orders given that escapees would be subject to imprisonment. They also knew that escape attempts organized by SHAEF had come under Russian fire.

Vlasov's Army

Stalag Luft 1 at Barth, Germany, was the last POW camp exchanged before the Soviets stopped all repatriation across the lines. The "exchange" for these American and British aviators was Stalin's former favorite general, A.A. Vlasov, who had been captured by the Germans in 1942. Within months of his capture, Vlasov had turned against Stalin, beginning a long and ultimately futile effort to convince the Germans to allow him to organize multiple divisions of anti-communist Russians to fight against the Soviet Union. A few months before their defeat, the desperate Germans finally gave Vlasov permission to form just two divisions.

Although the "Vlasov Army" was largely fiction, German intelligence "could tell how much anxiety this caused Moscow, for we rounded up many Soviet agents parachuted behind our lines with explicit orders to infiltrate that army at all costs and bring Vlasov back dead or alive into Communist hands."[5]

Once Vlasov and his men had been traded (to their certain death or imprisonment) for the Western POWs at Barth, exchanges along the line were halted by the Soviets. Two days later American, British and Soviet negotiators met at Halle, Germany, where they would haggle seven days before signing an agreement governing future prisoner exchanges.

The Negotiations

The American and British negotiators were led by U.S. Army Major General Raymond W. Barker, who was Eisenhower's acting G-1 chief of staff at SHAEF. The U.S. and British officers assumed the posture of a team whose mission was to ensure an agreement was reached to make it possible to conceal specific anti-communist, Russian-staffed units that had fought for the Nazis. Kennan's sifting recommendation had filtered down through the bureaucracy to the military negotiators as an order.

The Soviet posture was conversely that of a party determined to get back "all" Soviet citizens, as agreed to at Yalta, if the opposing party expected to receive all of their personnel.

The Russians arrived with 40 officers and an equal number of heavily armed enlisted men driving armored cars for the first meeting on May 16 at 9:40 p.m. They were led by the Soviet assistant administrator for repatriation, Lieutenant General K.D. Golubev, an NKVD (Soviet intelligence) general well-known for his huge size and small intellect.

Barker used the two-hour-and-twenty-minute opening session to establish that the American and British POWs held by the Soviets were actually hostages.

His strategy was to insist upon the fastest possible exchange, demanding that the Russians "promptly allow our airplanes to go into the Russian lines and bring out our people . . . also, while doing that, that we send back as many Russians as we can right at the same time." The hostage politics that had earlier plagued the diplomats was now on the military negotiating table.

Golubev countered by ignoring Barker's opening demand. Instead, he attempted to establish the number of Russians the West was going to return: Barker estimated 250,000, but Golubev said the Soviet Union expected 700,000 to one million.[6]

Golubev then spent the rest of the meeting emphasizing the Soviet hard line: They would not immediately give back all American and British POWs and simply trust the West, sooner or later, to give back all Soviet citizens as defined at Yalta. The West must rapidly repatriate everybody, according to the Russian general, noting "there possibly might be people who, for some reason or other, would not like to return home. They should also be returned."

Barker did not challenge Golubev on the point of forced repatriation. Instead, he insisted that U.S. airplanes be allowed to evacuate the American prisoners. The faster the American prisoners were evacuated, the less opportunity Moscow had to use them as hostages.

Golubev obviously failed to display enthusiasm for an air evacuation, responding that "the use of aviation as the main mode of transportation is not very feasible. The transportation should be carried out on a wide front" using trucks. "I agree with you 100 percent," Barker replied, but "I am afraid that the General does not appreciate what a magnificent effort our air force has made in moving prisoners of war within the past three weeks or so. Does he realize that we have transferred ... something like over 200,000 men. Does he realize that! That is a lot of men!"

Golubev kept insisting that airplanes would require too much improvement of airports. "You are talking about which program is quicker," Golubev said, "aviation or ground transportation. I believe the vehicles are quicker. The roads are good."

Barker continued to press for the use of planes, this time specifying POWs held hostage at Stalag 3A, Luckenwalde, a camp where U.S. rescues had been attempted in early May (see Chapter 1). He stated that "there are about 15,000 French, British, American and Norwegian prisoners [at Luckenwalde]. There is an airfield there which is serviceable and can be used."

Golubev replied that "while we are speaking here, these people are being moved to the front line." That wasn't true. Of the 9,500 American, British and Commonwealth POWs at Luckenwalde when the Soviets "liberated" it, 1,300 British and Commonwealth prisoners and 180 American POWs were still there when Golubev claimed they had all been moved.

At that point, Golubev finally revealed four sites where American and British POWs were being concentrated:

Wismar, Crivitz, Magdeburg and Dessaw. (Magdeburg would turn out to be the only point of the four from which American or British POWs were passed back to Western control.)

"Could I ask the General this?" Barker continued. "We have figures now where some British and American prisoners of war are located in Russian camps." (The figures presented were expunged from the transcript, but Golubev's response indicates that the U.S. knew the location of 32,000 American and British POWs that were under Soviet control east of the Elbe River in Germany. Two days later, SHAEF estimated that 40,000 to 45,000 were actually in the Soviet zone of Germany.)

"Thirty-two thousand?" Golubev mused. Then he quickly switched the topic: "But hundreds of thousands of Soviet citizens are still in France and they have been waiting for repatriation for about eight months."

Barker moved on, asking about four locations where U.S. POWs were being held: Neubrandenberg, Luckenwalde, Muhlberg and Muterborg, "where there are a good many thousands of Allied prisoners of war. There is a good airfield nearby," Barker observed.

Remarkably, Golubev simply claimed the men were not there anymore. "As soon as our Government had taken the decision to give the Allied prisoners of war over across the front lines, we set up some new assembly points which are located now in the region of the seven points which I have already mentioned."

"Our people are still there," Barker insisted. "An officer returned from one of them only three days ago."

"There was no camp at Muterborg and the camp at Muhlberg was transferred. There are only plains there now," Golubev insisted.

"Our people were at Luchenbach [Luckenwalde] several days ago. Our officer came from there and told us about them."

"What existed under the Germans does not now exist," Golubev angrily shot back. "We are moving [Allied POWs] to the front lines."

"Does the General say all of our people have been moved from [Luckenwalde] now?" Barker asked. "Yes." "And Muhlberg?" "Yes."

The first response was a lie, the second true. There were still U.S. and British hostages at Luckenwalde. But the POWs at Muhlberg had been moved to a point directly opposite the Halle negotiating site, where they were conspicuously held as hostages.

Seconds later, Barker accused the Soviets of violating the Yalta Agreement. "If the Russian Government had complied with the . . . Yalta agreement, we could have flown in there three weeks ago and our people would be home now–thousands of them."

Golubev tossed the Yalta argument right back, asserting that after returning thousands of Norwegians, Belgians and Frenchmen, "we did not get a single Soviet citizen in return. . . . These are facts." Golubev was clearly stating that such one-sided exchanges would end, and Barker got the point.

The next morning, he passed on the Soviet message in a memorandum to the SHAEF Repatriation Planning Group. "British and American prisoners of war, now in Russian custody, are being used as a bartering point in order to force our hand. Hence, these men are, in effect, 'hostages,' " Barker reported.[7]

The general's memo also revealed that he had been expressly limited by his government. The use of the word "all" to describe Soviet citizens, as used in the Yalta Agreement, was now "subject to such qualifications as may be imposed by the respective governments, with respect to citizenship and affiliated subjects, although this should not be incorporated in the paper."[8]

The U.S., British and Soviet governments were at this point debating three points: the status of Soviet citizens fighting for the Germans, the status of Baltic state citizens and the citizenship of several senior Cossack officers who had fought for the Germans but were legally citizens of Yugoslavia or stateless.

The day before the Halle negotiations began, the American Embassy in France assured the State Department by memo that Barker would make it "quite clear to the Russians that any discussions of [Allied POW policy and Soviet citizens] will be subject to reference to the proper authorities."

The State Department, probably the Special War Problems Division, was monitoring and controlling the portion of the negotiations not directly related to the simple mechanics of transferring millions of people across the U.S.-Soviet line.

Barker's memo also revealed that his instructions included the order not to reach an agreement permitting the Soviets to demand specific Soviet citizens in exchange for specific American and British POWs: "We must avoid anything which will commit us to an exchange on a man-for-man basis. The tenor of the agreement should be such that each Government will proceed with the repatriation of liberated personnel in their custody and that the rate and numbers of transfer will be based solely on the capability of each party to move and/or receive that personnel."

Barker knew when he wrote those words that some U.S. POWs would not be returned if this point prevailed, because it relied on the goodwill of all parties rather than strict accountability. And Golubev, the Soviet intelligence general, had clearly indicated that there would be no goodwill.

That same day, Churchill advised the British military not to destroy captured German aircraft. He would also keep 700,000 German troops under arms or with easy access to them–all as a precaution against Soviet moves.

The three negotiating sessions on May 17 produced nothing of substance. There was a firm effort by Britain's Brigadier General R.H.S. Venables to initiate an exchange of POWs at Neubrandenberg, Stalag 2A. This was passed to the diplomats, and an exchange occurred on May 18 and 19 without further discussion by the military negotiators.

On May 17, Barker also issued a three-page memo to SHAEF because of the "considerable anxiety and concern throughout the United Nations over the condition, care and treatment of prisoners of war in Germany, and the prospects for their early repatriation." The only POWs then still awaiting repatriation were those being held hostage by the U.S.S.R., and the "considerable anxiety and concern" were fully justified.

On the 18th, two major issues developed: The Soviets wanted the negotiations to result in a governmental agreement, and they wanted the phrase "all without exception" included in the verbiage to define who and how many would be repatriated by each side.

The debate began in a committee of negotiators appointed by Barker and Golubev to hammer out the wording and details of the agreement.

" 'All without exception' is redundant and discourteous," Brigadier General Stanley R. Mickelsen advised the Soviets.

"Why is it so? You will probably find some other English word which won't sound so discourteous which will mean just the same so that . . . all the French, American and English peoples will be returned to their countries," a second-tier Soviet negotiator responded in a thinly veiled threat.

The dialogue also focused on whether the generals were negotiating an "agreement" or a "plan." An "agreement" would be governmental in nature, a broader understanding that was strongly pursued by the Soviet delegation.

British General Venables summed up the American and British position: "Perhaps it is a play on words but an agreement by our various governments has been signed already. We do not need another agreement. We have one agreement. We want a plan to implement the agreement."

They agreed to disagree and went on to a paragraph by paragraph discussion of the Soviet proposal, where "all without exception" continued to dominate the discussion.

Mickelsen then diplomatically broached the subject of Soviet citizens who did not want to return. "It is very evident that we cannot agree on 'all without exception,' because it is known that some Soviet citizens are hiding in the woods, others will not make [their presence] known, and SHAEF cannot undertake the search of these people and arrest them and bring them under arrest to the reception centers in the Soviet zone. We cannot do this." (Actually, the Allies could and did search for Russians. When they couldn't catch them, the troops were sometimes ordered to shoot them.)

The junior negotiators arrived at an impasse over the "all without exception" phrase, and it was removed from the table until the head negotiators next met. They then moved on to exactly when the repatriations would begin.

The U.S. and British exploded when told the prisoner exchange wouldn't start until the 23rd: "We can argue all night if you want us to explain just what we mean," Venables said. "There are approximately 6,000 British and American soldiers at Reisa. We have sent trucks up to Reisa to collect these people on more than one occasion. There are no arrangements to be made, no organization necessary. Our people are there. Our trucks are ready. Our point is that there are some places which can commence operations now, at once. We can do it tomorrow morning at 0900 or earlier. We can send our trucks to Reisa to collect these people and it is not necessary to wait until 1200 hours on the 23rd of May."

But the Allies would have to wait because the prisoners they wanted to pick up were the American and British hostages being brought south from Stalag 4B by the Soviets to a point directly east of the negotiations. They were to be prominently displayed as hostages until an agreement was reached.

The negotiators argued all night. The meeting, which had convened at 9:45 a.m., ended the following morning at 4:45, when Barker and Golubev again took up the "all without exception" controversy.

Barker first advised Golubev that he "had instructions from General Eisenhower that the document which should be prepared here is to be a plan and not an agreement. That the agreement has already been made by our governments, and that it is the function now of the commander in the field to draw up a plan to put the agreement into effect."

The stolid Soviet general agreed to call it a plan, but went right back to the main disagreement.

"The first paragraph," Golubev began, " 'all without exception as prisoners of war, citizens, of the U.S.S.R. liberated by the Allied troops and all the people of the Allies without exception liberated by the Red Army should be handed through the line of troops to the corresponding military command.' This is the first paragraph. This article defines who are to be repatriated."

Barker firmly replied:

> I am not competent to, and have no authority to, accept such a provision, nor is General Eisenhower competent to accept such terminology. As General Golubev may know, there has been a great deal of correspondence between the governments on the subject of who is subject to repatriation. This subject is still under discussion between the governments and I understand that a final agreement has not yet been consummated. Therefore, as General Golubev

will see, if we vote this clause into our plan it may well occur that we will not be in a position to execute it. As General Golubev undoubtedly knows, there are many intricate questions of citizen[ship] involved with certain people. I am quite sure that full agreement will be reached on these questions by our governments before very long. The numbers of people involved are quite small, and by far, the vast majority of the people in question are liberated persons and have clear-cut status and it is my view that we should avoid this issue and go ahead with repatriation of these large numbers without waiting for the agreement [of the governments].

Twice in one statement, Barker made reference to an ongoing negotiation at the governmental level. A State Department political director had earlier assured the department that Barker had been properly briefed on the limited negotiating authority necessitated by those parallel negotiations: "the SHAEF delegation . . . was not authorized to touch on matters being dealt with on a governmental level."

Back at the negotiating table, Barker's view prevailed and the remainder of the bargaining process focused on finalizing the logistics of transferring people across the lines.

Barker and Golubev signed the plan on May 22, and it went into effect 24 hours later. Shortly after the military negotiators signed the Halle Agreement, the government-level negotiations resulted in the second, secret understanding.[9]

Section Four of this secret agreement "outlined the construction of the phrase 'Soviet citizens' as used in the U.S.-Soviet reciprocal agreement . . . [and] requires the following action by the U.S. [and Britain]:

a. The return to the Soviet Union of all Soviet military personnel held as prisoners of war by the Germans and liberated while in prisoner of war status from German prisoner of war camps. b. The return to the Soviet Union of all liberated civilians . . . who are Soviet citizens. The return to the Soviet Union of Soviet citizens captured in German uniform other than those who demand that they be retained as German prisoners of war, and thus come under the Geneva Convention.[10]

The secret governmental "agreement" and the military "plan" from Halle went together to form the outlines of the hostage deal. They defined how the American and Allied POWs would be returned and which citizens the Soviets would get back in return.

Forced Repatriation

Within 48 hours after the Halle plan and the secret government-level agreement were finally signed, British troops in Austria were ordered to use deception and deadly force in order to return 50,000 Cossacks to Soviet control. More than 100 were murdered in the process to demonstrate the British government's "good faith" in prisoner exchanges.

For months after, American and British troops would assist the NKVD in hunting down and forcibly repatriating all Soviet citizens not secretly saved by the Western recruitment of anti-communist Russians.

In his final report to Eisenhower, Barker observed that

there is every indication that the Russians intend to make a big show of repatriation of our men, although I am of the opinion that we may find a reluctance to return them all, for an appreciable time

to come, since those men constitute a valuable bargaining point.[11]

On May 24, Golubev gave a SHAEF officer written
permission to inspect the five southern-most of the seven
POW camps where the Soviets had said that all POWs had
been moved: Reisa, Torgeau, Dessaw, Magdeburg, Par-
chim, Crivitz and Wismar.[12]

When the officer "set upon his journey he was accompanied by a Russia Major, who stated he had the necessary
orders in his pocket. After visiting the first and nearest
camp" at Reisa, the officer indicated that he was ready to
go on to the next camp. At that point, the Soviet officer
"produced an order from Golubev which restricted our
officer's visit to this one camp only. No amount of per-
suasion would prevail upon them to extend the visit, in
spite of the promise of General Golubev."[13]

Reisa was the only camp SHAEF personnel ever inspected after the agreement was signed, and it was the
only camp from which American or British POWs were
returned after May 22. It was also where more than 10,000
American and British POWs from Stalag 4B had been
moved to be conspicuously displayed as hostages. By May
17, 6,000 remained, but only 3,000 were ever accounted for
in the returned POW ledgers at SHAEF.

No Americans would be allowed to leave Reisa until
May 25, two days after the Halle Agreement went into
effect. Then, a ceremony was performed, with the POWs
lined up in a field watched over by large pictures of
Roosevelt and Stalin.

4B alumnus Ted Perkins will never forget that day.
"American buses arrived with loads of Russian POWs and
Eastern bloc POWs. They were immediately formed up
and marched off. You could tell by looking in their faces
there was agony in coming back."[14]

The American and British POWs waiting in the field
watched as the Russian POWs were marched off to a

nearby rock quarry. Soon the NKVD machine guns "played a song for about ten minutes."[15]

When the American and British ranks stirred with anger at the mass murder they heard echoing from the quarry, the U.S. officer in charge warned them to: "Keep your heads down, your mouth shut and get on the truck."

There are no firsthand stories from Americans then held at most other camps discussed during the Halle negotiations. Of the 25,000 American POWs still under Soviet control during the talks, only 4,165 would return. The fate of the rest would soon be buried under an avalanche of false U.S. documents and disinformation.

Chapter 7

Austria and the Bitter Fruits of Halle

"To hand them [the Cossacks] over is condemning them to slavery, torture, and probably death. To refuse is deeply to offend the Russians, and incidentally break the Yalta agreement. We have decided to hand them over."
—Harold Macmillan, British resident minister to Field Marshal Harold Alexander's headquarters, May 13, 1945

As the war in Europe ended, the POW-hostage crisis spread to yet one more arena—Austria. And perhaps nowhere was the crisis more bitterly resolved.

In order to save a Ukrainian division filled with Nazis, needed by Allied intelligence for use in the coming Cold War, the British and Americans condemned innocent women and children, along with their own POWs, to Siberia.

In May 1945, General Eisenhower was in command in Germany, while the commander in Austria and Italy was British Field Marshal Harold Alexander. Though the U.S. and British for the most part acted concomitantly on all forced repatriation and hostage questions after Roosevelt died, their approach to the forced repatriation-hostage crisis was quite different. Eisenhower accepted governmental orders and carried them out to the best of his ability. Alexander, on the other hand, refused to become involved in forcible repatriation, forcing the British government to bypass him by using the British resident minister to Alexander's headquarters, Harold Macmillan, to convey government orders to the field commands.

Return of the Cossacks

The dispute centered on the Cossacks, a proud race of horsemen who had been fighting the Russian central government on and off since the czars. They hated the Soviet communists and quickly joined the German army when it reached the Kuban region, north of the Caucasus. As the war dragged on, the Cossacks, their families in tow, slogged along with the German retreat. After Germany surrendered, the Cossacks settled into an Austrian valley between Lienz and Oberdrauburg, on the river Drau.

On May 10, 1945, V. I. Tolbukhin, commander of the Third Ukrainian Army, headquartered in Austria, demanded that all Cossacks be returned to Soviet control,[1] and gave the British a list of those Cossack officers the Soviets were particularly anxious to have returned.[2]

Many of the officers on the Soviet list were exempt from repatriation under the Yalta Agreement. These men were not Soviet citizens, and some had lived abroad in places like Yugoslavia for decades. But they would still be forcibly turned over to the Soviets less than three weeks later.

On May 13, one day after the U.S. turned General Vlasov over to the Soviets, Harold Macmillan flew to Klagenfurt,

Austria, to meet with British Lieutenant General Charles Keightly, who commanded V Corps and had received the demand from Tolbukhin.

Macmillan advised Keightly to follow the American example and turn the Cossacks over to the Soviets in exchange for American and British POWs being held by the Red Army in Austria.[3] Macmillan's diary for May 13 reads: "To hand them [the Cossacks] over is condemning them to slavery, torture, and probably death. To refuse is deeply to offend the Russians, and incidentally break the Yalta agreement. We have decided to hand them over."[4]

Macmillan, representing Churchill's government, revealed in these lines the difficult and perhaps agonizing decision made at top levels of British government. He knew on May 13, when he penned those words, what was in store for the Cossacks if they were forced to return.

His statement that "we have decided to hand them over," written three days before the start of the Halle negotiations, indicates that the British diplomats assigned to handle the secret government-to-government side of the negotiations had been given authority to bargain away the Cossacks. The only question was whether the British would bow to the Soviets' May 10 demand that Cossack officers not covered by the Yalta Agreement be delivered as well.

On May 14, the Eighth Army sent the following suggestion to the Fifteenth Army Group: "Consider negotiations should be opened with Marshal Tolbukhin for the return of 28,000 [sic] plus Cossacks to Russian lines. This policy advocated by Macmillan when here...."[5]

The Eighth Army received a timely response and a day later advised V Corps that

> All Russians should be handed over to Soviet forces at agreed point of contact established by you under local agreement with Marshal Tolbukhin's HQ. Steps should be taken to ensure that Allied PW held

in Russian areas are transferred to us in exchange at same time.[6]

Sent one day prior to the start of negotiations at Halle, the British had already decided who was to be sacrificed to protect the Ukranian and Byelorussian forces needed for operations against the Soviet Union.

By May 16, the day the Halle negotiations began, Stalin had ordered all POW exchanges across the lines halted until a formal agreement was signed, which prompted the British to put the repatriation order on hold. The Cossacks were temporarily spared.

Two days later, Alexander wrote to Eisenhower:

> My earnest appeal to you is to come to my assistance as regards surrendered German armed forces including 87 Cossacks. I request urgently your agreement that these surrendered forces other than Austrians, Hungarians and arrestable categories be transferred to your area soonest at a point agreeable to you in status of surrendered personnel. The only alternative is that as a matter of operational and administrative necessity I shall be compelled to disband them, which would produce confusion in contiguous German territory under your command.[7]

Alexander was taking preemptive action by trying to pass the problem to the Americans and advising Eisenhower that if that didn't happen, he would not force the Cossacks to return.

The message was repeated to the Adjutant General War Department (AGWAR), the Combined Chiefs of Staff (CCS), the British Chiefs of Staff, the Fifteen Army Group Main and the Eighth Army. So the entire command structure now knew Alexander was not going to follow orders blindly. No one up or down the chain of command could doubt where Alexander stood on the question of forced repatriation. If the Cossacks were not moved away from the Soviet forces in Austria demanding their return, Alexander would disband the anti-communists to scatter at will throughout Europe.

The day before the Halle Agreement was signed, Alexander received a message. It came from the American Twelfth Army Group, signed Omar Bradley:

> Still at large in lower Austria are surrendered forces comprising approximately 105,000 Germans NOT yet totally disarmed and 45,000 Cossacks who are fully armed and may NOT submit to being disarmed until after evacuation. The latter are accompanied by an estimated additional 11,000 camp followers (women, children, old men) *who until segregated and disposed as DPs, will be given same treatment as forces they accompany* [authors' emphasis]. To assist AFHQ forces these groups will be accepted by 12th Army Group units which will be responsible for any necessary disarmament and turned over to control of Seventh Army which will designate an assembly area in its name for their reception."[8]

Circumventing the Geneva Convention

This seeming capitulation to Alexander's demands actually carried a death sentence for an estimated 11,000 women, children and old men. They were now to carry the same classification as the Cossack warriors—Surrendered Enemy Personnel (SEP), thus losing their rights under the Geneva Convention.

On the day the Halle Agreement was signed, Alexander ordered the Eighth Army, Fifteenth Army Group, and V Corps to evacuate all Soviet citizens to the Twelfth Army Group except those who "can be handed over to Russians without use of force."[9]

On the same day, Harold Macmillan returned from consultations with Churchill in London. He met with V Corps, which would have the responsibility for repatriating the Cossacks, and countermanded Alexander's orders to move the Cossacks out of Austria.

The secret government-to-government agreement, signed May 22-24, required the "return to the Soviet Union of Soviet citizens captured in German uniform other than those who demand that they be retained as German prisoners of war, and thus come under the Geneva Convention." Because the Cossacks had been declared SEPs, not POWs, they would not be given the opportunity to claim Geneva Convention safeguards as German prisoners of war.

All Allied officers who came into contact with the Cossacks (and other Soviet citizens who were to be sacrificed by being forced back to certain death or prison) were given written orders: "Under no circumstances will those captured serving in enemy forces be referred to as prisoners of war."[10] Only Soviet citizens valuable to the Cold War effort would be given the protection of POW status.

While the intent of the Yalta Agreement was "to repatriate to USSR all proved Soviet citizens irrespective of their wishes,"[11] the requirement of forcible repatriation had not been given to British forces in the field in Austria, at least not in a form considered a direct order.

So questions remained after Macmillan departed V Corps on the 22nd of May, and an inquiry was made to the Eighth Army:

> As a result of verbal directive from Macmillan to Corps command at recent meeting we have undertaken to return all Soviet Nationals in Corps area to Soviet Forces. Macmillan mentioned no proviso about the use of force and we have issued instructions that force may be used if absolutely necessary. Consider it quite impossible to guarantee to return

Cossacks and so in honour our verbal agreement with Soviet forces unless we are allowed free hand in this matter. Cossacks will view any move with suspicion as to destination. Consider therefore may be necessary use force to move Cossacks all from present area. . . . Request you confirm our freedom of action on this.[12]

That problem was resolved when the Eighth Army sent to V Corps the following "top secret" message: "Ruling now received 15th Army Group. All Soviet citizens including arrestable categories will be treated as surrendered personnel [SEP] and will therefore be handed over to Russians . . . Please take action accordingly.[13]

On May 23, the day the Halle Agreement went into effect, General Reinhart, Third U.S. Army, met with General Derevenko, Russian First Guards Army, in an attempt to implement the plan by trading the POWs in Austria.

Derevenko told Reinhart that the U.S., British and Commonwealth POWs in the Russian zone were held at Wiener Neustadt, approximately 75 miles northeast of Graz, deep inside Soviet territory.[14]

Wiener Neustadt is near Baden bei Wien, where "the center of the [Soviet] counterintelligence groups on the southwestern front" was located in May 1945. "Every villa in this once expensive and popular spa was now a prison. The cellars were full of prisoners brought here from all over, including even Czechoslovakia and Hungary.[15] (Germany had maintained a POW camp for British and Commonwealth POWs at that location, but all reference to his camp has been removed from maps and documents at the National Archives.[16])

Reinhart asked Derevenko for a count of U.S. and British POWs. He was told the number was not immediately available but would be provided.[17] The exact number of

American and British POWs held by Tolbukhin would be provided within 72 hours.

After orders were given on May 25 to forcibly repatriate the Cossacks, Macmillan departed once again for Britain. Churchill's representative certainly wanted to be as far away from the scene of the forced repatriation as possible. It would be very difficult later to place the blame on an overzealous military if Macmillan had been spotted at the scene.

General Alexander received the POW count promised by the Soviets and on May 26 went public with the POW-hostage-forced repatriation secret. Heretofore it appeared to have been handled on a back channel or oral basis. Alexander sent telegram FX-82606, dated May 26, 1945, to government representatives from each country that had POWs at risk, the U.S. Mission and Embassy, Canadian Embassy, Australian and New Zealand legations. The telegram stated:

> 1. Agreement with Russians at Graz only applies to handing over of Soviet citizens in British zone Austria. NO repeat NO reciprocal guarantee in respect of British POWs obtained apart from half hearted promise which so far has not been honoured. Evacuation to Odessa still continuing from this area. 2. Premature to plan on overland exchange on a local contact basis till Moscow issue directive to Graz commander. 3. Consider essential Moscow be asked to announce agreement to local overland exchange, as there are 15,597 U.S.A. account, 8,462 British account awaiting repatriation in this theatre.[18]

This telegram was designed to correct a War Department misunderstanding that Alexander had already reached an agreement with Tolbukhin to return American and British POWs under Soviet control.[19] The point of

FX-82606 was to tell the War Office it was in error, the Soviets were perfectly willing to accept their prisoners in the British zone, but not willing to transfer the 15,597 American and 8,462 British POWs to Western control. The message also told the War Office it was futile to attempt a reciprocal exchange until the British Military Mission to Moscow arranged to have the Soviets order Tolbukhin to make the trade.

Alexander, who was unalterably opposed to the forced repatriation order issued to his forces the day before, had now for the second time in May committed what would normally be considered gross insubordination. Louise Buchanan, "who in 1945 stayed with neighbours and friends of the Alexanders of Northern Ireland," recalled that "the return of . . . the Cossacks was mentioned and I remember being puzzled by hearing that 'Alex's' protests were absolutely ignored and how sick and furious it made him."[20]

The last week of May, the British began the bloody process of repatriating the Cossacks, and orders came down the line that "any attempt whatsoever at resistance will be dealt with firmly by shooting to kill,"[21] and those orders were followed. Hundreds of the Cossacks and their families and followers were murdered or committed suicide.

The effort was particularly brutal and bloody because the British government was trying to impress upon the Soviets that they could be trusted to comply with the Yalta and Halle agreements and return "all" Soviet citizens, when they actually had no such intention. Churchill wanted to maximize the political benefits of forcing back Soviet POWs, but not at the expense of turning over certain Russian-staffed Nazi formations most wanted by Stalin.

Saving the Ukrainian Waffen SS

The Ukrainian Waffen SS Division "Galizien" was en-
camped in the British zone of Austria. Its members were
considered essential to the anti-communist program. As
reported in "Blowback," the story of the U.S. effort to use
Nazis in the Cold War, the CIA "systematically sought out
Ukrainian SS and militia veterans because they were
thought to be well suited for rejoining their comrades still
holed up in the Carpathian mountains."

So the "Galizien" Division was secretly moved to Italy
on the day the Halle Agreement was signed. Members of
this division had been initially recruited by the Germans
in September 1943 and saw considerable action on the
Russian front. They were withdrawn from the front in July
1944 because of heavy casualties. As the Germans
withdrew from the Ukraine, they no longer needed their
Ukrainian police regiments, which were staffed with indigenous personnel. Eventually, some of these police regiments were integrated into the Ukrainian SS "Galizien"
Division. Many of the police units had "assisted the SS in
the extermination of Jews and Poles." Five regiments of
the Ukrainian police "were incorporated into the SS-
Division in the summer and fall of 1944 after the
withdrawal of the Nazis from Poland." It would have
seemed that these 9,000 men were certainly doomed for
forced repatriation to the U.S.S.R., since all of them were
Nazi SS troops and many were war criminals.

That was not to be the case, however. Instead of another
bloody, forced repatriation, they were moved en masse to
Italy and protected from the Soviet repatriation efforts. By
1947, 8,000 were quietly allowed to enter Canada. Many
would be recruited by British and American intelligence
and participate in the Cold War efforts to destabilize
Stalin.

By the end of June 1945, the bulk of the Cossacks had
been returned, but only 2,000 POWs, all British, were

received in exchange for the 50,000 Cossacks. There were still 5,000 to 6,000 British POWs waiting to be repatriated through Graz, Austria, as of June 7, 1945,[22] but only 927 British or Commonwealth POWs were repatriated from the entire European theater after that date.[23]

At least 4,000 British and Commonwealth POWs held by the Soviets at Wiener Neustadt were never returned. Except for 47 stragglers, none of the 15,597 Americans POWs held by the Soviets in Austria was repatriated. Nothing more was known about them until February 1946, when Hungarian Ben Kovacs saw a trainload of them headed for the Soviet border.

Chapter 8

Historical Myth

"There can be no greater myth than to suppose that historical myths cannot be created by design."

–George F. Kennan,
senior State Department Soviet expert, 1960

When the POW ledger from the European theater in World War II is finally reconciled, documents authorized by Generals Eisenhower and Marshall, two of the most prominent heroes molded from the war, prove that of the 25,000 Americans that Joseph Stalin held captive during the Halle negotiations, only 4,165 came home.[1] And, as another of General Barker's pervasive memoranda showed, the Germans were holding 199,592 British and Commonwealth POWs as of March 15, 1945.[2] Only 168,746 returned.[3]

American and British Cold Warriors had gambled and lost. They thought that a vigorous and bloody forcible repatriation would convince Stalin that they intended to honestly, if not honorably, follow the Yalta Agreement.

But Stalin knew the real intentions of the U.S. and Britain. He maneuvered them into committing atrocities against the expendable anti-communists, rewarding the Cold Warriors with some of his POW hostages.

Yet Stalin kept a reserve of American and British prisoners to trade for the all-important Ukrainian anti-communists. But in this final show-down, the West decided that keeping the anti-communist Soviets for the Cold War was more important than rescuing Western POWs still under Red Army control.

This secret and shameful decision, which marked the beginning of classified anti-Soviet intelligence programs that would continue for decades, had to be concealed, the participants well knew.

After the Halle exchange ended, the United States and Britain knew documents must be manufactured to downgrade the numbers. They had to provide a plausible explanation that would stand the test of time and permanently bury the 23,500 Americans and 31,000 British non-returnees.

So the American and British governments created documents at the end of World War II to reflect the official government position that:

☐ The Yalta Agreement on repatriation was almost an afterthought, negotiated on a military-to-military basis, which included verbiage that experienced diplomats would never have agreed to, thereby placing those governments in a precarious position with Stalin at the end of the war.
☐ Government officials did not know Soviet citizens would not want to return and would even violently oppose repatriation.
☐ There was no forced repatriation (later changed to limited forced repatriation carried out on an unauthorized basis by overzealous military personnel who misinterpreted orders).

☐   No hostages were ever held by Stalin.
☐   All POWs returned.

SHAEF outgoing message FWD-23059, from Eisenhower to AGWAR, June 1, 1945, was the cornerstone of the
American attempt to create a fictional version of history
that would permanently cover up the abandoned POWs
along with America's foreign policy mistakes. It attempted to explain away the problems that surfaced in
telegram S-88613, dispatched May 19, 1945, when General
Marshall demanded to know what action was being taken
to gain the release of 25,000 American POWs still being
held by the U.S.S.R. on the Western front weeks after the
Allies linked up along the Elbe River.

The U.S. Army secretary-general staff (SGS) was given
the responsibility for concocting an explanation that
would stand the test of time. The "Secret Urgent" work
sheet suggested the following narrative for FWD-23059:

> 1. Due to local transfers of US PW from Russian area
> to US control immediately prior to and during dis-
> cussions with Russians which ended 22 May, it is
> now estimated that only approximately 15,000 US
> PW were held by the Russians as of 21 May, and not
> 25,000 as quoted in our cable G 88613. 2. Of these
> 15,000 there have been transferred to US control
> 12,400 since 21 May. 3. It is estimated that not more
> than 2-3000 US PWs still remain in Russian hands.
> These no doubt are scattered in small groups as no
> information is available of any large concentrations
> of POWs in any one camp.[4]

Because only 1,500 American POWs were returned
under authorized local exchanges during the time frame
referenced in point one, the reduction from 25,000 to
15,000 could not be forthrightly explained. Instead, the
nebulous phrase "several thousands were in transit or

already under U.S. control and not yet reported on nominal rolls on 19 May,"[5] was substituted. Also false, but easier to defend and much harder to disprove.

In fact, the last POWs who returned before the Halle negotiations began were from Stalag Luft 1. U.S. Army Air Corps B-17s evacuated the men between May 12 and May 14. The POWs carried rosters listing the names of every man in camp since May 2 when the Soviets overran it. Their numbers began appearing on SHAEF data sheets within 48 hours and were fully recorded by the start of the Halle negotiations on May 16. That was a full three days before Eisenhower told Marshall that Stalin had imprisoned 25,000 Americans. As of the May 21 date listed in point one, all POWs that had been or were being transferred to American control were entered in the books.

SGS attempted to explain away an additional 7,200 POWs in point two, initially claiming that 12,400 had returned under the Halle Agreement (which went into effect on May 23, not May 21 as claimed). But only 4,165 actually returned under the Halle Agreement.

Proposed point three provides the irrefutable connection between the SGS work sheet and Eisenhower's June 1, 1945, fabrication (the italicized portion is the same in the proposed and final versions): "*It is* now *estimated that* only small numbers of U.S. prisoners of war *still remain in Russian hands. These no doubt are scattered* singly and *in small groups as no information is available of any large* numbers in specific camps. They are being received now in small driblets and being reported as received."

This false work sheet became the official statement of fact, a document that has concealed the truth until this book.

A second problem had to be faced. On May 30, a new document surfaced. Theater Provost Marshal Major General Milton A. Reckord released a memo estimating that 10,000 to 15,000 additional Americans would be released from Russian control and would need to be added to the shipping requirements for POWs being returned to the United States.[6] Yet another report surfaced on May 30 with the information that Eisenhower was attempting to bury. Lieutenant Colonel K.H. Clark signed a document entitled "Allied Prisoners of War," which once again revealed that 20,000 Americans remained under Soviet control.

Those numbers couldn't be the last word because in reality almost all the prisoners were to be home by now, and the Soviets released few Americans after May 28. The solution was to add 15,000 to the cumulative total of recovered prisoners of war during the month of June, even though only 147 stragglers filtered in after May 28.

Once the statistics were altered with document FWD-23059, it was then necessary to alter the historical records to reflect the return of an additional 15,000 POWs. The official Pentagon document on the repatriation, called the RAMPs report (for "Return of Allied Military Personnel), does, in fact, reflect this myth, stating that more than 92,000 Army and Army Air Force personnel were liberated and returned to American control from the European and Mediterranean theaters. The actual number of returnees is between 78,000-85,000.

The British began to fudge their numbers well before the end of the war, after their minister for POW affairs gave a speech in February 1945 alleging that 15,000 British and Commonwealth POWs had been liberated by the Red Army in Poland. But only 4,300 were returned. On April 18, 1945, the British Foreign Office sent telegram 1923 to the British Embassy in Moscow to cover the minister's indiscretion:

> For your information the War Office estimates that the three military districts over-run by the Russians held 68,537 men. We have now learned from the International Red Cross Committee that 64,520 British prisoners of war were evacuated from the

eastern zone by the Germans. As the Russians have recovered 3,399 there remains a balance of only 700 unaccounted for. Even allowing for a considerable margin of error it therefore looks as if the size of the problem has been over-estimated.[7]

Actually, six military districts had been completely or substantially overrun, not three. The Germans could provide the number of POWs they intended to evacuate, but had absolutely no ability to provide a count of those who remained under their control amid the confusion of the westward retreat from Soviet forces. Camps were broken down into smaller marching groups that frequently lost touch with the main body. POWs dropped out daily from injury, sickness or attempts to escape, and roll call was seldom if ever taken after leaving camp. Four days after the first bogus report was sent, British authorities issued message 87814 to SHAEF and AFHQ, which had an accurate appraisal of the situation in Poland:

"Owing [to] large scale transfers of PW by [the] Germans from the battle zones [it is] impossible [to] make any reliable estimate [of the] numbers of British [and] Commonwealth PW likely to fall into Russian hands."[8]

The first message, 1923, has been sitting in the British archives for many years misleading researchers. The second message was hidden from the public until August 1990 when it was unearthed by the authors under the Freedom of Information Act from the American National Archives.

As the POW-hostage crisis in Germany spread to AFHQ in Austria, the Mediterranean area commander, Field Marshal Harold Alexander, was faced with a dilemma: Go-along-and-get-along with government orders to brutally repatriate Cossack men, women and children, in effect delivering them to their death, or refuse to follow orders.

He refused to follow orders, and on May 26, 1945, Alexander went public with the anti-communist Russians-for-POWs secret, forcing the American and British governments to create yet another set of cover-up documents. That day Alexander sent his infamous telegram that revealed that the Soviets were holding 15,597 American and 8,462 British POWs and weren't giving them back.

Alexander, the only senior ranking officer who attempted to thwart the government-ordered forced repatriation, caused a political crisis demanding the very best in damage control. On June 1, the same day Eisenhower's cover-up was released, the myth-making began in Britain, with the assertion that FX-82606 actually referred to 8,462 Russians held by the British forces in the AFHQ zone of operations and 15,597 Russians held by the Americans.

That was a lie. Actually, British intelligence documents show that 72,000 Russians were in Austria under British control awaiting repatriation, not 8,462. And, the United States held 35,000 Russians, not 15,597.[9]

The British secretary of state for war, Sir James Grigg, four days after FX-82606 was dispatched, confirmed that the 8,462 were British when he told Parliament that "About 8,500 [British and Commonwealth POWs] are in the part of Austria controlled by the Red Army. . . . "[10]

On June 11, 1945, SHAEF's G-1 PWX Branch admitted in a four-page memo entitled "Repatriation of British, U.S., and Other United Nations Prisoners of War as of 7 June 1945" that 4,000 to 6,000 British and Commonwealth POWs were still awaiting repatriation through Graz, Austria. The memo also revealed that 4,400 British and Commonwealth POWs had been returned through Graz, so at least 8,400 British POWs had been held in Austria by the Red Army, just as Alexander's May 26 message said. The numbers prove that Alexander was actually talking about American and British POWs being held hostage by Tolbuhkin and not Russians waiting to be repatriated.

Although 199,592 British and Commonwealth POWs were "registered" as prisoners of war of the Germans as of February 1945, the British initially wrote off 25,000, claiming that only 175,000 were expected to return by the end of the Halle negotiations. But even this number was optimistic; only 168,746 returned home. Thirty-thousand eight-hundred and forty-six British and Commonwealth POWs "liberated" by the Red Army, known by name, rank and serial number, were never returned.

Chapter 9

World War II GIs in the Gulag

"Assure your constituents that the Department of State has no information indicating that there are American soldiers from World War II being held in Soviet labor camps."
—July 1950 letter from Thruston B. Morton,
Assistant Secretary of State
to Senator John W. Bricker of Ohio

"This [POW] information . . . could be expected to cause serious damage to the national security."
—May 1992 Army letter
refusing to release 1946 records on
Americans imprisoned in the Soviet Union

One cold snowy evening in early February 1946, eighteen-year-old Ben Kovacs was crossing back to Hungary after a smuggling trip into Czechoslovakia.

He and his friends were passing the railroad station at Novo Mesto, a town on the Czech side of the border, when a train bound for the Soviet Union approached. As it slowed to a stop, gun-toting Russian soldiers jumped off and established a cordon around the train.

Remembering what the Soviets had done to civilians in Hungary, Kovacs and his friends hid, laying flat on the ground in the snow a few meters from the train, which included 40 to 50 boxcars completely enclosed except for small windows covered with barbed wire.

"We could see that there were soldiers in the cars," Kovacs remembered, "what we thought were German and Hungarian prisoners. But my friend told me, "They're not German, they're not Hungarian.' We knew that much. They were speaking English."

Kovacs doesn't know if the prisoners were American or British, but "there was only one way [for the train] to go." This was the rail line from Austria, where thousands of American, British and Commonwealth POWs were held hostage in May 1945, to the Soviet Union.

By June 1945, the Pentagon had created paperwork to cover the loss of more than 20,000 Americans during World War II. Information on American POWs from World War II continues to be highly sensitive and often secret. Thousands of pages sought by the authors have been classified or "misplaced" by the U.S. government. But the fraction of reports that has leaked out draws a chilling portrait of Americans condemned to slavery in the gulag.

As early as May 1945, three U.S. paratrooper veterans of D-Day were imprisoned in a Soviet camp near Dresden. Corp. Bucki Okhane, Private Billy Hafers and Private First Class Olen Taylor were reported by a German returnee named Friedrich Grzybeck. The German even brought U.S. military intelligence a signed picture of Taylor in U.S. uniform. The men were later believed to have been shipped "east" on railroad cars.[1]

An American GI named Victor Boehm, whose picture was also smuggled out, had been taken from a German POW camp and shipped to Siberia in July 1945, according to another German. Boehm was reported working at a tank factory with 200 Americans and about 900 Allied POWs, mostly French and English.[2]

And in the summer of 1945, an Italian diplomat, Primo Levi, saw "negroes in American uniform" held by the Soviets in a POW camp in Byelorussia.[3]

On December 10, 1945, message S-34414 was sent by U.S. forces in Europe to the American Embassy in Moscow:

> Information received here that as of 30 August 1945 the Russians were holding prisoner approximately 45 American enlisted men and two officers, one captain and one lieutenant, at Rada near Tambov in the Stalingrad area. Prisoners were reported in barbed wire under guard.

Eight days later, an OSS document entitled "U.S.S.R. POW and Internee Camp Near Tambov" was written. In it was another story of Americans, along with French, British, Dutch and German prisoners, being held captive near Tambov:

> 1. Informant, a Pole forced to serve in the German Army was taken prisoner by the Russians in 1944. . . . At the end of 1945—April, he escaped and tried to get to Europe. He was, however, arrested by the NKVD after he had got beyond Moscow, and placed in the P.O.W. and Internee Camp in TAMBOV . . . . The prisoners numbered, in informant's estimation, well over 20,000; they were both military and civilian, most likely over-run by the Russians during the offensive.[4] When informant left the camp there were . . . Englishmen and several score Americans. . . . When he was leaving these Englishmen and

Americans asked him urgently to notify the Allied authorities of their plight.

The Pole notified the American government, but a thorough search of State Department files reveals no effort to obtain the release of these men. The presence of U.S. POWs in that camp was confirmed by the Russian government in June 1992.

Keeping Quiet

Yet even in 1945, the Pentagon knew full well that the reports were true, according to Superior Court Judge Carl Heinmiller of Haynes, Alaska, who was transferred in 1945 from a combat zone in the Pacific to the Army's Special Information Project at the Pentagon. One day he came across documents reporting specific numbers of Americans abandoned behind the Iron Curtain after the war was over. The records referred to POW camps in northeast Germany that had been overrun by the Red Army at the end of the war.

"I talked to a couple of other officers ... and asked, 'What does this mean?' "

"These people had gone somewhere in Russia," he was told.

"I asked whether we are making any effort to get them back." The State Department was handling the problem, Heinmiller was informed. He was also directed to keep quiet about American POWs in the Soviet Union.

"I got slapped on the wrist for even talking about it" with another officer, a colonel who later landed on General Douglas MacArthur's staff in Korea. "He was a really easy going kind of guy, but we were talking about it, and he said, 'There are some things you better not talk about idly or otherwise.' "[5]

The presence of American POWs in the Soviet Union was kept secret for compelling reasons. Telling the truth would have required the Pentagon to reveal the World War II hostage crisis and the retention of anti-communist Soviets.

The military might even have had to discuss such remarkable cases as that of General Reinhard Gehlen, Hitler's top military intelligence expert on the Soviet Union.

After he defected to U.S. forces in May 1945, Gehlen and many of his subordinates were hidden by the Pentagon, which even removed their names from lists of POWs, thereby violating the Yalta pledge to give the Russians such German officers involved in "eastern area activities."[6]

Gehlen's organization, with agents throughout Russia, soon became a leading U.S. intelligence source on the U.S.S.R. Obviously, Gehlen's agency would have been in a prime position to gather proof of U.S. POWs in the Soviet Union but revealing that intelligence would have exposed the treachery that allowed Gehlen and his men to stay in the West.

The result: America's top human intelligence network targeted against the Soviet Union had a strong vested interest in covering up the presence of U.S. prisoners in Russia.

The Truth Leaks Out

Yet the truth continued to escape. On December 1, 1946, the *Wisconsin State Journal*'s page one lead story was entitled "Iron Curtain Shrouds Lee's Fate, Parents Believe Russians Hold Him With 20,000 Other Yanks."

Frank Lee, the son of Wisconsin residents Mr. and Mrs. C.E. Lee, was shot down over Austria shortly before the war ended. The Lees and other families whose sons were on the same plane began receiving information about them from Europe.

In Scarsdale, New York, James Thomas and his wife "began to get mysterious messages from abroad saying that their son, pilot of the B-24, was among a group of prisoners in Austria." In December 1945, the Thomas family received "a letter from their sources abroad saying their son had been moved from a Linz, Austria, hospital on April 25, 1945, further north in Austria," to an area overrun by the Red Army a few days later. A "friend connected with the Federal Bureau of Investigation later claimed that records in Munich bore this out."

The newspaper also located a former POW who confirmed part of the story. Tom Tierney had been liberated and held hostage by the Russians but managed to escape. He recalled that "those who tried to escape and were caught or involved in some offense against Russia were shipped to other camps farther inside Russia.

Yet the article failed to prompt any action by the U.S. government. And by 1948, the government had apparently given up trying to recover its missing servicemen from World War II.

In a September 28, 1948, letter to the director of Army intelligence, who was apparently pushing for action, Moscow Embassy attaché Major John W. O'Daniel discussed the "internment of 20 American officers and enlisted men in an MVD [Soviet secret police] camp at Kaliningrad, East Prussia."

The men couldn't be positively identified, O'Daniel wrote, but "several previous reports have been taken up with the ministry of Foreign Affairs by the Embassy. In each case the reply has been a categorical denial that there are any U.S. prisoners of war in the Soviet Union. Therefore, the Embassy feels that no useful purpose would be served in bringing this matter up again unless complete data is available on the individual being held illegally by Soviet authorities."

The embassy was concerned that English-speaking Europeans might try to pass as Americans in order to get out of Soviet prisons.

But some Soviet prisoners were clearly U.S. servicemen. An American major, still wearing his U.S. Army uniform, was reported in 1949 to be alive in the Vorkuta prison complex, serving a 25-year espionage sentence.

A German source who had been in Vorkuta with the American reported that he'd been "kidnapped by the Russians" shortly after the U.S. and Soviet armies met at the Elbe River. He was described as being 5'9", dark blond hair, blue-gray eyes, slim figure, broad shoulders, mustache and a long last name.

"The Major . . . was constantly questioned by the Russians about German and American industrial installations."[7]

An Austrian returned from the gulag where he had met an American Air Force lieutenant only two months before. The American had been shot down over Germany in 1945. He was "liberated" by Soviet forces from a hospital, then shipped to the Soviet Union. The Soviets sentenced him to 25 years of hard labor. In 1950 he was described as being forty years old, fair, slim build. His parents owned a farm or estate in New York.

Two Japanese returnees, who had been in Karaganda, Camp 99-13, reported that an American GI from World War II was at that camp in 1948. "The repatriate 'heard' that the American was an 'ex-GI' who was captured in Europe near a large river [probably the Elbe] after being lost from his unit during the last war. He had received a 15-year sentence for espionage."[8]

A second American, captured by the Russians "somewhere in Germany," was also reported. "The American was quartered in the same room with the interrogee for three days," and was also sentenced for espionage. Badly treated by other prison inmates "who blamed the United States for their predicament,"[9] he may have been unfortunate enough to be in a prison camp with anti-communist Russians the United States had forcibly repatriated to the Soviet Union at the end of World War II.

In 1950, a "reliable German source" reported seeing about 30 Allied prisoners from World War II, including one or two Americans, at prison Camp 6 near Odessa, U.S.S.R. He identified one of the POWs as Harry Lepselter, 1284 St. John's Place, Brooklyn, 13 New York. A family with the last name of Lepselter did, in fact, live at that address in the 1940s.[10]

A German who returned in December 1953 said that Joe Miller, a "U.S. Air Force Bombardier shot down over Berlin in 1945," had been liberated by Soviet forces and then "transported directly to [the] USSR." The Chicago native was last seen by the returnee working at a coal mine in Karaganda, U.S.S.R., which was a location frequently referenced by returnees who told of Americans from the Korean War that had been shipped to Siberia.[11] The report says Miller was single, and was born in Chicago, Illinois, where his mother, father and sister were living before he was shipped off to the Soviet Union.

According to the report, Miller had been badly beaten by the Soviets, but he refused to renounce his belief in American democracy.

In July 1955, another Austrian returnee reported that William Bizet "was taken prisoner by the Soviets in 1945 in Korea where he was serving with the U.S. Navy or Sentry Patrol." The Austrian believed that Bizet was an officer, probably a lieutenant. Bizet's name at birth was Wasiljevski. His mother married a professor named Bizet, who worked at the University of San Francisco. Professor Bizet adopted him. William was married and had a child. Serving an eight-year sentence, he was last seen in mine pit No. 40, at Vorkuta, in 1952.[12]

Fritz Bauer was a German prisoner of war captured by the U.S.S.R. who returned from the gulag in 1955 and contacted the American consulate in Hamburg, Germany.

Only nine months before, he had met an American, William George Robertson, at International Camp 6062/XIII located at Kiew-Darnizza. Robertson told Bauer that he had been captured by the Germans during World War II. The Russians liberated the POW camp in which he was held and took all of the "liberated" Americans to the U.S.S.R. along with the German POWs. He told Bauer that the German POW camp had been near Dresden, well inside the Soviet zone.

Three camps are located in that area, according to a recently declassified map found in the National Archives Red Cross files dated February 28, 1945: Oflag 4B at Konigstein, Stalag 4A at Hohenstein and a hospital near 4A. A National Archives study says that only four POWs returned from Oflag 4B, and 243 from Stalag 4A. No report has ever surfaced giving the numbers at the camps when the Red Army arrived.

Robertson was reported to be a native of New Orleans, the son of a lawyer. He wore glasses and was talented at drawing. From 1945 to 1949, he was held in a camp in Leningrad; from 1949 to 1950, he worked as a laborer in a coal mine in Stalino; and in 1950 he was transferred to the International Camp in Kiev, government documents show.

In 1962, an American returned from visiting the U.S.S.R. A "source in Erevan [U.S.S.R.] claims to have seen American soldier Gunner Zigerman of Philadelphia and 'many other Americans' in Siberia camp in 1955." These Americans had been "imprisoned in Siberia after World War II."[13]

Also in 1955, returning Austrians stated that they had been a slave labor camp with two Americans who had escaped from a Japanese POW camp to the Soviet Union during World War II. They were arrested and enslaved by the Soviet Union.

Major Wirt Thompson

Perhaps one of those men who had escaped the Japanese was Major Wirt Elizabeth Thompson, an American missing after a World War II plane crash in Asia. In 1954, Dr. Anton Petzold, a German returnee described as "intelligent and cooperative" by U.S. intelligence, told the Army that he had been imprisoned with an American, Air Force Major "William" Thompson.[14]

The American was arrested by the Russians after a forced landing in 1944. He was subsequently sentenced to 25 years imprisonment for espionage. From 1944 to 1948, he had been incarcerated in the Budenskaya (probably Butyrskaya) prison in Moscow, and had then been transferred to Tayshet, Compound 026. (Tayshet has frequently been identified as a location where Americans from World War II and Korea were held in the 1940s and 1950s.)

Thompson had "once mentioned that his home had been in San Antonio, Texas," Petzold told American officials. The report went on to describe Thompson as "about 38, height 1.85 meters [6'], slim build, thin features, fair hair, blue eyes."

Upon checking, the U.S. government learned that the major's full name was Wirt Elizabeth Thompson Jr., born August 8, 1920, in Italy, Texas. He lived at 123 Eleanor Street, San Antonio, and attended high school in Italy, Texas. Thompson enlisted in June 1941 when he was living in North Little Rock, Arkansas, and he had been stationed at Sedalia Army Airfield in Missouri.

He departed Myitkyina, Burma, on December 4, 1944, for a bombing mission over Kunming, China, and went down over enemy territory. According to Major Edward F. Witsell's December 6, 1945, letter to Wirt Thompson's father, his son had gone down on a combat mission, and the wreckage of the aircraft was spotted on a mountain peak east of Myitkyina exactly a year before. "A ground party was immediately sent to investigate," but after "several weeks they returned without having been able to reach the wreck. Another party was then dispatched, and in March still another. Both of these parties were unsuccessful in their attempt to reach the wreckage."

Thompson's sister, Juanita, said the Army told the family that Major Thompson was flying a plane overloaded with airmen who were escaping Japanese forces about to overrun their base camp. It crashed because it was overweight, which is consistent with the forced landing story that Thompson told the German returnee.

The U.S. government admitted internally, but never revealed to the Thompson family, that "there is a strong likelihood that the man in the Soviet Union is Major Wirt Elizabeth Thompson." Secretary of State John Foster Dulles cabled the embassy in Moscow to say that "Major Wirt Thompson may be known to Sov Gov as Major William Thompson, name used by returning POWs," just as Petzold had said.

A message was sent to the Soviet government requesting Thompson's release, but the Soviet response was predictable. In essence, they ignored the request; they could neither reveal information nor release a World War II prisoner because of the inevitable Pandora's box that would open if they did.

So what happened to Wirt Thompson and the other American POWs from World War II? Reports of their survival diminished in the late 1950s, as fewer and fewer foreign prisoners were released from Siberia. But fragments of information continued to arrive in the West.

"The story about dozens of American soldiers interned by the Soviets in Ostrava and later reported as missing was circulating in Czechoslovakia during the Prague Spring in 1968,"[15] wrote Ilya Gerol of the *Ottawa Citizen* of Ontario, Canada.

According to Gerol:

Up to the 1960s there were camps in the Soviet Union where English speaking prisoners were held. It was confirmed by many Soviet authors in their written and oral accounts of the time they spent in these camps. Since there are no English-speaking minorities in the Soviet Union, one would suspect that the prisoners were brought from foreign countries.

The Big Red One

In 1967, John Weatherly, a young British sailor, was released after a short sentence from the Soviet camp at Potma, where he said Americans were then being held.

Ten thousand American and British POWs were still alive as of 1982 in the Soviet Union, according to one Soviet whose story was described to the authors. The source even possessed a picture of a Siberian reunion of the "Big Red One," a famed U.S. infantry division that saw heavy action during World War II.

There can be no doubt that in 1945, with the full knowledge of the American government, U.S. POWs from World War II joined the millions of other prisoners held in the Soviet Union. And they were soon to get more American company as the Cold War heated up.

Chapter 10

Life in the Gulag

"He was missing his motherland terribly. He wanted to return but he didn't know how."
> *—Villager describing "Uncle Neal the American," an unidentified U.S. prisoner exiled outside Moscow from 1953-82*

"There is a law in the [Gulag] Archipelago that those who have been treated the most harshly and who have withstood the most bravely, the most honest, the most courageous, the most unbending, never again come out into the world. . . . A part of your returned POWs told you that they were tortured. This means that those who have remained were tortured even more, but did not yield an inch. These are your best people. These are your first heroes, who—in a solitary combat—have stood the test."
> *—Alexander I. Solzhenitsyn[1]*

When the Soviet guard entered the East Berlin prison cell, Sidney Ray Sparks smashed him over the head with a chamber pot. Overhearing the scuffle, two more guards rushed into the room, tackling Sparks and thwarting his escape attempt. "Then they beat the hell out of me," Sparks remembered. "One caught me over the eye and busted open my eyebrow," giving him a scar he still bears. His escape attempt dashed, the country boy from Georgia found himself in solitary confinement for the first, but not last, time in his fifty-three months behind the Iron Curtain.

Unable to face the prospect of dying in Soviet captivity, Sparks settled on suicide, and with a running start smashed his head against his cell's concrete wall. Before he could make a second attempt at the wall, prison officials bound him hand and foot. There was no cheating Soviet justice. Sidney Ray Sparks would serve his sentence in Siberia.

On December 4, 1951, just days before his nineteenth birthday, U.S. Army Private Sparks made the mistake of his life. Rather than face a court-martial for robbing a taxi driver of $4.95, he escaped the stockade with two other Americans, Charles J. Scott and David Schultz, and made for East Berlin.

Sparks didn't know where he was going. "Hell, I was just running. They were older. I really wasn't that damn smart, didn't finish high school. I didn't know what a damn communist was. If I hadn't escaped, I'd of probably gotten out of it [the original charges]." In the end, Sparks earned not only a punishment more horrible than anything the U.S. Army could devise, but also a dubious place in history.

Thousands of American POWs have entered the Soviet prison system since 1945. To our knowledge, not one has ever escaped. But other American servicemen and civilians—men like Sidney Ray Sparks—did return from the gulag after being imprisoned because of varying combinations of bad luck, stupidity and criminality. Sparks and other Americans who came home brought word of the grim realities of Russian prison life. Here is their description of the fate no doubt endured by many American soldiers of misfortune.

At first in East Germany, things didn't go badly for Sparks. He was a defector who copied in long hand a communist-written statement denouncing capitalism and the United States. He also answered questions from the Russians, who requested a full autobiography and asked about military matters, a subject in which Sparks had little knowledge and even less interest.

Soviet intelligence also demonstrated an intense interest in American slang, something in which Sparks was quite proficient. Sparks was given plenty of time to read and exercise, and on his birthday, a Russian major gave him a bottle of wine along with cheese and crackers. Finally, Walter Ulbricht, East Germany's communist party chief, offered Sparks a chance to go to school and work in East Germany.

He accepted and within a few days had a new suit and home in a hotel for Allied defectors in Bautzen, East Germany. By April 1952, the East Germans had put him to work in a cognac factory. "It was good stuff," he recalled–he often drank it himself. But he just couldn't stay out of trouble. He and another American broke into a railroad boxcar at the factory where he worked. Sparks said he had no intention of burglarizing it, that he was just unloading it, but when he and his American accomplice got in, the guard slammed the door shut. The two deserters nearly suffocated before being rescued by the police. Remarkably, Sparks received only a one-year suspended sentence for the crime, but his good luck had run out. Within ten days, the Soviets arrested him again and hauled him off to prison.

After Sidney Ray's attempted suicide, he faced Soviet justice in the unsmiling form of a three-man military tribunal. Like many others, Sparks was judged by the

Special Conference of the MVD, or OSSO (Osoboye Soveshchaniye). Created in 1934, the tribunals had served as the main instrument for the Soviet purges and later saw heavy duty condemning foreign prisoners to sentences in the gulag.[2] "Almost never were the prisoners of war present at the proceedings, which seem usually to have taken place in Moscow. Judging by statements made by these ex-prisoners of war, the Conference imposed sentences of ten years or more, despite the statutory restriction limiting its authority to sentences of 5 years or less," reported U.S. military intelligence.[3]

Article 58

The main charge used by the Soviets was Article 58, which outlawed crimes against the state, no small category in a society with limitless views of the national interest. It covered everything from praising foreign consumer goods–implicitly understood as slanderous of collectively produced Soviet goods—to planning insurrection. "In all truth, there is no step, thought, action or lack of action under the heavens which could not be punished by the heavy hand of Article 58," wrote Alexander Solzhenitsyn, himself convicted under the statute.[4]

Sparks said he too was convicted for espionage on a trumped up charge supported by the testimony of two other Americans the Soviets had captured in East Berlin. They had never seen nor heard of Sidney Ray before they denounced him, but a trip he took to West Berlin to visit his girlfriend was proof enough that he might be working for American intelligence.

"Ninety percent of the people I met, if they weren't Russian, they were charged with espionage," Sparks remembered. An American officer from an Air Force reconnaissance plane that was shot down by the Russians on June 13, 1952, was held under the same statute. Government documents say the man "was observed in October 1953, in a Soviet hospital north of Magadan . . . at a place called Narionburg. This officer stated that he had been convicted, wrongfully, under Item 6 of Article 58 of the Soviet Penal Code."[5]

Even Americans who had been prisoners of war had no protection from the Soviet penal code. The Soviet Union, while not a signatory to the 1929 Geneva Convention, did sign the 1949 Geneva Convention—with one major exception: "The Union of Soviet Socialist Republics does not consider itself bound by the obligation" of Article 85, declared the Russians and eight of their communist allies. Article 85 guaranteed POWs rights even if convicted by their captors for acts committed prior to their capture. "If the retention of a prisoner should be desired for political, intelligence or economic reasons, the term 'war criminal' need only be expanded and the prisoner would be deprived of his rights under the [Geneva] convention," U.S. officials concluded.[6]

The Soviets made wide and cynical use of the "war criminal" category during and after World War II. Germans had been convicted as "war criminals" for fixing the shoes of German troops—thus allowing them to march into Russia; playing music for troops—thereby inspiring martial spirit and atrocities; and blowing up a bridge—destroying the property of the U.S.S.R. And woe to the GI who happened to be of Russian ethnicity. According to the Soviet prison system, once a Russian, always a Russian.

In 1950, a German watchmaker spent time with a husky American named Frank in the Soviet prison of Vologda. Frank, from Pittsburgh, had been a sergeant working at an Army motor pool in Berlin. The Soviets arrested him on U.S. territory in Berlin, and the soldier was convicted of espionage and sentenced to ten years of labor "for the sole reason that he was born in the USSR from where his parents had emigrated to the US in 1931."[7]

"Based on Soviet examples during World War II . . . it may be assumed that Communist nations will render lip service to the principles of international agreements in regard to prisoners of war but will continue to base their actions in this regard on a policy of maximum exploitation as the time and the situation demand," the U.S. Army concluded in a 1954 study.[8]

Railroading

In more ways than one, the Soviet penal system railroaded its victims. Sparks, like millions before him, rode to his Soviet prison on the "Blue Express" passenger train providing daily service between Berlin and Moscow. Soviet prisoners traveled in the infamous "Stolypin" railroad cars, named after a czarist official and designed especially for inmates. On the first leg of his trip, Sparks's railroad car had twenty-three cages holding sixty-seven men and women. Three prisoners shared one cell little more than a yard square. In the annals of the gulag, that was first-class travel. Prisoners on another trip were packed so tightly that for days one inmate's feet never touched the ground until guards created more room by removing the dead passengers.[9]

For food, Sparks and so many other prisoners had mostly salted herring. The fish produced a powerful thirst, and during some trips the guards would withhold water to torture the inmates. When the water finally came, the prisoners would fight over who drank first. Since there was only one cup, no one wanted to drink after the prisoners with tuberculosis and syphilis.

Sparks learned that stops in prisons along the way offered little relief. In one cell, bed bugs tormented the prisoners. This too was a common experience in the Soviet camp system.

"I stared at the whitewashed wall. It was not white anymore. A mass of black insects was migrating down the wall. I screamed and jumped off the bunk," recalled Alexander Dolgun, a U.S. State Department worker who spent years in Siberia after being kidnapped on a Moscow street.[10]

Dolgun could find no escape even by sitting up all night. As another American inmate recalled, the bugs "literally rained down on you, a steady cascade of insect life showering down on you from the wooden framework over your head."[11]

Diversions

But even the Soviet prison system provided some diversions. At one stop in Sparks's trip, the men had little work and plenty of time for chess and dominoes. At some camps where the prisoners were allowed to roam freely around the compound, the prisoners played softball, handball and soccer. "We could move around all we wanted to and go visit each other," he recalled.

Sparks also learned about the "parasha." Literally, that was the name of the urine barrel. As the place where rumors were shared, parasha also became the term for the prison telegraph. At every chance, prisoners would exchange information on people they had met in their travels.

Information was also spread by another method soon learned by Sparks—the use of numerical code to tap out messages from one cell to another. "You got better and better at the tap language, until you hardly felt handicapped at all—after a month or so at it, every time you tapped you thought you heard your voice doing it and not the piece of soap you used against the wall, " wrote U.S. prisoner Victor Herman, taken to the Soviet Union as a child and later arrested. "It was the same way with what you heard–they were not taps any longer, they were the voices of men speaking–and you could hear every nuance in their speech, every hint of character that distinguished one speaker from another. "

There was another type of gulag code. Upon boarding a train or entering a new cell, a prisoner might see a white handkerchief or towel sitting on the slop next to the urine barrel. If he stepped over the cloth, an inmate identified himself as a political prisoner–thus marked by the others for robbery. But if an inmate stepped right on the white cloth, he pronounced himself one of the "urki," or professional criminals.

There were other, permanent, marks of the "urki." The men were known for their tattoos. Some were light-hearted: a prisoner with a cat on one buttock and a mouse on the other—when he walked, the cat chased the mouse. Several men boasted inscriptions on their penises reading "Shalun"—or little rascal. Motherhood was a popular theme: Many had "Mother" on the backs of their hands; one carried the message "I would die for my mother." Politics also appeared. One inmate's forehead advertised: "Slave of the Communist Party." Another inmate's chest tattoo represented more typical, highly conservative "urki" politics. It was a portrait of Stalin, worn with great respect until prison officials ordered it blacked out.

Most common criminals within the gulag system had little affection for those opposed to the Soviet state. They called political offenders "fascists," mercilessly robbing "beavers," rich prisoners, of their baggage and food. Yet the "urki," professional criminals, had their own rigid code. Americans Alexander Dolgun and Victor Herman both made friends among the criminal class, although Herman had first to prove his fighting ability. Both men later earned respect as camp storytellers, repeating the plots of American movies, and in Dolgun's case, an expanded version of "Les Miserables." Such friends of the criminals could expect life-saving favors, but fiercest enemies of the "urki" were other criminals who cooperated with the guards. Stool pigeons were killed, often by beheading. In some cases, the killer would present the severed head to the nearest guard, then wait calmly for shipment to a punishment camp.[12]

Dolgun writes that when a 1953 law introduced the death penalty for such offenses, "urki" executions simply went underground. The lights in the barracks would go out, and a representative of the "People's Council of Justice" would pronounce the sentence. Muffled thrashing would follow, and guards with torches would soon arrive to find the body, still warm, in bed.[13]

Slave Labor

It was this life the boy from Georgia found himself living in 1953. His new home was Vorkuta, a coal-mining complex in Siberia sixty miles from the Arctic Ocean, and he was soon at work in Mine No. 13. The mine, one of forty in the Vorkuta area, stretched four levels and almost a quarter-mile under the earth. The shafts were barely two feet high, so inmates had to work sitting or on their backs. There were many accidents. It was the same in all gulag mines across the U.S.S.R. Dolgun recalled the accidents he saw at the Dzhezkagan copper mine. Workers with crushed fingers were sent back to work, after being given aspirin.[14] A man with a crushed leg or arm might have to wait hours until a shift change before being allowed to leave the mine. Terrible occupational diseases ran rampant. "The work in the mines was a nightmare," Solzhenitsyn wrote. "The maimed and badly injured were constantly being hauled off to the camp hospital."

At Vorkuta, the mines were worked twenty-four hours a day. Two-hundred workers per shift had eight hours to make their 1,200-ton quota. Failure to reach the quota meant a cut in rations. Never did Sparks see a shift achieve its quota, and conditions were much the same at other camps. According to Dolgun: "If you made your norm you were given a basic ration, known as 100 percent, and this was sufficient to keep you going. If you dropped below your norm, you got a lower ration. With lower rations you would be too weak to maintain whatever percentage of the norm you had been achieving, and so your ration would be lowered again. Finally, it would be reduced to the starvation ration. At that point, without some supplementary food, a prisoner would simply starve to death."[15]

The food wasn't any better than the working conditions. Sparks lost twenty-four pounds during his time in the gulag on a diet of cabbage soup and black bread, a little borscht and something called kapushka, a red cabbage salad. During harsh times, gulag inmates ate horses, dogs and even the bodies of the dead. Victor Herman survived on rats. He ate his first one raw. "I undid the trap door and pulled him out of there and . . . with my fingers I stripped him as best I could and then I just tore away and ate him."[16] Camp managers judged inmates' health, and their value as workers, by their buttocks. At one point, starvation shrank Dolgun's buttocks so much it was painful for him to sit.[17]

Sparks started his sentence with the job of handling a giant drill that cut holes for dynamite charges in the shaft walls. After a work error, however, he was assigned to sawing support timbers for the mine ceilings. He always worried about the unsafe working conditions, and when several Ukrainian inmates advised him not to work because he was an American, and perhaps not being a Soviet citizen able to get away with it, he stopped working.

"They told me not to go to work. I went down into the coal mine a couple of times. Well, I didn't like it and I told them I wasn't going back," he remembered in a thick Southern drawl. So "they locked me down [in solitary confinement] for a few days, then let me back out. Then I might go down again for a day," but eventually Sparks always wound up staging a one-man strike and frequently found himself in solitary confinement.

While Sparks may certainly have brought upon himself a lot of extra attention from his captors, it would seem that many parts of his experiences were similarly encountered by his fellow inmates. Though something of a troublemaker, Sparks and what he endured likely were a mirror of circumstances taking place in much more secret camps.

For months, Sparks shuttled between solitary and the punishment brigade, where workers were stripped of their privileges and slept on the floor. Although he was earning little or no pay, he was able to survive because other prisoners from the Ukraine and Baltics liked Americans and shared their food and money with him.

Americans were not the only foreigners subjected to Soviet abuse. In February 1954, German prisoners went on strike, demanding to be sent home.

The Soviet camp system was filled with foreigners, many captured during and after World War II. "Following World War II," a CIA economic intelligence report says, "a large but unknown number of foreign nationals became prisoners of war in the USSR. These prisoners came from virtually every country in Europe, the Middle East and the Far East, and estimates of their total have ranged from a few hundred thousand to several million."[18] Sparks ran into all of them—French, Belgians, Germans, Japanese, Chinese, Filipinos, Austrians, Arabs, Poles and Ukrainians. In fact, a Czech and a Bulgarian Sparks met had worked for the American Office of Strategic Services (OSS) during World War II. One of them gave Sparks a message to take to "Wild Bill" Donovan, the flamboyant, pistol-packing OSS chief, a message that Sparks stashed in the lining of his coat until he was able to pass it on to CIA authorities in Berlin upon his return to U.S. control.

As Sparks learned, foreign slave labor had its drawbacks for the Soviet system. A CIA report concluded that "the foreigners created serious disciplinary problems. They were the nucleus of dissidence when thrown with native

prisoners; they frequently refused to work."[19] The strike
that Sparks witnessed was just one in a series of disturban-
ces that began in 1953. While it did not get the Germans
home, the 1954 strike did produce minor improvements
in camp life, but not for Sparks, who was incorrectly
fingered as a leader of the strike. That, plus his continued
malingering, earned him a trip down to the next rung in
the Soviet penal system. On the 15th of April, 1954, Sparks,
along with two Germans who actually helped lead the
strike, boarded a prison train, landing in Vladimir prison
four long months later.

There, the cell lights never went off and the schedule
never changed: head-count three times a day; prisoners up
at 6 a.m., in bed by 10 p.m.; a bath every ten days. In many
ways, Sparks appreciated life at Vladimir. The prisoners
could get food from home.

In August 1954, Soviet officials separated all foreigners
in the prison system from the Russian inmates, putting
Sparks in a cell with one Pole and three Germans, including Guenter Robisch, a leader of the February 1954 strike
in Vorkuta. The Germans received food packages from
home, sharing them with Sparks. Life in Vladimir was not
so bad compared to Vorkuta and other camps to which
Sparks could have been sent. In October 1954, Soviet officials even replaced the striped prison uniforms with black
trousers and jackets.

Medical Care

But any doubts Sparks had about the nature of his
captors was dispelled in December, when he reported to
the prison hospital with a stomach problem. The female
Russian surgeon diagnosed appendicitis. While two Red
Army soldiers held Sparks down, the doctor cut out his
appendix using a straight razor and no anesthesia. "They
don't believe in it," Sparks later said. "They told us it
makes you a drug addict. In them camps, they do what the

Life in the Gulag

hell they want to." Sparks remained conscious for the entire operation and was in such pain he could not sleep for three days.

In reality, Sparks was lucky. The doctor who operated on him apparently had medical training. In some camps, medical personnel were self-taught. Alexander Dolgun, the American kidnapped from a job at the U.S. Embassy in Moscow, became the assistant to a real doctor. But he soon found himself forced into practice. One day, a worker appeared with a leg shattered in a mine accident. While the worker waited, Dolgun rushed to the next room and frantically leafed through a medical textbook. After some quick practice on a cadaver, Dolgun returned to his office and successfully amputated the man's leg. He also once performed an appendectomy on another inmate.[20]

Back at Vladimir, Sparks had soon recovered enough from his operation to cheat in a dominoes match with his German buddy, Robisch. That started a fight, and Sparks was packed off to solitary confinement and was soon on the move again.

Relocation

On June 17, 1955, he was put on a train with German prisoners going to a camp at Potma, what would seem to be a positive development since it was a repatriation facility for foreigners. Unhappily, however, he and the other new arrivals soon learned they were not headed home. While everyone else in camp had been freed and going home, Soviet authorities told Sparks and his German friends that they would become the new prison work force. "Me and two Germans and a Jewish fellow did a little work putting a roof on the barracks," he said, work for which he was supposed to be paid. "I never did get a damn nickel," Sparks recalled. "The boss wrote it up so I wouldn't get any money," so Sparks's Ukrainian friends jumped him and beat him up.

While frustrating, this turn of events wasn't as bad as it first appeared. Although still technically an inmate, Sparks received the same privileges as the foreigners scheduled for repatriation: trips to a nearby village, which allowed them to buy booze surreptitiously, and freedom to mingle with the camp's female inmates.

Sparks was soon sharing the bed of a German woman named Magda Schmidt. Even the horrors of forced labor camps could not kill romance—or at least sex. "I have some medical experience and I know all that is written in books about hard work preventing people from thinking about sex. But I know that is not true," said Vasily Ivanovitch, a former medic in the camp system.[21]

The annals of the gulag include the X-rated. Sordid episodes of rape and prostitution occurred in almost every camp. For example, while masturbating male inmates peeped through holes in the wall, an emaciated woman named Masha in the next cell did a strip tease in exchange for a few bits of the camp tobacco called "makhorka."[22]

And a mutual need to escape into sensuality often brought inmates together voluntarily. At one camp, female inmates went on strike for the right to grab some anonymous sex in a men's camp.[23]

"Men and women met where and when they could. I saw couples making love in the snow at 40 below zero, in caves, cellars, attics, dugouts," one inmate recalled.[24] The camp system even included special wards for babies born out of wedlock.[25]

Sex may have been a common gulag diversion, but it was also a good excuse for the camp commander to get rid of Sparks and his German buddies. Seizing upon the fact that prisoners were not allowed to associate with free persons, the commander sent Sparks and his friends packing on another train. Later that day, the group arrived at Yavas. Inspectors there found a knife that Sparks was hiding, but there was no punishment. Many prisoners carried a "moika," or knife, often home-made.

At Yavas, the Soviets assigned Sparks to Camp No. 11, home of 1,600 political prisoners, half of them foreigners. The camp provided workers for furniture factories and wood-making shops. Sparks quickly tired of the work and began hiding. His decision to avoid work grew firmer when the Soviets repatriated all the camp's German prisoners, including Spark's best inmate friend, Guenter Robisch.

Because he did little work, Sparks received little pay. Once again, friendly inmates aided Sparks because he was an American. Some gave him money and food. But a Lithuanian doctor gave Sparks something even more valuable—a gift that could mean the difference between life and death—a sick slip.

Mastyrka

Inmates would do almost anything to avoid assignment to certain jobs or camps that meant almost certain death, such as a uranium mining camp. One tactic, called "mastyrka," was self-inflicted injury to get out of work. Some methods were ingenious. Alexander Dolgun saw a man coat a thread with plaque from in between his teeth, attach the thread to a needle and then run it through the skin of his leg. A terrible infection soon rose up, preventing the inmate's reassignment.[26]

A friendly doctor helped Dolgun infect himself by transferring puss from a boil on his back to a slit on his arm. The medic took care of the entire procedure except the last step. "My professional ethics won't let me infect a wound. But you can. I'll look away."[27]

Other means of "mastyrka" were even more crude. Swallowing the aluminum teaspoon provided for eating lunch would help a prisoner avoid transfer for as long as it took the camp medical section to cut him open and remove the spoon.[28] One inmate blinded himself by putting pencil dust in his eye.[29] Another nailed his scrotum to a bunk. But once the guards pried the nail loose, he was shipped out anyway.[30]

There were even some remarkably inventive methods. For example, shoving a piece of garlic up one's rectum was known to produce a fever high enough to win a respite.[31] But most forms of "mastyrka" had the blunt simplicity of desperation. Men routinely hacked off their fingers and toes. And when that failed to disqualify them from work detail, some removed both of their arms or legs.[32]

Sparks never went to the extreme of making himself sick; his tactics leaned more toward simple malingering or defiance.

Letters

In October 1955, he got a letter from the United States. Two girls in New York had read about him in the newspaper, a bit of ink that probably saved Sparks from a life sentence in the Soviet prison system, because an American citizen publicly known to be in the gulag created major problems for both the Soviet and American governments.

Most such publicly identified Americans eventually won their freedom. Sadly for thousands of others, the United States withheld information from the families of POWs who did manage to smuggle out information to some level of government on their enslavement. Without public knowledge creating pressure, little or nothing would be done by the United States to effect a release.

Responding to infrequent complaints by the U.S. government, the U.S.S.R. reduced its population of American prisoners, not by releasing them, but by stripping them of their U.S. citizenship. Dolgun, the American State Department official assigned to the U.S. Embassy in Moscow, had to sign an agreement before being released from a labor camp into internal Soviet exile:

It declared that during my years in camp I had been naturalized [without his knowledge or consent] as a Soviet citizen. That if I went to Moscow I must undertake never to try to contact the American Embassy. That if I did try to make that contact or try in any way to leave the Soviet Union I would immediately be put in a closed prison, not a camp, for life. No trial, no privilege of review. That I would be under constant surveillance by the KGB.

The American Embassy

After his release from the prison system in 1956, Dolgun somehow conned the KGB into letting him go to the American Embassy, escorted by a KGB officer, in order to collect his clothes and pay that had been held since his kidnapping years before. When they arrived at the Embassy, one might have expected a warm reception for Dolgun along with an unceremonious expulsion of the KGB agent, but that didn't happen. An embassy officer very coldly approached them, gave Dolgun his clothes and money, and then showed him to the door without further inquiry. His family in the United States was never told that he was alive.[33] Why no one took the opportunity to rescue him then is unknown. There are reports of similar instances of U.S. indifference or incompetence, along with pleading letters concerning missing POWs sent by Americans to the U.S. Embassy but never returned. Thus, with Orwellian flare, the Soviets transformed American citizens into Soviet subjects, with the active assistance of the U.S. government.

It would be several years before Dolgun was able to make contact with his family, who then forced the U.S. government to reverse its shameful abandonment of him and negotiate his release.

Sidney Ray Sparks was luckier. The world knew he was a Soviet prisoner and the U.S. government couldn't claim it didn't know about him. The American authorities, using the same note in which they asked for WWII POW Major Wirt Thompson (who was never returned), asked for Sparks's return.

The attorney general of the U.S.S.R. reviewed the Sparks case, and his conviction for espionage was reduced to suspicion of espionage, punishable by five years in captivity. Because of time already served, that made Sparks eligible for amnesty. So, after nearly five years in the gulag, Sparks was headed back to the West—but not before the Soviets made one more attempt to keep him in the U.S.S.R. Soviet officials asked him if he would like to stay in Russia as a free man. He refused. "I never did give up hope," he says now. If he had, he believes, he wouldn't have survived. "I was never afraid," he said. Sparks always told his Soviet captors, "I was born in Georgia, I'm going to die in Georgia."

Other Americans

Many other Americans were not so lucky. Until 1982, a man named Nikolai Mikhailovich Skorodinsky lived and worked in the village of Lashma about 330 kilometers outside Moscow. Skorodinsky was a sawmill worker, well-respected but with a reputation as a bit of a drinker. Not unusual for a Russian. But Skorodinsky was no Russian. He was really an American.

According to friends from his village, who told their tale to co-author Sauter, Skorodinsky was born around 1923 in New York City, the son of Ukrainian immigrants. His American name was something like Neal Goch. In 1945, while serving with the U.S. armed forces in Austria, he was arrested by the Soviets and spent eight years in a Soviet prison before being released into the village outside Moscow.[34]

During the next three decades, he married and became a popular villager, even helping send one of his wife's relatives to school. But he never learned to speak Russian very well. And he desperately missed his sisters Mary and Kate in New York City. But Neal Goch was under some sort of control by the KGB, most likely a form of internal exile. His letters to the U.S. Embassy were never returned, and may never have even been delivered. As one of his friends told us: "He was missing his motherland terribly. He wanted to return but he didn't know how." For as long as he lived, the villagers called him "Uncle Neal the American." He was buried in his Russian village in 1982.

Part II

Silent Screams

Chapter 11

The First POW Activist

"I have had the matter investigated thoroughly, but without success. The Embassy has no record of a report, either official or unofficial, of any of these men [WWII POWs] ever having been heard of in the Soviet Union."
—*Letter from U.S. ambassador in Moscow to Mrs. Ida Mae Reitz Stichnoth, mother of U.S. POW in U.S.S.R., July 1947*

"Will you please help get Tech. Sgt. Lawrence Reitz home . . . ."
—*Letter from Mrs. Stichnoth to President Dwight D. Eisenhower, December 1960*

The document was carried from the White House gate to a Secret Service man, to a secretary, and then into the files in December 1960. "The attached papers were left at NW Gate," the cover letter said. In all her years of fighting, it was as close as Ida Mae Reitz Stichnoth ever got to the men who had written off her son. You can almost see her–a tormented soul approaching the building, clutching a letter that combines all the rage and sorrow and love one person can hold. She starts her letter to the president with the easy part: "Lawrence Reitz.... He was born in Hoopeston, Illinois . . . September 1, 1920 . . . . Enlisted July 29, 1940. Ploesti Oil Field raid, Rumania, 30th mission. Captured by Germans, August 1, 1943."

But then comes the hard part–the part that nobody will talk about—the true but secret part that they believe mothers are not supposed to know: "Prisoner ever since . . . Russian hospital . . . coal mines . . . Vladivostok . . . Odessa."

Then comes the crazy part, the truth hidden and twisted so long that her dreams are now the closest thing to reality: "I met my son . . West Berlin . . . 1956. . . . A man was walking with Lawrence who had power over him . . . I saw burns on his face and fainted. . . . He motioned for me to follow but I could not then."

And finally back to reality, the really insane part. She knows they will never do it, but somehow she must ask just once more. Because this is the White House and she is an American. And she prays the president himself will read just this one letter left at the Northwest Gate: "Will you please help get Tech. Sgt. Lawrence Reitz home. . . . "

She might as well have flushed her letter down the toilet, because her government will do nothing. She will never see her son again.

The indifference and deceit of the U.S. government probably helped drive Ida Mae Reitz Stichnoth into madness, but we will never know for sure. All that can be said with certainty is that it took the bureaucrats many years to break her will. Of the many who tried to smash through the cover-up, this one housewife came closest. She did it for her "Ritzy," Air Force Technical Sergeant Edward Lawrence Reitz.

Lawrence Reitz had soft blue eyes and long straight fingers. His mother lovingly described him as hard working but not strong, a quiet, good boy who never smoked or drank at home. Reitz joined the Air Force and on August 1, 1943, his bomber, the "Damfino," took off to attack the Axis oil fields at Ploesti, Rumania. This was Germany's principal source of oil, and sheets of anti-aircraft fire reached up to greet the planes as they approached the target. It was Reitz's last mission. He was almost 23. At first, the Pentagon told his mother that "Ritzy" was missing. Then, after the war, they said he was dead—consumed in a ball of flames along with the rest of his crew. Ida Mae didn't believe it. Call it a mother's intuition.

A 12-Year Journey

So Mrs. Stichnoth began a 12-year journey throughout the United States, Europe and the bureaucracy in Washington to find her "Ritzy" and get the government to bring him home. She would thereby become America's first POW activist and suffer the consequences of an active government disinformation program to discredit her reputation and destroy her personally. Her odyssey began in 1947, by which time she had come across enough evidence of her son's survival to begin actively and aggressively pursuing the case. She had located former POWs that had seen her son at Stalag 3B in eastern Germany. Others told her that he was taken to Luckenwalde's Stalag 3A and was at the camp on April 22, 1945, when the Red Army "liberated" it.

True enough, Stalag 3B POWs had been moved to 3A in February. But for the State Department, which handled the case until it faded from the files, no amount of evidence would ever cause them to pursue the case with vigor. Instead, a concerted effort was made to ignore solid evidence that Reitz was one of the men who never made it home from Luckenwalde.

Having no success with her own government, Mrs. Stichnoth then approached the Soviet ambassador in

Washington in July 1947. The same month that President Truman's ambassador in Moscow was telling her that her son was dead, she "talked to the Russian Ambassador, Mr. [K.V.] Novikov. I visited with him one hour. . . . Mr. Novikov told me it was only a matter of politics that [the] U.S. was holding their men and Russia [was] holding some of ours."[1] Novikov was referring to the hostage politics the two governments had engaged in at the end of the war. Mrs. Stichnoth began to believe her son was a pawn in a strategic postwar power struggle between the United States and the Soviet Union. She and Novikov agreed, however, that it was lamentable that the World War II Allies had become such bitter enemies.

In 1947, she also received information that "a higher up in Turkey had a Russian come over and talked to him of my son."[2] A flimsy piece of evidence, but nevertheless another clue in the mounting evidence the State Department ignored. Meanwhile, Germans returning from the gulag wrote Mrs. Stichnoth about "several thousand of our American [World] War II men . . . [in] those prison camps northeast of Moscow."[3] Once again, her information was correct. Tambov, where OSS reports had placed at least two groups of American POWs in late 1945, is northeast of Moscow in an area riddled with slave labor camps.

But the U.S. government did nothing—except deny her evidence. In July 1947, the U.S. ambassador in Moscow wrote: "I have had the matter investigated thoroughly, but without success. The Embassy has no record of a report, either official or unofficial, of any of these men ever having been heard of in the Soviet Union. The Military Attache has a record of every man ever reported a prisoner of war in the Soviet Union." Edward Reitz, the State Department averred, was dead.

Then, in 1953, as the State Department was telling Senator Thomas Kuchel that "Mrs. Stichnoth's mind has been affected by her loss," Ida Mae got the first major break that could threaten the cover-up in Washington that had abandoned her son. She heard from a German named Bruno Jacobsen who apparently knew something about Edward. From the French sector of Berlin at 16 Klinnerweg, Jacobsen wrote, "permit me to inquire whether your son Lawrence Reitz . . . has returned from being a German prisoner of war. I would be happy to learn whether his comrades Rolf Kolb and John Kraft from the same Air Force unit have also returned."[4] The letter didn't say why he was making the inquiry, but the government insinuated, incorrectly as it turned out, that he was really interested in being paid for the information, which would taint him as a source.

Six weeks later, the State Department revealed that it had interviewed Jacobsen. In 1945, he had owned a house in Berlin, and one of his boarders was a Gestapo agent handling American and British POWs. According to the May 11 dispatch, the agent fled the city before the Russians moved in, leaving some files. "Mr. Jacobsen, looking through one of the files which contained the names of approximately 45 English and American airmen captured in Rumania, noticed the name of Lawrence Reitz. As this was the name of an old friend of his who emigrated to the United States some 30 years previously, he jotted it down, thinking that it might be one of the children of his old friend." Jacobsen "also noted down the names of Kraft and Kolb because they sounded German and he thought that he might notify their parents." Altruism, not money, had moved Jacobsen to contact Mrs. Stichnoth.

Going Through the Motions

The State Department began to go through the motions that would, over the years, become the bureaucratic trademark for POW matters. They would dutifully approach the Soviet Union "even though the Department of the Army believes there is no doubt that Sergeant Reitz was killed." On May 29, 1953, the State Department asked Soviet officials if they knew anything about Reitz. Up to this point, Mrs. Stichnoth hadn't made much progress beyond strongly believing that her son had been a POW at Luckenwalde where, unbeknownst to her, 9,000 American and British POWs had been held hostage by the Red Army and from which 3,000 had disappeared into the gulag.

On March 30, 1954, Walter J. Stoessel, the acting chargé of U.S.S.R. affairs at the State Department, wrote to Mrs. Stichnoth:

> I deeply regret to inform you that the Soviet government has now informed our Embassy in Moscow that "the necessary measures have been taken to determine whether your son is in the Soviet Union but that nothing has been learned regarding him." [5]

Four months later, in September, Congressman Ray Madden took up Mrs. Stichnoth's case, as well as that of Mrs. Kraft, mother of one of the other airmen. That's when the State Department first began its program to discredit Mrs. Stichnoth's efforts. They alleged that her entire effort was based on mistaken identity. Assistant Secretary of State Thurston Morton wrote, "notwithstanding the fact that the records of the Department of Defense appear to prove conclusively that Sergeant Reitz and Lieutenant Kraft were killed at the time the plane was shot down, Mrs. Stichnoth and Mrs. Kraft believe that they were captured alive by the German forces and were later liberated to the Soviet Army." After all, Morton wrote, "Mrs. Stichnoth bases her belief . . . on a picture which appeared in a Prisoner-of-War bulletin of January 1944. . . . An interview" with one of the subjects in the photograph shows "that the soldiers in this picture were not Sergeant Reitz and his crew." [6]

That may have been true, but Mrs. Stichnoth wasn't basing her case on the photograph, the one small clue about which she may have been mistaken. Mrs. Stichnoth had uncovered the basic truth from World War II that the government had attempted to expunge from history: The Soviets kept hostages, and the United States and Britain brutally forced Russians to return to communist control. When Congressman Madden gave her a copy of the State Department letter, she wrote across the bottom, "I have talked to many men now come home who knew and talked to members of our crew in Stalag IIIa."[7]

A Bombshell

Then she dropped a bombshell in a "To Whom It May Concern" letter dated October 4, 1954:

> October 15, 1953, I received a letter from GERMAN RED CROSS that they had traced my son from the day they captured him August 1, 1943, through their prison and work camps to April 22, 1945. This is the day RUSSIA TOOK them, as per Jacobsen report. THEREFORE HE DID NOT DIE AT THE TARGET AS I HAVE BEEN CONVINCED MANY TIMES IN REPORTS I HAVE GATHERED FROM SO MANY OTHERS.[8]

Predictably, the State Department did not ask for a copy of the German Red Cross letter, even though she offered one. Confirmation of its contents would offer conclusive proof that the Germans notified the U.S. government that Reitz was a POW. The Germans were meticulous record keepers, and if the German Red Cross had Reitz's records, so did the American government. "NOW," she wrote, "MAY I GET A GENUINE HONEST DEMAND BY THE U.S. GOVERNMENT FOR HIS RELEASE."[9] The State

Department ignored this information about the Red Cross as well. But that didn't stop the tenacious Mrs. Stichnoth.

Ten months later, on June 29, 1955, she gave the State Department more proof that Sergeant Reitz had been a POW. Larry Turner of Fullerton, California, formerly a POW at Stalag 3B, read an article in the local paper and recognized Reitz as a friend at that camp. Turner had told his acquaintances that "Lawrence Reitz was a good kid and he knew him very well as they were both in Stalag 3B at the same time and did sleep in the same quarters."[10] Moreover, Mrs. Stichnoth wrote, "I, Lawrence Reitz' mother, asked if Lawrence Reitz was crippled from the plane crash and capture [at] the Ploesti oil fields? He [Turner] remarked [that] Lawrence Reitz walked around like any one else."[11]

But when Congressman James E. Utt brought this information to the attention of the State Department, Morton again denied the government had any information on Reitz. The department had "pursued every lead which might disclose information about Sergeant Reitz, [but] no information has ever been received which substantiates Mrs. Stichnoth's belief that her son is alive," he wrote on August 8.

The *Fullerton News Tribune*, a Southern California newspaper, gave Mrs. Stichnoth her next break on June 18, 1956, in an article headlined, "Ex-POW Verified Former Airman in Prison Camp. Some Escaped but Reitz Left in Russ Hands." Don Keller, a reporter for the paper, tracked down a former POW from Stalag 3A at Luckenwalde named Henry Kirker, who resided at 11111 E. 16th St. in Garden Grove.[12] According to Keller, "A Garden Grove man who saw Reitz in a prison first maintained by the Germans, then taken over by the Russians as the war neared its end told his story exclusively to the *News Tribune.*"

Kirker, now a mechanic, kept a diary for his 22-month stay as a POW, and his entry for September 12, 1944, recorded that he "talked to some new boys today." As the diary soon revealed, "Eddie Reitz," probably with Kraft and Kolb, had arrived at Stalag 3A. On the 14th, Kirker's diary shows he "talked to the new boys, Eddie and some other flyers." Two days later Kirker recorded that "Reitz was here getting [a] haircut by Joe."[13]

Kirker wrote that on "many occasions he played cards with Reitz," and the POWs frequently took turns making Nescafe for a "Koffee clutch." They lived in the same barracks until Kirker was sent to another unspecified camp on September 24, from which he escaped the next May. But not from the Germans. Like the POWs who were forced to flee Russian "liberators" at Luckenwalde, Kirker fled as Red Army soldiers were trying to shoot him in the back.[14]

Twelve days after the *Fullerton* article appeared, another piece of information about Reitz surfaced, this time from a POW that had been interned with Reitz at Luckenwalde. According to a confidential dispatch from the American Embassy in Bonn, Sergeant First Class William M. Lacy, a Luckenwalde alumnus captured by the Hermann Goering Division at Anzio, "saw and learned to know the American prisoner of war named 'Reitz' who he has unequivocally identified before us as being the one and the same person whose picture appeared in the 'Stars and Stripes' issue mentioned" in a sworn affidavit Lacy filed with the Embassy.[15]

Lacy had met Reitz while roaming the camp "in order to trade various articles, including cigarettes, on behalf of various prisoners of war and myself located in the tent,"[16] his affidavit says. "I saw Reitz on an average of once or twice a week and sometimes perhaps three or four times a week during a period of eight weeks, from approximately the 15th of February, 1945, until on or about the 10th or 12th of April, 1945, at which time I ceased traveling into other compounds because of executions of prisoners." Lacy also testified that the "features in the picture [from

Stars and Stripes] and those of the man I knew as Reitz are so identical that there is no question in my mind that these belong to one and the same person." Moreover, Reitz told Lacy "that he was a member of the Air Force, in fact, as I recall it, the other American prisoners of war referred to him as 'fly-boy.' " Lacy said he even remembered Reitz "cutting or picking his name into the wooden side, that is, the inner wall of the barracks" and that "if I could return to that barracks today, I believe I could locate that name."[17]

Lacy, described by a military officer as "a big, quiet, genuine man whose statements carry distinctions necessary to presenting the facts and whose recollection of details is excellent," had nudged the bureaucracy. In describing the subject of the dispatch from Bonn, the bureaucracy finally admitted the "Probable survival of Technical Sergeant Lawrence Edward Reitz."[18]

This, however, was not an admission they would ever make outside the department. As far as Congress and Mrs. Stichnoth were concerned, the Army declaration of death was undoubtedly correct. In fact, eleven months later, they were still saying that "all available evidence indicated, unfortunately, that he was killed during World War II. . . .[19]

They also claimed that "Over the years Mrs. Stichnoth has sent the Department reports concerning persons who allegedly had evidence concerning her son. All such reports have been investigated with negative results."[20] *Stars and Stripes* isn't the only place in which a photo of Reitz appeared and was identified. According to a United Press dispatch, Mrs. Stichnoth "found in wartime issues of the *Red Cross* magazine two photographs which remain convincing to those who have seen them."

By this time Mrs. Stichnoth, who was trying to raise the Iron Curtain itself, had moved to an apartment in West Berlin and was keeping a daily "vigil . . . in the stark reception hall of East Berlin's Soviet embassy. . . . I know my son is still alive," she told a United Press reporter. "I will never give up. I am staying in Europe until I get my boy."

The *Red Cross* photos provided some interesting detail: One showed a group of unidentified American patients at a Rumanian hospital, taken in late 1943. The patients, some of them wearing striped hospital pajamas, bear a strong resemblance to the faces in a wartime picture of the "Damfino's" crew, including Reitz. The second photograph was taken some months later and showed unidentified prisoners at the huge German camp for Air Force POWs. Even allowing for the graininess and soft focus of wartime German film, one of the prisoners appeared almost certainly to be "Ritzy," and other members of the bomber crew seem to be in the group.

The dispatch also revealed another man who knew Reitz after his transfer from Stalag III-B to Luckenwalde: Dr. Hermann Thalhammaeir. Mrs. Stichnoth then unearthed yet another eyewitness, ex-Luftwaffe Captain Hans Buller, a German officer stationed at Luckenwalde until the day it was "liberated" by the Red Army.

Four months after the department had taken Lacy's affidavit, Buller gave Mrs. Stichnoth a written statement about her son. "I knew Lawrence Reitz very well as a prisoner in Luckenwalde in 1944 to April 22, 1945," he wrote. "Reitz was a skinny little fellow with cheeks all sunken in and very thin all over his body. A walking skeleton."[21]

The State Department, now faced with overwhelming evidence that Reitz hadn't been killed over Ploesti, said it would attempt to determine whether Buller had been at Luckenwalde by getting Lacy to identify him. The records don't show the results, but it was an anemic effort at best because the United States possessed all German war records and could easily verify Buller's statement.

On August 7, 1956, the State Department received yet another letter from a former POW at Stalag 3A who remembered Reitz.[22] Surprisingly, the department admitted that information was pouring in from California, Austria and Germany "from persons who state that they saw Sergeant Reitz in prisons in Germany or in the Soviet Union." The department also said that they were once again approaching the Soviet government and asked an inquiring senator not to give that information publicity "in the interest of Sergeant Reitz."[23]

The next salvo fired in the war of words over Edward Reitz was an Associated Press dispatch in 1956 reporting that "a determined American mother got encouraging word today that her long missing airman son may still be alive in Russia. Mrs. Ida Mae Reitz Stichnoth said she found a German former war prisoner who said he spent two years with her son in a Soviet labor camp from 1952 to 1954 and heard from him as late as last year." Apparently, the West German newspaper *MorganPost*, which had published a story on Reitz, "received scores of letters from Germans released from Russian prisoner camps last year and early this year."

Of particular significance was a letter from Hans Joachim Balfanz. When Mrs. Stichnoth contacted him he told her, "Reitz? Yes. I knew him well. I was with him and two Americans in the Vorkuta Camp, Shaft One, from August 4, 1952, until the spring of 1954. As camp barber, I shaved Reitz twice a week and cut his hair once a month. He taught me a few bits of English."[24]

Balfanz said Reitz was transferred from Vorkuta to a camp in Vladivostok in 1954, from where Reitz sent a letter to his former prison mates. Before Balfanz was released from the gulag, Reitz wrote another letter from Odessa on the Black Sea, where about 24 smaller camps were located, noting that he and others were to be released.[25]

This was not the first report that Reitz had been seen in Odessa. Three Austrians who had returned from the gulag in 1956 reported they had known Reitz in a Soviet camp near Odessa, along with two other Americans,[26] identified as Bob Goldman and Jack Koarelsky.[27] When Reverend Kenneth Goff of Englewood, Colorado, wrote to the State Department about the story, the department admitted it was already aware of Koarelsky. He had gone to the Soviet Union in the 1930s and had advised the United States Embassy that he, like many other communists, had renounced his citizenship. They had no prior record of Goldman, but his name appears in a declassified secret government report called "American Citizens Detained in the USSR."

As for Reitz, the department said: "The United States Government has investigated exhaustively in the United States and in Europe every report presented by Mrs. Ida Mae Stichnoth, Sergeant Reitz's mother, or other persons which might lead to information about Sgt. Reitz's fate. These reports appear to be based on mistaken identity."[28] In response to another inquiry, the State Department stated: "It has been learned that practically all these reports are based on rumors."

When Senator Kuchel brought forth yet another man who claimed to have known Reitz in Luckenwalde, he got much the same answer, with one small difference: "the Department has instructed the American Embassy in Moscow to inform the Soviet Government concerning the information which we have received indicating that Sergeant Reitz was seen in a German prisoner of war camp and the further information indicating that he is now imprisoned at Vorkuta." On September 22, 1956, the department delivered a note to the Soviet Foreign Office at 2:16 p.m. local time, asking for "an expeditious investigation on the basis of the above information with the view to learning the whereabouts in the Soviet Union of Sgt. Lawrence Reitz and restoring him to his family and friends."[29]

The problem was, the note was full of errors that would not have been made if any care or effort had been put into it. It said Reitz was in Vorkuta until 1954, but didn't mention that he was transferred to Vladivostok and then to Odessa, where he was heard from by letter and seen in 1956. More glaringly, the note said he had been a POW at "Stalag IIIB in Luckenwalde." Stalag 3B was at Furstenburg. Stalag 3A was at Luckenwalde. The note also errs in saying Reitz was last seen in Luckenwalde in March 1945, when he was last seen under Soviet control on April 22, 1945.

The State Department could have also told the Soviets it knew Reitz was held by them because he had been on a roster smuggled out of Luckenwalde on May 3, 1945, by Edward Beattie. It could have mentioned the hostage situation under which Reitz was held at Stalag 3A. The officials could have, but they didn't. Whether the Soviets had any intention of seriously looking for Reitz is doubtful, but the State Department note effectively told them it was not necessary. On October 20, the Ministry of Foreign Affairs reported that the "competent Soviet organs have no information" about Reitz.

Over the Edge

It's not hard to imagine that government disinformation eventually drove Mrs. Stichnoth over the edge. The story of her efforts to force the bureaucracy to face up to its responsibilities in an honorable manner fades from the files after May 20, 1957, when Senator Kuchel was told that "all available evidence indicates, unfortunately, that he was killed during World War II." The department reinstated its multi-year disinformation statement: "Mrs. Stichnoth bases her belief that her son is alive on a photo published in a January 1944 prisoner of war bulletin," and added the claim that "although there is little to support Mrs. Stichnoth's belief that her son was in the Soviet Union," they did their best to help her.[30]

Tragically, the years of fighting the government had taken its toll on her mental state, and the Department of State used it to advantage, advising Kuchel:

> She frequently informed the United States Mission in Berlin that she had seen her son in numerous places in Berlin but that he was under guard and was not permitted to speak to her. In the hope of relieving her mind, an officer of the Mission escorted Mrs. Stichnoth to each place where she had alleged her son is held. She was given an opportunity to talk to the people in charge and to investigate the premises. After this Mrs. Stichnoth informed the Mission that she was convinced that her son was not held captive in the alleged places. The next day, however, she returned to the Mission and reported that her son had been returned from Berlin to the Vorkuta mines in the Soviet Union and was now a prisoner there. I have outlined the information in the case at length in order that you will be able to understand the nature of Mrs. Stichnoth's allegations and the measures which the Department of State and other offices of our Government have taken to assist her.[31]

The department's simulation of concern as they aggressively discredited an old woman is to the government's everlasting shame. America's first POW activist, after twelve long years, had at long last been beaten by the bureaucracy, and she died without victory. She was the first in a long chain of government victims turned back by bureaucrats defending a new type of American government in which American POWs, and the truth, could be sacrificed for classified foreign policy goals.

Part III

The Korean War

Chapter 12

Secret Prisoners of the Forgotten War

"We don't have any evidence that anyone was transported from Korea to the Soviet Union."
—Public statement by Pentagon POW/MIA
spokeswoman Captain Susan Strednansky,
June 1992

"These reports [of U.S. POWs being transported from Korea to the Soviet Union] came in great volume through the earlier months of the war."
—Secret Pentagon report,
February 1953[1]

In the fall of 1951, Korean War POW Lieutenant Warren L. Polk was beaten to death by Russian soldiers. In some ways, he got off easy.

The last man to see Polk alive was Marine Billie J. Lessman. In September 1951, Lessman, Polk and other U.S. prisoners captured by North Korea set out on a death march to POW camps in the north. Weighed down with seventy-five pounds of grain and marching more than ten miles a night with no shoes, many of the POWs dropped out and were shot along the route.[1]

"Lieutenant Polk was very sick, so I put my arm around him to help carry him along. We [had] seen Russians go by us in Russian jeeps and they yelled at us in Russian," reported Lessman after the war.

One Russian asked Lessman whom he was carrying:

> I said an officer who was sick. He asked me if he had ordered me to carry him, I said that he was my countryman and that I would help him. The Russian then hit me and the Korean guard struck me with his bayonet. . . . The Russian then called his other friends over and they beat up Lieutenant Polk by turns, until he was out, and then they drove off. Lieutenant Polk died the next morning.[2]

In June 1951, Air Force Staff Sergeant James Mullens parachuted safely from his plane only to be captured by Soviet anti-aircraft troops. One Russian "jabbed him in the ribs several times with a rifle butt, causing severe pain and several broken ribs. Mullens added that the Russians would have continued to mistreat him in this manner if he had not been ordered to stop by a Chinese officer who was present at the time."[3]

It was North Korean police who captured U.S.M.C. Captain Charles Martin after his plane went down over enemy territory in November 1951. Martin soon learned that some captured Americans, especially aviators, were a valuable commodity on the battlefields of Korea. The day after his capture, while suffering the abuse of North Korean troops in an Army garrison, Martin was rescued by a visitor. "I did not realize that he was a Chinaman at the time. He just came walking into the compound. He just pushed the Koreans aside and indicated that I should follow him," recalled Martin.[4]

Secret Combatants

While marching to a prison camp farther north, Martin and his Chinese captors ran into a force of more than 1,000 Russian troops manning a motor pool and 20 anti-aircraft positions. The Soviets

> gave me this political business, kept calling me "Truman" and kept pushing me around. . . . They tried to persuade the Chinese to turn me over to them. But the Chinese wanted me as much as they did and they refused to do so and we continued on our way.

Martin would suffer badly under the Chinese, but he was lucky to have escaped the Russians. Even those beaten, perhaps even those killed, by the Soviets were lucky in a way, because up to 2,000 other American prisoners from Korea, selected for use as spies, technicians and slaves, would face a lifetime of imprisonment in the Soviet Union.

If the Korean conflict is the "forgotten war," then the war's forgotten enemy must be the Soviets, who provided America's North Korean and Chinese enemies with thousands of troops, supplies and Russian-piloted jet fighters.

"As a political entity, North Korea was purely a Soviet creature," concluded a November 1953 White House record.[5] Many leaders of the North Korean regime were former Red Army officers, and in some cases they had even been born in the U.S.S.R. and held Soviet citizenship. North Korean President and Communist party chief Kim

Il Sung had served in the Russian military. One-time Soviet citizen Nam Il, reported to have been born in Siberia and fought as a Soviet officer during the World War II battle of Stalingrad, served as North Korea's army chief of staff, foreign minister and senior Communist delegate at the peace talks. At lower echelons, Soviet-Koreans served throughout the North Korean government. U.N. forces even captured documents ordering the 1950 North Korean invasion, documents written in Russian. Soviet advisers and troops took key combat roles in the ground fighting and flew MiG fighters from bases in Manchuria. Russian troop strength peaked in the spring and summer of 1951 as up to 20,000 Russians advised North Korean units, ran anti-aircraft facilities and provided technical support.[6]

Soviet Captain Evarest Buklemishev, company commander in the Tenth Anti-Aircraft Searchlight Regiment, arrived in Antung, China, in May 1951. There, his regiment became part of a Soviet air defense system, including fighters and anti-aircraft guns, spread along the Chinese border and into Korea. The 10th Regiment helped down "dozens" of U.S. planes, recalled Buklemishev. "One B-26, a very rare incident, was destroyed by a searchlight. Lieutenant Spector's platoon lit it, the pilot threw the aircraft to the side and hit the mountain."[7]

Soviet leaders, however, wanted to keep the light off their involvement in the Korean War. Russian troops were ordered to destroy identification numbers on their equipment and wear Chinese uniforms. "The idiocies of secrecy reached the heights of requiring pilots to conduct radio transmissions in fluent Korean," the Soviet officer recalled.

One reason for all the camouflage was the "secret policy" of Soviet troops in Korea–the policy of capturing Americans and shipping them to Russia. "We hunted for the wreckage of [U.S.] planes for the equipment of the enemy and for downed pilots," recalled former Red Army officer Colonel Gigori Dzhagarov, who earned a Red Star for his then-secret efforts.[8]

Yet Russia's role was not a secret to American officials, who believed that Soviet support allowed China and North Korea to continue the war. President Harry Truman even mused in his diary about a direct challenge to Stalin. "Now do you want an end to hostilities in Korea or do you want China and Siberia destroyed? You may have one or the other which ever you want. . . . You either accept our fair and just [peace] proposal or you will be completely destroyed," wrote the president.[9] But the president never communicated his threat to the Soviets, instead allowing large numbers of Americans to be killed or captured by the U.S.S.R.

Soviet intelligence officers controlled the overall communist POW system. A 1953 White House record, classified until 1992, outlined the command structure:

> The Secretary General of the top [POW] secretariat was a Soviet officer named Takayaransky, Director General of the POW control bureau was a Colonel Andreyev, USSR; its Deputy Director, Lt. Col. Baksov, USSR; for the North Koreans, General Kim Il [reportedly a former Soviet citizen]. . . . The Chief of the Investigation Section [one of the three component sections in the bureau] was a Colonel Faryayev, USSR.[10]

Americans captured during the Korean War ended up in one of three POW systems: "peace" and "reform" camps in China and "normal" POW camps in North Korea.[11] Only the last set of camps has ever been officially acknowledged by the U.S. and communist governments–because only prisoners from the "normal" camps were allowed to return at the end of the war. As the CIA put it, "Normal prisoner of war camps, all of which were in North Korea, detained prisoners whom the Communists will exchange.

Prisoners in the peace and reform camps will not be exchanged."[12]

Day to day operations at the "normal" POW camps were run by Chinese and North Koreans. According to the Pentagon, those North Korean camps were under the direct control of North Korean official and one-time Soviet citizen, Kim Il, assisted by Russian advisers.[13] A CIA report indicates that Kim Il and the other North Korean and Chinese camp officials ultimately reported to a Russian "Colonel No-men-ch'i-fu, an intelligence officer attached to the general headquarters of the Soviet Far Eastern Military District." The colonel's Pyongyang POW office employed several English-speaking Soviets, according to the CIA report.[14]

Returned U.S. POWs reported numerous contacts with those English-speaking Russians. In the area around the North Korean capital, "Russian advisers were frequently seen and a Russian Air Force intelligence officer was directing the establishment of a North Korean interrogation center."[15]

Interrogation

Ranger Sergeant Martin R. Watson had been a POW in World War II. So he kept his cool when a blond foreigner in a conservative suit began interrogating him at a North Korean camp:

> Sgt. Watson was asked by a Russian if he spoke any Polish or Russian and he replied, "I might." The Russian then asked if he knew who he was. Watson replied, "Rooski." At this point both the Russian and the North Korean snickered. The Russian offered him a cigarette and proceeded to question him. He asked if he was hungry, and was given food which was placed on the desk in front of the pictures of [then Soviet leader] Malenkov and [Chinese dic-

1. *Joseph Stalin, Franklin Roosevelt and Winston Churchill at Yalta, where the post-war world was shaped and where the fate of American and British POWs was decided. Churchill became the odd man out because of his fears of Soviet expansionism and his secret plans to retain anti-communist Soviets to fight the coming Cold War.*

2. Harry Hopkins, in 1943, on the grounds of the Russian Embassy in Teheran. From left, two unidentified Russians; Hopkins; an interpreter, Stalin; V. M. Molotov and E. Vorshilov.

3. *In June 1945, Harry Hopkins returning from his special mission to the Soviet Union where he met with Joseph Stalin for the last time. Four decades later Oleg Gordievsky, a former KGB agent, stated that Hopkins had been a Soviet agent. Hopkins was the second most powerful man in the United States, FDR's closest aide.*

4. *Roosevelt greets Henry Morgenthau, then Secretary of the Treasury, whose aides formulated his plan to punish Germany for World War II.*

5. *Harry Dexter White, the notorious Soviet spy, helped conceive the Morgenthau plan. White died mysteriously while on a trip in South America.*

6. *Roosevelt and Secretary of State Cordell Hull. Hull opposed forced repatriation of Soviet citizens, but he was not in Roosevelt's inner circle, and his views went unheeded.*

7. *President Roosevelt and British Prime Minister Winston Churchill at the Quebec conference in 1944, where Roosevelt convinced Churchill to accept the Morgenthau plan, the creation of a Soviet agent. The plan would have "pastoralized" Germany.*

8. *Secretary of War Henry Stimson (left), a Republican, opposed forced repatriation of Soviet citizens. On his right is Army Chief of Staff George C. Marshall.*

9. Generals Dwight D. Eisenhower and George Marshall, celebrating V-E Day and Ike's return home. These two generals sealed the fate of more than 20,000 American GIs trapped in POW camps on June 1, 1945 with SHAEF Memo FWD 23059. When he was President, Eisenhower similarly wrote off American POWs left behind after the Korean War.

10. American and British POWs standing around in Stalag 3A after the April 22, 1945 "liberation." Little did they know about their liberators' intentions.

11. American POWs in the town of Luckenwalde after their "liberation" from Stalag 3A. One of their Russian "allies" stands in the foreground at left.

12. POWs at Tent City, Stalag 3A, after their "liberation." Photos from Stalag 3A are extremely rare.

13. A Navy PBY-4 Privateer of the kind that carried American intelligence officers to their captivity in the gulag in the late 1940s and 1950s.

14. *Above is Maj. Wirt Thompson. Thompson's family was told that he died in a plane crash in 1944. A German returnee saw Thompson in a Moscow prison in 1948. His family was never informed.*

15. *Above is Olen Taylor's snap shot which was smuggled out of the gulag in 1947. Taylor was a slave laborer with 200 other Americans at a tank manufacturing plant.*

16. *Below, Sergeant Edward Reitz, who was shot down over Rumania, taken from Stalag 3A and tranferred to the Soviet Union where he was sighted by numerous witnesses.*

17. Major Robert Brown was shot down over North Vietnam in 1972 and immediately sent to the USSR. Brown was an expert in the space program and within two years of his capture his expertise appeared in the Soviet space program.

18. Below is Ike's intelligence officer Philip Corso, taken in 1953. He reported to Eisenhower that American POWs in Korea were being shipped to the USSR; Ike said to "cover it up."

19. Rear Admiral Ronald F. Marryott, the man who as Deputy Director of the Defense Intelligence Agency told a congressional subcommittee in June 1990 that the Pentagon had "no such evidence" that American POWs had been kidnapped by the Soviet Union. Official Navy photo by Robert Lucier.

tator] Mao Tse-Tung. While eating the food, he had his picture taken by the Korean. After he completed eating, he was questioned again. With the repetition of previous questions he became irritated and informed the Russian that he was tired, and that he would not answer any further questions. He had barely completed his statement when the Russian whipped out his pistol and hit him across the nose.[16]

The Soviet official interrogated Watson for two days. At this interrogation center, Watson shared a cell with a Captain Hal (Harold) Beardall, a U.S.A.F. B-26 pilot. When Watson was leaving the cell for the final time, Beardall expressed doubt that he himself would ever make it home. Watson then left for another camp. Beardall never returned.

While most Americans who returned from the "normal" POW camps were questioned by Chinese and North Korean officials, evidence of the content and brutality of the treatment could be traced back to Soviet direction. "This was not hapstance [sic] but what I feel was purposeful direction by Russian political cadres. The attempts at breaking down prisoners, their treatment of prisoners, coincide with Pavlovian techniques and established Russian practices," testified former POW Marine Major Gerald Fink.[17] "[I]t was pretty definite that a lot of these questions that were being asked were being prompted by Russian advisors," said Martin, the Marine captain.

Sifting for Information

It was also Soviet practice to sift the North Korean camps for U.N. prisoners with certain skills and/or attitudes. "Cooperative prisoners were being transferred to peace camps," many of them secret facilities in China.[15] Soviet intelligence officers also selected U.S. prisoners with specific technical abilities, according to the former director of the Defense Intelligence Agency, Lieutenant General Daniel Graham. "They'd come with a list of specialties and find out whether such specialties existed among the U.N. prisoners in the camps in North Korea and China . . . and then they would ship them off" to the Soviet Union, according to Graham.[18]

"When we first got to [POW] camp #1, all radio men, telephone operators, and other communication personnel were taken for questioning at Panmunjom. We never saw them again," reported one returned American.[19] "Numerous young aviators who were shot down after January 1952 were not seen or heard from again although they came through the camp for interrogation," recalled another.[20] A friendly Chinese who had served in the Chinese Nationalist Army helped Master Sergeant John T. Cain and other U.S. POWs. "He also told of one (1) helicopter pilot with rank of Second Lieutenant being taken to Russia in March 1952," Cain reported when he returned.[21]

There seems little doubt that some of the 389 Americans the U.S. government acknowledges did not return from North Korean POW camps ended up in Siberia, but they were just a fraction of the American POWs abandoned during Korea. Not counting the secret camps in China, even in the so-called "normal" camps, secret U.S. government records indicate yet more POWs who did not return. In 1955, the chairman of the Joint Chiefs of Staff was given a list of eleven Navy personnel who were shot down and known to be alive on the ground. None of these eleven was on the original list of the "normal" camp inmates given to the communists for an accounting, and there were undoubtedly still others.

Without a Trace

Far more than 389 Americans disappeared without a trace into the secret "peace" and "reform" camps and from there directly into the Soviet gulag via the Manchurian railway system that winds north through Manchouli, China, into Siberia. Peace camps detained prisoners with pro-communist leanings and "were characterized by considerate treatment of the prisoners and the staging within the camps of Communist rallies and meetings," reported the CIA. Reform camps "contained anti-Communist prisoners possessing certain technical skills. Emphasis at these camps was on reindoctrination of the prisoners."

The secret camps held many of the giant ghost army of more than 4,000 Americans who simply vanished off the battlefields of Korea. Sergeant First Class Lewis Sowles was one. According to government documents, "Available evidence indicates that many of the casualties which are carried on the records of the Department of Defense as missing in action in South Korea were actually captured and transported to North Korea where they subsequently died; however, specific information is lacking as to the number, identity or circumstances surrounding their disappearance."[22]

Contrary to repeated statements by the Pentagon, most of those men were not known to have been killed in combat. Nor were they reported by any of the several thousand Americans who returned from "normal" POW camps in North Korea. Instead, many of them were apparently shipped directly to secret camps in China and then on to the Soviet Union.

In March 1951, the U.S. Far East Command received a message relaying intelligence from the French military. According to the report, up to 3,000 American POWs had been moved to the Korean border with China by December 1950. The report said 1,200 wounded POWs had been placed in a communist hospital in Manchuria.

U.N. officials knew and publicly confirmed that communist forces moved large numbers of South Korean and other U.N. prisoners into Manchuria and then elsewhere in China, starting in the fall of 1950. A captured Chinese lieutenant "described in detail a prisoner-of-war processing center in Harbin to which he had helped escort captured United Nations personnel." The camp reportedly held over 1,000 prisoners, including Americans.[23] CIA documents on these secret camps list the names of American prisoners in their Chinese transliterations, plus details on communist plans for the men.

Two Letters Postmarked: Canton, China

Marjorie Joyce Morgan received two letters from her husband, Sergeant Tommie Lee Morgan, in early 1951. The letters were postmarked "Canton, China," where the CIA had reported a secret camp. Sergeant Morgan never returned from captivity in Canton.[24]

At a camp in Shanghai staffed by Chinese and English-speaking Soviets, 78 U.S. POWs were forced to study communist doctrine. The CIA obtained a list containing the last names of ten prisoners written in their Chinese transliterations. "Hein-man" had been the company commander, First Company, Ninth Regiment, Division 2; "Lai-mi-shi," of the Fifth Regiment, Division 24; and "Ma-erhk-o," who was extremely homesick (the Pentagon refers questions on the fate of these men to the CIA. The CIA won't comment).

In the Chinese town of Mukden, 400 U.S. prisoners, of whom 300 were black, studied communism. "All prisoners held here, with the exception of three second lieutenants, were enlisted personnel. The prisoners, dressed in Chinese Communist Army uniforms, with a red arm band on the left arm, were not required to work." An Army report said prisoners in Mukden were "to be given short-term training pending transfer to Soviet Union on order of central authorities."

While large numbers of U.S. prisoners were taken to Manchuria and other parts of China, a 1954 Senate investigation revealed that only a handful ever returned. As for the rest, some were probably retained by the Chinese; most were shipped north to Siberia.

"These reports came in great volume through the earlier months of the war . . . " reported CCRAK, the Combined Command for Reconnaissance Activities, Korea, a joint Pentagon-CIA operation. The shipment of U.N. POWs out of the war zone and on to Russia had continued throughout the conflict. "A compilation of reports indicate that during the past two years several PWs have been transferred from PW Camps in North Korea to points in Manchuria, China and Siberia."[25] "[R]eports state PW who are moved to the USSR are technical specialists who are employed in mines, factories, etc."[26]

On to Siberia

Other U.N. prisoners were shipped to Russia to "be specifically trained at Moscow for espionage work. PWs transferred to Moscow are grouped as follows: British 5, Americans 10, Canadians 3, and 50 more from various countries."[27]

Many U.S. prisoners were known to have been shipped on trains from China to Siberia. The CCRAK intelligence on one rail shipment of 63 Americans to the Siberian city of Chita was so strong the Air Force "immediately called off any air strikes in that corridor so the train wouldn't be bombed," said retired Army intelligence officer Mel Gile.

Despite their knowledge of American POWs in the U.S.S.R., U.N. negotiators pressed the Communists for the return of only POWs in the "normal" camps in North Korea. At the end of the Korean War, the U.S. never even asked for its prisoners being held in China and Siberia–no doubt an irony not lost on the chief communist negotiator representing the North Koreans, General Nam Il, who as a Soviet citizen would have certainly known about them.

Instead of fighting for the return of all American prisoners, the U.S. simply signed a truce on July 27, 1953, and began warning the bureaucracy that some Americans would not be returning. "The U.S. Government believes that some American and other United Nations military personnel, held prisoner by the Chinese and North Korean Communist forces in Korea, will not be returned to friendly control," said an August 1953 State Department memo.[28] "UN prisoners retained by the Communists will not necessarily be held in Korea, Manchuria or Eastern Siberia, but may be retained elsewhere in the Soviet orbit. The U.S. Government is anxious to obtain any information concerning these captives," wrote Secretary of State Dulles.

Beginning in late 1953, the Pentagon began declaring that all U.S. MIAs were dead. Yet even as the bureaucrats were writing off the prisoners, new proof was emerging that many of them were alive in the Soviet Union. In early 1954, Soviet intelligence agent Yuri Rastvorov defected to the U.S. Embassy in Tokyo. He confirmed that American POWs had been shipped on trains to the Soviet Union, where they had been forced to renounce their citizenship.[29]

Later that year, the U.S. Air Force attaché in Hong Kong sent a remarkable report to Washington. "This office has interviewed refugee source who states that he observed hundreds of prisoners of war in American uniforms being sent into Siberia," read the report, entitled: "American POWs Reported en Route to Siberia."[30] At the Chinese-

Soviet border town of Manchouli, the source saw two shipments of seven railroad cars each during the spring and summer of 1951. Many of the prisoners were black. During one shipment, the refugee got a good look at three American Air Force sergeants eating at the station restaurant. "POWs appeared thin but in good health and spirits, were being given what source described as good food. POWs were talking in English but did not converse with guard."

At the station, Asian guards herded the Americans from the Chinese cars onto a Russian train manned by Soviets in dark tunics. The source had a Russian friend at the station whose job was numbering the railroad cars each time a POW train passed through Manchouli. The source claimed that "these shipments were reported often and occurred when United Nations forces in Korea were on the offensive."

Faced with such evidence, the American government finally decided to act. On May 5, 1954, the U.S. Embassy in Moscow delivered a note to the Soviet Government:

> The Embassy of the United States of America presents its compliments to the Ministry of Foreign Affairs of the Union of Soviet Socialist Republics and has the honor to request the Ministry's assistance in the following matter. The United States Government has recently received reports which support earlier indications that American prisoners of war who had seen action in Korea have been transported to the Union of Soviet Socialist Republics and that they are now in Soviet custody. The United States Government desires to receive urgently all information available to the Soviet Government concerning these American personnel and to arrange their repatriation at the earliest possible time.[31]

A week later the Soviets responded: "The United States assertion . . . is devoid of any foundation whatsoever and is clearly contrived, since there are not and have not been any such persons in the Soviet Union."[32]

Escapees from the gulag told a very different story. First- and secondhand reports from a number of returned gulag prisoners placed American POWs in the Potma, Irkutsk, Taishet and Omsk prison complexes. American prisoner Alexander Dolgun "heard rumors of an American colonel captured in Korea who was supposed to be somewhere in Dzhezkazgan but I had never been able to find him."[33] Another American in the gulag, William Verdine, heard "rumors on numerous occasions to the effect that US soldiers captured in Korea were being held by the Soviets," according to his debriefing report. John Noble, an American who returned from the gulag a year after Verdine, heard repeated stories of American POWs from the Korean War being shipped to Irkutsk, Taishet, Omsk and Magadan.

Perhaps the most compelling description of the Soviet fate of U.S. POWs from Korea came from an entirely open source–a 1953 article that was denied by the Pentagon then but is now supported by recently released government documents.

In early 1952, Zygmunt Nagorski Jr., then general manager of the Foreign News Service, which specialized in gathering news from behind the Iron Curtain, developed sources with extensive information on American, British and South Korean POWs being shipped to the Soviet Union.

Nagorski, writing for *Esquire* magazine in 1953, reported that "large numbers of Americans are now living in camps scattered in the various Republics of Russia." The headquarters for the Soviet operation was in the city of Molotov, formerly called Perm. There, "Soviet political police" interrogated the American POWs. Northeast of that city, in northwestern Siberia, "Americans have been seen in at least six camps, and other American POWs have been reported from camps situated on the Pacific Coast of Siberia, in Khabarovsk and in the towns of Chita and Omsk."[34] (Both those cities were connected by the trans-Siberian Railroad, which is linked to China by way of Manchouli, where hundreds of American POWs were observed in transit to Siberia.)

All non-Asian POWs were first sent to camps near the Yalu, "where they are interrogated by Chinese and Russian officers who speak perfect English. These officers conduct the first screening. American Air Force officers, artillerymen, tank specialists and other technicians are separated from the rest and sent to special camps."

In June 1952, Nagorski obtained descriptions of two of the camps. "At that time about nine-hundred non-Korean P.O.W.'s, mostly Americans and some British and Turks, were housed at the two camps." These were apparently the peace camps described in CIA documents. The POWs remained there only for a few weeks, were well fed, were offered courses in the Russian language and were visited by various communist peace organizations. Once the POWs were softened up,

> the Communists are ready for further screening and for work on their victims. . . . The political officers, who formerly led discussions on world events, now begin conducting daily interrogations. Within a day or two they know which prisoners they want. . . . They are marked as dead on the official P.O.W. lists.

Those considered to be "especially valuable, are flown directly to Russia. Their first stop is at Poset," a naval station on the Soviet-China border. Other Americans agreed to cooperate fully and were sent to a "luxurious" place near Chita called "Shivanda." "The selected few stay in the camp for a period of four to five weeks. At the end of that period they either graduate and receive an assignment, or fail and return to the labor camps." Most of those who graduate "start their work by giving lectures on new American weapons, strategy, political trends and psychological warfare to selected groups of Red Army officers."

Other U.S. servicemen selected from the secret Manchurian camps were shipped to "transit camps directly north of Korea at Khabarovsk and Komsomolsk," where further interrogations and culling took place. At those camps and others, the "Communists start talking force," telling the Americans they had been declared dead. The POWs were then given two choices: cooperate and enjoy a reasonable standard of living, or resist and go to a slave labor camp. Camps for Americans who make the latter choice are at Kudymkar, Chermoz and Gubakha. "There are four camps in Chermoz, three of them labor camps and the fourth a disciplinary prison camp." About 200 American POWs were assigned to one camp near Chermoz, "where they were working on the local railroad."

While the Soviet system seems to have created several slave labor camps composed exclusively of POWs from the Korean War, long after Nagorski's report many American military personnel also turned up in camps where World War II-era prisoners were kept. A German prisoner named Otto Herman Kirschner had been imprisoned with American POWs in the Kirov camp prior to January 1955. The nine Americans, all captains and majors, were in civilian clothes and were fliers from the Korean War.[35]

During a Military Armistice Commission meeting in 1957, U.N. representative Major General Homer L. Litzenberg once again asked the Chinese and North Koreans about American MIAs removed from the Korean battle zone by the Chinese and Soviets. "Were they taken outside of your side and turned over to other jailers. Were any of them turned over to the U.S.S.R.?" the general demanded.[36]

Of course, the Pentagon knew the answer to that question. Reports of Americans from the Korean War in the Soviet prison camp system, many apparently still classified, continued to arrive throughout the 1950s. One "source released from internment in Russia stated he knew of two Americans captured in Korea who were presently interned in Siberia." At least two other returnees from the gulag reported U.S. POWs from Korea in the slave labor complex at Bulun.[37]

For years after the end of the Korean fighting in 1953, U.S. intelligence continued to collect information on U.S. POWs. Until the late 1950s, the Air Force intelligence's "Project American" was collecting information on "a large number of personnel . . . [who] may still be alive" in communist custody. Exactly who those prisoners were and where they were held has never been made public. Recently declassified records indicate only that the project was suddenly canceled in 1959, and the Air Force now says it has lost the "Project American" files.[38] As for the prisoners described by *Esquire* writer Zygmunt Nagorski Jr., according to his sources, 1,000 of the men were still alive through at least the late 1950s.

In April 1959, Rita Van Wees received word from anti-communist activist Nicholas Sheikin, a White Russian operating in Europe, that her son Ronald, a Korean War MIA, was alive in the Soviet Union. The message, smuggled out of the U.S.S.R. on the margin of a Soviet newspaper, read: "They have seen your friend R. [Ronald] in September 1959. He is alive, healthy and works as a tractor driver together with his countrymen in the District of Krasnoyarskays Oblast near Turinskaya Kultbaza."[39]

When Van Wees took her evidence to the White House, the Eisenhower administration denied that any U.S. POWs had been taken from Korea to the Soviet Union. As of this writing, more than 30 years later, that is still the official U.S. government policy.

Chapter 13

===

China and North Korea

"We learned that the Chinese and the North Koreans, like the Communists in Russia, had refused to return all the prisoners they captured. Why the Reds refused to return all our captured personnel we could only guess. I think one reason was that they wanted to hold the prisoners as hostages for future bargaining with us."

—General Mark Clark,
commander of U.S./U.N. forces
in the Korean War[1]

"The Chinese side settled the issue of American prisoners of the Korean War long ago . . . all the POWs were treated in a humanitarian manner. None of the POWs under Chinese control was transferred to a third country or to the Chinese territory."

July 1992 statement from
the People's Republic of China[2]

In August 1951, communist troops put Captain John Hindman and other American POWs on display in a North Korean town near Sunchon. "A young American GI, flanked by several Chinese soldiers, came down the street," Hindman would later state under oath. "He was dressed the same as them and was speaking Chinese with them. They were laughing and playing. When the American noticed us they all came over and the American talked to us."3

The GI claimed that he had been captured during the Chinese offensive in November 1950, while serving with the Army's Second Division. The American said he had joined the communists as a truck driver for an artillery unit and, after a four-month stay in China, had volunteered to serve in Korea. He said such service paid five times as much as duty in China. His only complaint was that the Chinese had "promised him a new American truck [to drive] but gave him a Russian truck instead." Soon the American wandered off with his Chinese comrades.

That truck driver may have been U.S. POW Richard Desautels. Returning Americans reported that Desautels had worked closely with the Chinese. "He drove their trucks, attending to firing boilers and learned to speak the Chinese language fairly well," according to Army intelligence.[4]

Official History

According to official Pentagon history, only 21 Americans (but not Desautels) definitely remained in North Korea and China at the end of the Korean War. They were the so-called "turncoats," the Army said, men who accepted communism while imprisoned in North Korean camps. While their defection shocked many Americans at the time, official spokesmen explained that the 21 represented only a tiny fraction of American POWs. The U.S. is still quick to note that after the war, most of the turncoats quietly slipped back into the United States.[5]

Those 21 defectors, however, appear to have been part of a much larger number of U.S. servicemen who remained in China and North Korea after the war. Some, such as the GI truck driver, had apparently switched their allegiance to communism. First Lieutenant John Adams, an Air Force MIA, was described by a fellow prisoner as "procommunist . . . [and] had spoken many times against the American form of government."[6] Like other Americans with similar views, Adams appeared to be alive and well in Chinese captivity but never returned, and he was not listed as an official "turncoat."

Other Captives

As for Gerald W. Glasser, "Sixty-six returnees reported that subject was a prisoner. The statements indicated that he was in prison Camp No. 1, Chang-Song, N.K. In the spring of 1953 he was taken away in a jeep by Chinese officers. He was in good health at the time and there was nothing to indicate that his removal from camp was in the nature of an arrest as he and his camp companions were given candy and cigarettes before leaving."[7]

Many other U.S. servicemen were kept in China against their will. During the Korean War, some of them fell directly into Chinese hands. Second Lieutenant Paul Joseph Jacobson, an Air Force pilot, disappeared during a dog fight over Sinuiju, near the North Korean-Chinese border. Chinese soldier Wang Ing Rwa later saw a U.N. pilot brought into nearby Antung, Manchuria. Hundreds of Chinese watched as officials denounced the foreigner as a "crook of the air" and "stripped [the] pilot of [his] clothes and gave him a Chinese uniform." U.N. forces later captured the Chinese witness and matched his report to the disappearance of Lieutenant Jacobson, who never returned from Manchuria.[8]

At about the same time, the Chinese had captured at least two other fliers:

> On 18 January 1953, a plane of Navy Patrol Squadron 22 with thirteen aboard was shot down off the southern coast of China. . . . A U.S. Coast Guard PBM dispatched from the Philippines rescued eleven of the survivors, but it also crashed and sank on take-off. One Navy officer and five enlisted men of the VP-22 and one USCG officer and four enlisted men of the PBM were reported missing. According to information received via the Associated Press . . . two American fliers were captured and taken to Swatow, China, where they were forced to participate in an anti-American parade.[9]

The Chinese later put the two Americans on display in bamboo cages. The report, linked to Navy airmen William F. McClure and Lloyd Smith Jr., came from communist prisoners captured by Nationalist Chinese forces during a raid on Swatow. While there is inconclusive information that the two aviators died, it is certain the Chinese Communist government has never accounted for them.

Most American prisoners, however, did not initially fall into Chinese hands, but got to China the hard way, on the ground and through the Korean War prison camp system. After the intervention of the People's Republic of China (PRC) in late 1950, the Chinese began to operate POW camps in North Korea. At the end of the war, 389 Americans, reported alive and in enemy hands, never returned home. Hundreds, probably thousands, of other U.S. servicemen held in secret Manchurian prison camps (described in Chapter 11) also failed to return.

A secret camp in Canton held more than fifty Americans. "These prisoners were sent to Canton because the Chinese Communist authorities hoped to obtain military and medical supplies from the United States

Government in return for their release. They planned to demand U.S. $100,000 worth of supplies for each prisoner released," according to CIA Report SO-66740.

The Chinese wanted not only hostages, but also Americans with technical skills ranging from the ability to drive U.S. trucks to knowledge of high-tech radar systems. Private First Class Gildo Rodriguez remembered a Chinese officer carefully screening U.S. POWs for their skills. "He didn't seem as interested in me as he was in the men who were from motors and maintenance sections."[10]

Another POW was told "we were heading for China to be used as laborers in factories."[11]

"The treatment there was mental torture. You just more or less lived in suspense—they would just come in one day and take a guy out for sabotage or something and that was the last you saw of him," testified former POW Homer Richardson.[12]

When Lieutenant William Lewis complained to his Chinese captor "that I was not treated according to the Geneva Conventions, he laughed at me and said you're not a prisoner of war, you're just a political prisoner." Neither China nor North Korea had signed the Geneva Convention by the beginning of the Korean War (and the U.S. had not yet ratified it). Communist treatment of American POWs reflected a total disregard for international law and an equally contemptuous view of America's will to recover its fighting men.

Dozens of U.S. servicemen were reportedly taken from Korea to the secret Chinese prison camp in Harbin, Manchuria (which, as the reader has seen elsewhere in this book, was known to U.S. officials). At Harbin, U.S. prisoners were executed after being subjected to horrible medical experiments, which included comparisons of how much pain blacks could take versus whites. The experiments were allegedly supervised by Soviets from the Red Army medical corps, according to a July 1992 *Los Angeles Times* report.

The Chinese and North Koreans were confident that they could do whatever they wanted with captured Americans.

The case of First Lieutenants Gilbert Ashley, Harold Turner and Arthur Olsen, Second Lieutenant John Shaddick and Airman Second Class Hidemaro Ishida is a chilling example. On April 22, 1953, a pro-U.N. guerrilla unit operating behind North Korean lines reported ambushing an enemy truck and liberating five U.S. airmen who had been captured by the communists. Via radio transmission with the guerrillas and the Americans, U.S. officers "identified positively" that the men were crewmen of a U.S.A.F. B-29 bomber shot down on January 29, 1953.[13]

Operation Green Dragon

A month after making contact with the airmen, the U.S. launched rescue operation "Green Dragon." "Voice radio ... was used with Lt. Ashley directing the pilot to ground station," but as the rescue aircraft arrived, enemy machine guns opened up from at least two directions. The rescue was aborted. Rescue officials soon determined the aviators were actually under control of communist troops, who were using them to get supplies and equipment. The officials continued to keep in touch, careful not to reveal they knew that the operation had been doubled and that Ashley was apparently being forced to work for the North Koreans.

Finally, the Korean War ended. The next day, U.S. officers sent a message to the American airmen:

> To Ashley: request your captors to turn you into the nearest POW camp for exchange. You have been used by communists as bait in a planned scheme complete rpt complete details of which are known here. Your names and evidence of well being are

being given to the Armistice Commission in compliance with the Armistice Agreement which was signed at 271000 Communists cannot plausibly deny you are alive and must arrange your exchange or be charged with violation of armistice.

A reply was received on August 6:

Many agents were killed to rescue and guard the aviators. We were awakened from your deadly murderous action. We will not work anymore for you. Furthermore we resolved that in case you don't give us an answer regarding this message by 1700 hours 4th August we will self surrender to NK [North Korea] after we killed the five aviators in revenge." A report later noted that "This last message was interpreted by individuals who had intimate knowledge of this project as confirmation . . . that the airmen were alive on 4 Aug 1953." The men never returned.

Other Americans remained in North Korea and China after being sentenced by communist courts. Many of the men were prosecuted for fighting communist indoctrination and harassing the numerous American collaborators, most of whom returned to U.S. control.[14] First Lieutenant George W. Patton was sentenced July 1, 1953, to two and a half years for assaulting a fellow prisoner. "The sentence was not to be affected by repatriation."[15] First Lieutenant Robert L. Martin "was sentenced to one year for hitting an interrogator." Major Kassel M. Keene had been awarded the Soviet Order of the Red Star for service to World War II ally U.S.S.R., but that was not enough to get him off the hook during a communist trial in North Korea. "Subject was sentenced to 2 1/2 years for assaulting a fellow prisoner. He was sentenced in July 1953. According to the sentence, he was not to be affected by repatriation."

Obscure Reasoning

The Chinese and North Koreans kept other Americans for even more obscure reasons. The Air Force had eyewitness evidence of live Americans about to be repatriated in September 1953 who were suddenly held back by the communists. "Listed in the Nielson-Henderson list of USAF personnel known to be in Kaesong awaiting repatriation" but never returned were: Captain Jack V. Allen, Captain Harold Beardall, Second Lieutenant William J. Bell, Airman Third Class John C. Brennan, Staff Sergeant Joseph S. Dougherty, Technical Sergeant Robert F. Gross, First Lieutenant Edward S. Guthrie Jr., Tech Sergeant Robert W. Hamblin, Captain Luther R. Hawkins Jr., Second Lieutenant Frederick R. Koontz, First Lieutenant Waldemar W. Miller and Captain Fred B. Rountree. First Lieutenant Donald Bell also came within days of freedom, but was mysteriously held back at the last moment.[16]

Despite such galling evidence that the communists were keeping American prisoners, even the U.N. commander could do little but curse the enemy. So negotiations were tried. On September 9, 1953, the United Nations demanded an accounting of 3,404 troops, including 944 Americans (reduced by subsequent intelligence and graves registration work to 389), believed to have been in communist hands but never returned. "The list contains only the names of people who: (1) Spoke or were referred to in broadcasts from your radio stations. (2) Were listed by you as being captives. (3) Wrote letters from your camps. (4) Were seen in your prisons."[17]

"We now demand that you return these people to us or account to us for each of these individuals," declared the U.N. negotiator.

The communists responded:

As a matter of fact, it is precisely your side that has forcibly withheld a considerable number of captured personnel of our side who insist on repatriation. Everybody knows that the South Korean government of your side has forcibly retained 27,000 captured personnel of our side.

That comment referred to Communist Chinese and North Koreans who elected not to return, even though their governments had demanded that they be forcibly repatriated.

The United States had good reason to believe that North Korea and China held Americans who wanted to come home. "At the time of the official repatriation, some of our repatriates stated that they had been informed by the Communists that they were holding 'some' U.S. flyers as 'political prisoners' rather than prisoners of war and that these people would have to be 'negotiated for' through political or diplomatic channels," the government wrote.[18]

A "reliable" newspaper in Taiwan even reported that U.S. and British POWs were being moved deep into China in early November 1953, weeks after all Americans were supposed to have been returned.[19]

That came as little surprise, given earlier CIA reports that China would hold U.S. prisoners to trade for medical supplies. In addition, the Chinese had already established a practice of demanding ransom for American civilians in their hands.[20]

Then, in late November 1953, three South Koreans escaped from the North. They brought word that one hundred other men in their unit alone were being held against their will. Two other escapees later corroborated the claims, but the communist side refused a U.N. request for an independent investigation, saying they held no prisoners. On the 17th of August, 1954, a communist representative claimed "there are no captured personnel of your side for whom our side has to give additional accounting."[21]

American generals knew the communists were lying and ordered a worldwide intelligence effort to support "clandestine action" to recover imprisoned GIs. As of December 1954, at least thirty-four men "positively identified as remaining in the hands of the Communists at the termination of BIG SWITCH," the last POW exchange had not returned.[22]

The U.S. government, however, continued to publicly downplay the POW situation, especially regarding the fliers. "Due to the fact that we did not recognize the red regime in China, no political negotiations were instituted, although State did have some exploratory discussions with the British in an attempt to get at the problem," according to a Pentagon record.[23]

Bargaining Chips

By 1954, most missing Americans had been declared dead; but in June, the Chinese admitted to an American diplomat that they were holding sixteen fliers–fifteen Americans and one Canadian. The Chinese, eager to exploit the bargaining power of the American prisoners, soon upped the ante. "The situation was relatively dormant when, in late November 1954, the Peking radio announced that thirteen of these 'political prisoners' had been sentenced for 'spying.' This announcement caused a public uproar and a demand from U.S. citizens, Congressional leaders and organizations for action to effect their release."[24]

The Chinese claimed that eleven of the fliers had violated Chinese territory. Since that was a violation of Chinese domestic law, Peking said, the men were common criminals, not prisoners of war. By August 1955, intense negotiations had won the release of 15 American airmen, and in return the Chinese got something they dearly wanted: direct diplomatic contact with the U.S. The Chinese had played their bargaining chips well.

The Writing on the Wall

China, however, may have been banking some chips for a later game. The U.S. airmen who returned from China in 1955 claimed other Americans were still captive. Crew members saw other Caucasian prisoners who appeared to be American. Captain Elmer F. Llewellyn, the navigator aboard the downed B-29, saw written evidence of other U.S. POWs at the Peking prison. Drawn on his cell wall were "three or four numerical designations of possible U.S. military units," numbers that the officer had forgotten by the time he was released. Although the numbers were not complete unit names, Llewellyn "reasoned that the writers [had] attempted to convey a message of their existence without exposing themselves to possible punishment if detected." Also on his wall was the name "Heber," along with a date, which the captain could not recall.

He once caught sight of a U.S. Marine Corps officer's uniform drying after a wash, and later, at a second prison, he saw the name "Captain Brown" etched on the latrine wall. Llewellyn erased the name and replaced it with his own, but the next day his name was gone and Captain Brown was again on the wall. This pattern continued for several days. The Air Force officer who took Llewellyn's statement correlated the observations with the case of MIA Captain James B. Brown, USMC, lost on May 30, 1953, and apparently kept forever by China.[25]

Radio operator Steve Kiba saw other possible American captives while in prison. The Chinese admitted holding other Westerners at the time: missionaries, spies and others, most later released. But according to Kiba, one of the men he saw was Lieutenant Paul Van Voorhis, a fellow crew member on his ill-fated B-29. "In my early interrogations the Chinks told me that they had captured two of our crew as they hit the ground on the night we were shot down [January 12, 1953]. They also boasted that they had captured thirteen of us." Kiba said he saw Van Voorhis on at least four occasions between the 20th and 29th of July 1953, but when the Chinese put the crew on trial in October 1954, they said Van Voorhis and the other crewman died in the crash. China returned only eleven from this crew, and the United States accepted the Chinese explanation, even after Kiba was debriefed in August 1955.

"Now when I came home and reported this to the Air Force intelligence and to the CIA and to the State Department, they all told me to forget about it . . . that I didn't see them and that I should never talk about it."[26] The Pentagon kept denying Kiba's reports for decades–until Russia admitted in June 1992 that the Soviets had interrogated Van Voorhis, proving that he had been alive, and abandoned, in a Chinese prison.

Stonewalling

The government also didn't want to talk about the other lost Americans. President Eisenhower refused to meet with the relatives of Korean War POW/MIAs, continuing the long U. S. government tradition of stonewalling the demands of family members for action on the prisoner issue.[27] Secretly, the American government had already admitted defeat in the fight to recover lost Americans in China and North Korea.

"We have been unable, under existing national policy considerations, to bring about an accounting by the Commies on the original 944 list," wrote Pentagon POW expert James Kelleher in 1955. The study concluded the Pentagon should do a better job of encouraging soldiers not to be captured.[28]

Of course, avoiding capture is easier for a Pentagon bureaucrat than for troops on the front lines of the Cold War. At least two crewmen on a Navy reconnaissance plane discovered that in 1956. "A P4M-1Q electronic warfare plane and its entire crew of 16 men were lost approximately 32 miles off the Communist Chinese coast after reporting an attack by Red Chinese aircraft. Carrier and land-based aircraft, along with surface ships, conducted a search. They found aircraft wreckage, empty life rafts and the bodies of two crewmen."[29]

American intelligence knew that two of the crewmen had survived the shoot-down by a Russian piloted MiG. Patrol Boat No. 4 of the Chang-Tu Island Detachment rescued the men, taking them to the Third Ward of the Paoting Army Hospital. A nurse at the hospital reported in mid-September that one of the Americans had already recovered fully and the other was expected to be fine by the end of the next month. "After full recovery both probably will be transferred to Peiping. . . . Fact they are receiving medical care at Paoting Army Hospital closely guarded secret." So secret that the U.S. government never asked the Chinese to return the Americans.[30]

The U.S. did, however, maintain some contacts on the POW issue. The haggling at Panmunjom sputtered on. Between 1955 and 1957, the American ambassador to Czechoslovakia met in Geneva 77 times with Chinese representatives.[31] The Pentagon prominently mentions those meetings in its public relations POW "fact sheets" from the Korean War, but U. Alexis Johnson, the American representative at those meetings, was far less impressed with the U.S. efforts to account for lost Americans in China and North Korea. When he raised the POW issue in 1955, the Chinese representative said it should be discussed at Panmunjom. "In this, he was technically correct, though there was nothing to forestall our raising it at Geneva. In fact, this issue of the 450 MIA's was a poor one and, as far as I was concerned, I raised it at Geneva only for the record."[32]

By 1956, attempts to recover lost Americans through peaceful means had broken down. Early that year, at a Military Armistice Commission (MAC) meeting, the North Korean and Chinese side returned its final accounting of troops alleged by the U.N. to have been held by the communists and never returned.[33] Opposite each name was a notation in Korean. Most of the names had "no data" written by them. In some cases, the communists said the men had been killed in captivity. Next to other names, the Chinese wrote inconsistent or incredible fates. For example, Captain Harry Moreland was listed as "escaped," even though when last seen alive he was a double amputee.

Despite their obvious failure to account for the missing Americans, the communists demanded to know the fate of the 98,739 Chinese and North Korean troops last known to be in U.N. hands. For various reasons, U.N. negotiators were unwilling to make a complete accounting for those men, and it became clear that the MAC meetings were never going to solve the POW/MIA issue for either side.[34]

U.S. intelligence continued to collect information on "a large number of personnel . . . [who] may still be alive" in communist captivity. The operation, run by the Air Force in Asia, was called Project American. "Through information collected from repatriated U.S. and U.N. prisoners of war, Japanese repatriates, foreign refugees, and numerous intelligence reports, a strong possibility emerged that a large number of personnel listed as 'missing in action' may still be alive and interned in Communist prison camps." The objective of Project American was "to investigate the identification of as many of these men as possible . . . by the exploitation of all possible documentary and human sources."[35]

By 1960, the Chinese said it was pointless to discuss "minor matters" such as the release of four American civilians (and, presumably, the POWs) until the Taiwan issue was settled. The State Department concluded:

> The Chinese Communists demand in effect that the United States abandon its mutual defense treaty commitments to the Republic of China on Taiwan, withdraw its armed forces from the Taiwan Strait area, and permit the Chinese Communists to attempt to seize Taiwan by any means including the use of armed force. This Chinese Communist demand is obviously not an acceptable basis for negotiations toward freeing the imprisoned Americans.[36]

But Peking still held on to its human bargaining chips. Chinese defector Wu Shu-Jen saw 70 to 80 Americans during a 1961 trip to a machine tool factory in Qingdao, China, and again in 1967. "[I] also saw the American peoples in the factory.... [The] manager of the factory told me it was American peoples from the Korean War."[37]

Soon the Chinese had a new opportunity to seize Americans: the Vietnam War. The Chinese government reportedly has admitted dispatching over 300,000 combat troops to Vietnam. More than 4,000 reportedly died at the hands of U.S. and Allied forces. As in Korea, the Chinese inflicted their own casualties and captured their own prisoners, who never returned to America.

Lieutenant Junior Grade Joseph Dunn, flying a Navy A1H attack plane, was shot down off Hainan Island, China, on February 14, 1968. Before being driven off by Chinese MiGs, the crewmen on a second U.S. plane watched Dunn descend under a fully opened parachute with his manual UHF emergency beeper sounding. Eight hours later, a surveillance plane picked up a beeper signal from Hainan, but Dunn never returned. The Chinese have denied any knowledge of his fate.

On April 12, 1966, Chinese aircraft downed a U.S. Navy KA3B tanker carrying Lieutenant Commander William Albert Jr., Lieutenant Junior Grade Larry M. Jordan and enlisted men Reuben Morris and Kenneth W. Pugh. The plane probably crashed on or near the Luichow Peninsula, Kuangtung Province, China. On December 16, 1975, the PRC returned the ashes of Kenneth Pugh but failed to account for the other three crewmen. They are still missing.

Lieutenant Colonel Dean A. Pogreba went down near the Chinese border on October 5, 1965. Radio Peking announced that Pogreba had been captured, but he was not returned at the end of the war. His family claims he has been seen alive in communist captivity north of Hanoi.

Lieutenant Junior Grade Terence M. Murphy, Ensign Ronald J. Fegan and their F4B Phantom fighter were lost in an engagement with Chinese aircraft near Hainan Island on April 9, 1965. The Chinese have never accounted for them. Others include Lieutenant Commander Forrest Trembley and Dain V. Scott, missing from an August 21, 1967, air mission near the Chinese border.[38]

Perhaps the clearest case from the Vietnam War in which the Chinese still owe an accounting involves Lieutenant Commander John Ellison and his navigator, Lieutenant Junior Grade James E. Plowman. They were flying a carrier-based A6A Intruder on the 24th of March, 1967, when they disappeared near the North Vietnam-China border. POW Robert Flynn, who returned from China in 1973, saw a photo of Plowman, who was in the front row of a formation of American POWs three wide and at least four rows deep. Next to him was Ellison. Neither man has returned, and the Air Force has refused to release information on Flynn's evidence, saying it is still classified.[39]

Some evidence of Chinese involvement with U.S. POWs in Indochina, though, has been declassified. Chinese officials took charge of American POWs at the Lam Thao superphosphate plant in North Vietnam. By 1966, 20 Chinese and several Russians were at this center. "Two U.S. Pilots were taken to the debriefing point at one occasion in 1965, eight in 1966, and an unknown number in 1967," according to a CIA report. When pilots arrived, "a Soviet, a Chinese and a Vietnamese greeted the pilots and led them into the building. The pilots remained in the building for several hours. When they emerged they had changed from uniforms into civilian clothes." The men were taken away, and the source "did not know the destination of the prisoners."[40]

The National Security Agency had evidence that Chinese units in Vietnam captured and retained at least seven and perhaps up to 22 Americans. "We were convinced that Americans were taken" to help with China's aircraft production programs, said former NSA analyst Jerry Mooney. According to Mooney, the following men probably ended up in China: James Barr, Ralph Bisz, Willie Cartwright, James Dooley, Hugh Fanning, Stephen Knott and Charles Lee. Mooney said a source claimed to have seen American POWs in a Shanghai factory in early 1975.[41]

There were also reports that communist forces moved American POWs from North Vietnam into China. "Evidence that the Chinese have been acting as 'bankers' for one of North Vietnam's major bargaining assets, the 600 U.S. POWs, has been building up strongly in Moscow," read an article in the *London Evening News* in 1973.[42] The Chinese allegedly housed the Americans in Yunan Province, just across the border from North Vietnam. The POWs were far enough from Vietnam to be safe from rescue operations and bombing raids, but the North Vietnamese guards told the American POWs that they were still in Vietnam. Victor Louis, the author of the article, has been identified by intelligence experts as a "KGB agent of disinformation," yet he was the first to reveal the downfall of Nikita Khrushchev.[43] According to the article, the Pentagon did not flatly deny the story. "A Pentagon spokesman in Washington said there had been a number of reports of American POWs being held in China, but had no evidence to confirm it."[44]

North Korea was also reported to have obtained U.S. POWs from Vietnam. According to a heavily censored CIA document, two Americans were sighted on the outskirts of Pyongyang, the North Korean capital. "[A]bout 10 military pilots captured in North Vietnam were brought to North Korea," the CIA reported.[45]

The CIA report was supported by other evidence, according to the *Associated Press*. A diplomat saw what appeared to be American prisoners in Pyongyang on several occasions during the 1960s, the AP reported.[46]

And the Pentagon had its own information on the prisoners. "The reports were taken so seriously that U.S. officials from Seoul and Washington met secretly in Hawaii shortly after the war ended in 1975 to plan a possible prisoner release through North Korea," a reliable source who was at the talks told the AP.[47]

On June 5, 1979, Private First Class Ryen Sup "Roy" Chung, a Korean-American, was reported AWOL from his unit, Troop C, First Squadron, Second Armored Cavalry Regiment, in Germany. "The commander's report of inquiry into the absence revealed no evidence or indication of foul play, drug use or defection."[48]

Private Chung, a devout Christian, later surfaced in officially atheistic North Korea, according to the Foreign Broadcast Information Service. After refusing for many weeks to answer questions regarding this case at the Panmunjom talks, the Pyongyang authorities declared in August 1979 that Chung had escaped to the Democratic People's Republic of Korea because he could not "stand the life in the aggressive imperialist US Army." While at least five American soldiers did defect to North Korea, Private Chung's family and human rights experts think he was kidnapped.[49]

About the same time Chung was meeting his fate in North Korea, a visitor to that country spotted what many believe was a large group of American POWs.

In October 1979, Rumanian engineer Serban Oprica, employed at a North Korean factory, was on a bus trip through the countryside three hours from the North Korean capital when they stopped at a village. "By source description, the village appears to have been an agricultural collective," reads a highly censored and previously "secret" Defense Intelligence Agency report on the Oprica story.

As the bus passed a village, the passengers spotted 50 or more people, in traditional North Korean farm clothes, working in a rice paddy beside the village. Suddenly, Oprica locked eyes with a man ten feet from the road. The man was white.[50]

"Source [Oprica] was positive that the man had light colored eyes, possibly blue or gray, and appeared to have been 50 years of age or slightly older." As he watched from the bus, "About eight or ten men ... raised their heads and stared curiously towards the bus. None of these appeared to have been Korean. Rather they were also white, in their 50s, and taller than Koreans."

Other Rumanians on the bus "were sure that these were Americans, 'American prisoners of war.' Several who had been in Korea longer behaved as if such a sighting were neither strange nor uncommon. They said they knew about the 'existence of American prisoners of war in Korea and that it was normal in a communist country.' "

The Pentagon apparently believes North Korea is still holding U.S. prisoners. During a June 1986 phone conversation with Robert Dumas, Lieutenant Colonel Henry Land (then the No. 2 man in the Pentagon's POW office) discussed the presence of living U.S. prisoners in North Korea. "The bottom line," Land said, "is that until the North Koreans get to a position and they want to release prisoners and the remains that are up there, they will do it when they feel it is to their advantage." While the Pentagon has since claimed Land merely misspoke and that there is no evidence of live POWs in North Korea, a tape recording of the conversation leaves no doubt that the officer was referring to living Americans.[51]

Dumas claims that two other Pentagon officials and one former CIA agent have confirmed that U.S. POWs remained alive in North Korea at least through the early 1980s. Dumas, on good terms with the normally reclusive North Korean diplomats assigned to the U.N. in New York, claims they have admitted that discussions concerning living U.S. POWs in North Korea could one day occur.

That, however, is one subject the Pentagon doesn't want to talk about. "POWs in North Korea is not a current issue," Department of Defense spokesman Lieutenant Commander Ned Lunquist has declared. "We look at that as a graves registration issue."[52]

The U.S. government has apparently even pressured the Red Cross to avoid the issue of live Americans in North Korea. In September 1990, the American Red Cross wrote to the relative of a Korean War MIA, revealing that "the Democratic People's Republic of Korea has recently advised them [the International Red Cross] of their willingness to accept tracing inquiries [for POWs]."

But the Red Cross "recommends this not be done. They caution us about the delicate nature of the MIA issue and support the handling of this case through official U.S. government channels." Of course, even after 40 years, those "official channels" have failed to win the release of even a single U.S. POW from North Korea.

In June 1992, Ambassador Ho Jong, North Korean representative to the United Nations, said he could not rule out the possibility that current or former U.S. "war criminals" from the Korean War could be alive in his country. He said the U.S. had never asked North Korea to account for such individuals.

The U.S. also failed to ask the Chinese the right questions about U.S. POWs. When Beijing was ready for concessions in 1973, the U.S. did remember to negotiate for imprisoned CIA agent John Downey. But Henry Kissinger seemed to have forgotten all about the U.S. fliers and other servicemen kept by the Chinese.

"On March 12, 1973, Downey was released, clearing the slate at last of the human legacies of the period of hostility between the United States and the People's Republic of China," Kissinger wrote in his memoirs.[53]

That same month, Brent Scowcroft, then-military assistant to President Nixon, replied to a mother who had written to Kissinger asking for help in recovering her Korean War MIA son. Scowcroft responded: "As you know, we have discussed the question of American prisoners with the Chinese on several occasions, and we have no evidence that the Chinese are holding any prisoners from the Korean War."[54]

During a 1990 interview with co-author Sauter, then-U.S. Ambassador to China James Lilly (a former CIA official serving as of this writing in a high Pentagon position) dismissed questions about American prisoners, refusing to read them and tossing onto the ground CIA documents listing by name U.S. servicemen never returned by the Chinese.

In September 1991, Congressman John Miller took to China the names of American POWs kept by the communists after being convicted of crimes. "In reply, Minister Tao said he could state authoritatively that not a single POW from the Korean War was being held in China. . . ." But Tao agreed to check the list. And U.S. Ambassador J. Stapleton Roy promised: "I can assure you that we will continue our efforts to seek an accounting for any Americans that may have been in China at the conclusion of the Korean War."

But despite such promises, the Bush Administration has been unwilling to put any real pressure on the Chinese to account for American POWs. Soon after the Administration learned in 1992 that U.S. POWs had been medically tortured to death in Harbin, President Bush gave Beijing most-favored-nation trading status.

And the Pentagon has told Congress there is "no evidence" that China held American POWs after the Korean War.

Part IV

The Cold War

Chapter 14

Cold War in the Air

"[A] small number of Air Force crews... are probably held by the Soviet Union.... Your attention is again invited to the undesirability of providing any information through any source which might lead the next of kin of these armed forces personnel discussed herein to assume or believe that these personnel might still be alive and held unless the communists are prepared at some point to document such information."
                              —Secret memo from the Pentagon
                    to the State Department, September 1955

"[I] was serving a twenty-five year espionage sentence and had been a member of a downed United States aircraft."
            —U.S. airman seen in Siberian coal mine, 1950

A relaxed Captain John Roche had just lit a Pall Mall cigarette and co-pilot Captain Stanley O'Kelly had broken out coffee and sandwiches when 20-millimeter cannon fire began smashing into the number one engine of their RB-50 reconnaissance plane. The attacker, a Soviet MiG 15, screamed over the RB-50's wing and "climbed high and half-rolled to the left, his red stars clearly visible," recalled Roche.

As his damaged plane lurched to the left, Roche grabbed the controls. "Feather number one," O'Kelly barked. With the left aileron shot away and an engine belching smoke, Roche pulled back on the throttle to feather the dying engine, while the machine-gunner started hammering back at the enemy. Then another MiG entered the fray, pouring fire into the right wing and engines. O'Kelly sounded the alarm for the 16 crew members to bail out, and as it rang through the plane, the right wing tore free, ripping off the tail and slicing toward the sea 21,000 feet below.

The wounded plane's fuselage lurched up and then down. "I was thrown across the plane," recalled Roche, "bounced head-first off the instrument panel into the nose, was rammed in the stomach by the nose-wheel steering bar and jammed upside down between the auto-pilot stabilizer and the nose glass."

"John!" O'Kelly screamed. "Don't just lie there. You've got to get the hell out." Snapped out of his daze, Roche crawled back into the cockpit. By then, the engineer and a navigator had bailed out. As the RB-50 neared impact, Captain Roche dove through the nose hatch into the howling slip stream, so close to the ocean that his parachute barely had time to open. "I smelled smoke and looked up to see if my chute was on fire. It was open and there was nothing wrong with it. Then my feet touched the water." Roche plunged into the 58-degree water and came up to the sight of a sea on fire, ignited by his plane's burning wreckage. It was 6:30 a.m., July 29, 1953, a new day in the secret air war between the U.S. and U.S.S.R.[1]

Buoyed by a "Mae West" life preserver, Roche paddled to a floating mattress. Bobbing up and down in lonely waters forty miles off the coast of Siberia, the raw bone of his skull stung by brine from the Sea of Japan, Roche called out over pitching swells for other survivors. About an hour later he heard the voice of O'Kelly. "You look real pretty," Roche said as he swam over to meet his badly wounded crew mate. "You look real pretty too," came the reply.

The two officers spent that day and night together. His stomach ruptured and hemorrhaging, Roche fought agonizing cramps and vomited blood into the ocean. Their only company was a big shark. "He didn't try anything, so neither did we," remembered Roche.

The survivors attracted other predators as well. Soviet aircraft and twelve Russian patrol boats beat U.S. forces to the crash site. It wasn't until about 5:50 p.m. the next day that a U.S. aircraft dropped the first life raft to a group of four survivors. Rescuers also spotted a second group of three airmen one-half mile east of where the life raft was dropped.[2] When last seen, seven survivors were headed for the lifeboat, along with nine of the Soviet patrol boats.

Ten minutes later, Roche saw "the most beautiful sight in the world," an Air Force B-29. He fired a flare and spread his yellow dye-marker, but the plane continued on. Minutes later it returned, dropping a raft 100 yards upwind of Roche. Fighting the wracking cramps and vomiting, Roche reached the raft and climbed aboard, but he was too exhausted to start the engine. O'Kelly had drifted seventy-five yards away. Roche could only watch his friend impotently splashing in a feeble attempt to swim to the raft. Too weak even to return Roche's calls, O'Kelly finally flipped over on his back, cupped his hands over his face and disappeared beneath the waves. "He just ran out of steam," recalled Roche nearly half a century later.

By now it was growing dark. Fog obscured the view and Soviet jamming blinded the electronic eyes and ears aboard U.S. aircraft. By 4 a.m., the U.S. destroyer Picking had arrived at the scene. It found only one survivor, Captain Roche.[3] Two bodies were recovered several months later, but the remainder of the crew disappeared.

More than one hundred American lives and twenty U.S. airplanes have been lost in action during similar peacetime reconnaissance operations since 1945.[4] Those numbers are culled from the documents that have been declassified so far and include incidents involving the Warsaw Pact nations, China and North Korea. The figures are probably too low because information on many reconnaissance flights is still classified and because the reconnaissance operations were so pervasive: "One day, I had forty-seven planes flying all over Russia," remarked Air Force General Nathan Twining in the 1950s.[5] Air Force planes not only flew intelligence missions, but also dropped CIA-trained agents deep inside the Soviet Union.[6] Any loss from these flights would be still classified, and a State Department source says it is likely that some of these crews were indeed lost. In addition, the Air Force has admitted that sloppy record-keeping makes it impossible to locate crew lists and other documentation from some downed planes.[7]

The First Spy Flights

The Cold War in the air began when the United States and Soviet Union were still allies on the ground. Even as they fought side by side against the Nazis in early 1945, the two powers had already begun an air war that would span four decades. By March 1945, the British and Americans had launched a massive aerial mapping project over Eastern Europe, where many thought the coming war between America and the Soviet Union would be fought. During operations "Casey Jones" and "Ground

Hog," U.S. and British aviators tried to photograph two million square miles of Soviet-held territory.

As expected, the Soviets defended their airspace. Among the early face-offs, on March 18, 1945, the Russians lost six fighters during an attack on U.S. bombers flying over Germany's Oder River. April 2nd saw several engagements, including one fight in which an American P-51 was shot down.[8]

For a time, the Soviets tried to ban Allied aircraft from the U.S.S.R. through the use of diplomacy. In August 1945 alone, Russian officials lodged 366 complaints concerning Allied violations of Soviet airspace.[9] Communist sensitivity to violations of their airspace was a "reflection of their deeper concerns about the power of the Anglo-American air forces and, perhaps, the capability of those air forces to position Allied intelligence and subversion agents in their territory."[10] From the first days of the Cold War, the Soviets drew a hard line on flights over their territory. They would force down or shoot down any foreign aircraft caught inside their borders. Soviet pilots appear to have also operated under instructions to enforce this policy when aircraft "approach close to Soviet territory without waiting for an actual violation to occur," according to State Department records.[11]

While the Soviet Union made the penalty for "overflights" clear, the Western Allies, hungry for intelligence information on Soviet capabilities, were willing to take the risk. As a result, "almost forty aircraft were lost along the Iron Curtain or on the Berlin air corridors in the period 1945-1947," according to one author.[12] Recently declassified American records appear to contain information on some of those incidents. Heinz Peter Kaldonek, a German returnee from Soviet captivity, told U.S. intelligence that he had been imprisoned in Dresden with an American aviator named Lieutenant Kah, who was shot down over East Germany in August 1945.[13] In 1948, four U.S. airmen were seen in the Soviet Union's Karaganda labor camp.

An Austrian returnee had attempted to smuggle out photographs of the four, but they were confiscated by the Soviets.[14]

By the late 1940s, the United States learned that the Soviet Union had developed an atomic bomb and a delivery vehicle that would threaten all of Europe, and even the U.S. on one-way flights. The bomber was a copy of the U.S. B-29, engineered from American bombers the Soviets had interned during World War II.

Concerns about the Soviet Union's growing offensive punch accelerated the U.S.'s own intelligence offensive. Agents infiltrated the country by parachute and submarine. The CIA floated camera-equipped balloons across the U.S.S.R., and the Air Force engaged in photographic overflights. They even used a converted bomber to carry a small jet to the Soviet border where it was launched for a quick dash into Soviet territory.[15]

Pictures and spies, however, provided a limited spectrum of information. The military was developing a growing appetite for an invisible type of intelligence electronic signals. Radar signals could disclose the type, location and capability of Soviet defenses, but before spy planes could monitor the signals, the Soviets had to turn them on. The process used to provoke them to flip their switches is called "ferreting." Frequently, shallow penetration of Soviet territory was required on these ferret flights in order to accomplish that task.

Electronic warfare had played a role in World War II, but the capability had withered in the immediate postwar era in the absence of military conflict. The Navy even sold much of its electronic gear, so two chief electronic technicians were dispatched in civilian clothes to buy back equipment sold to junk dealers. They "purchased all the intercept receivers, direction finders, pulse analyzers and other electronic reconnaissance equipment they could locate," according to a Navy history of the era.

The Early 1950s

The Navy then repaired and installed the equipment in PB4Y-2 Privateer and P2V Neptune aircraft "for the high priority electronic reconnaissance or 'ferret' missions around the periphery of the Sino-Soviet bloc nations, and particularly Russia."[16] It was a Navy ferreting mission that suffered the first widely known U.S. loss in the Cold War's air war.

Jane Reynolds was too ill with morning sickness that spring morning to get up and make her traditional pancake and sausage breakfast for Lieutenant Junior Grade Bob Reynolds and his crew before they left Morocco's Port Lyautey Navy base for a mission to Europe. She would later feel somehow guilty for not making that breakfast, even though the young mother, pregnant with her second daughter, did get up to kiss Bob good-bye. It was the last time she would ever see the strapping Annapolis graduate.

On Saturday, April 8, 1950, Reynolds's "Privateer" reconnaissance plane, Bureau Number 59645, took off from the U.S. Air Force base at Weisbaden, West Germany. The plane and its ten-man crew were flying what the military would, twenty-five years later, admit was a "special electronic search project mission." The text of the classified Navy investigation insisted that "the scheduled flight plan of the subject aircraft did not include any routing over foreign territory."[17]

When the plane failed to return, the U.S. military launched a massive search over the Baltic Sea that eventually involved more than twenty-five aircraft. At first, the searchers found no evidence of the missing spy plane. But they did detect significant Soviet activity, including submarines.[18]

The day after, the Soviets protested the overflight of their territory by an American aircraft. An American B-29 bomber had penetrated twenty-one kilometers into the

Soviet Union, claimed the diplomatic note. When Soviet fighters demanded that the B-29 land, it opened fire. The Russians returned the fire and "the American airplane turned toward the sea and disappeared."

On April 21, 1950, the Soviet government, in *Pravda*, warned of the consequences of overflying their territory, saying such incidents would result in the aircraft's being forced or shot down. The president of the Supreme Soviet even decorated the four pilots who downed the Privateer.[19]

The U.S. search continued, hampered by the Soviets' electronic jamming. Two life rafts were eventually recovered. One was fully inflated and the second was partially burned. Both were of the type carried by the Privateer. Swedish fishermen began to pull pieces of the aircraft off the floor of the sea and eventually located where the substantially intact aircraft was resting, at a depth of 150 feet. Unfortunately, the Soviets won the race to salvage the Privateer and its electronic equipment.

It was clear to officials that the Soviets had shot down the plane. The crew members were declared dead on April 9, 1951, and evidence strongly suggests that eight of the ten survived and were incarcerated by the U.S.S.R. The wife of another crewman told Jane Reynolds that Polish fishermen had watched as the smoking plane came down for a flat landing on the Baltic. Eight crewmen emerged onto the wing. Soon, a Russian submarine surfaced and captured the men. A "fairly reliable" CIA source confirmed that "The American flyers were saved, but they will never be repatriated."[20]

By 1954, the Navy concluded that the Soviet Union had salvaged and was operating electronic equipment from an American plane, probably the Privateer. "In view of the successful salvaging and operation of the electronic equipment, there exists the possibility that some or all of the crew were taken into custody and are being held by the Soviets." They then requested that the necessary "collection requirements" be issued to determine whether any members of the crew were captured.[21]

In 1955, John Noble and William Marchuk, two American citizens who had been imprisoned in the Soviet gulag for years, were released.[24] From different sources, both had learned the same thing: that the crew from the Privateer had been captured by the Soviets.[22] Intelligence officials could or would not corroborate those claims, but reports of surviving U.S. aviators from the plane continued to escape from behind the Iron Curtain. One German who returned from Soviet captivity reported "a man who could have been aboard the PB4Y-2." Another German said he had met an American lieutenant from Pennsylvania. "It is believed it [the report] could refer to Lieutenant John H. Fette," from the Privateer, wrote a Navy official.[23]

In late 1952, a Japanese prisoner at Inta was assigned to a street-cleaning detail with a Caucasian who was sentenced under Soviet espionage laws. The Japanese prisoner was told that the white man was "an American airman of NCO rank" who had "been downed along the German USSR border." Another American was also reported to be at the camp.[24] A CIA report quoted an "intelligent and cooperative" source who "reports having seen an American at a prison in Lemberg [Lwow] sometime in the spring of 1949 [a date that may have been confused] who was being held by the Soviets as an American spy."[25]

He was described by the source as: "Name not recalled; Age: between 33-35 years; Hair: light brown; Weight: approximately 180 lbs; Height: approximately 5'8"; Peculiarities: had a dry eczema condition all over his body; had the words 'U.S. Navy' tattooed on his chest, with the picture of an anchor; Language: English." A German prisoner at Lemberg told this source that the American held the Navy's equivalent of a sergeant's rating. The American was transferred from Lemberg prison and never seen again by the source. The CIA report also indicated that the agency might have information about Privateer crew member Joe Danens.

Years after the Baltic incident, "an escapee from East Germany appeared in West Berlin and claimed to have been released from the infamous Soviet prison coal mine at Vorkuta, above the Arctic Circle. He stated that one of his fellow prisoners had said he was 'ensign Roberts' of the U.S. Navy and had been a crew member of the lost Privateer." It is possible the escapee was referring to Baltic MIA Lieutenant Junior Grade Robert Reynolds.[26]

In July 1955, Secretary of State John Foster Dulles updated President Eisenhower on the case. "We have also received a number of reports from returning European prisoners of war that members of the crew of the U.S. Navy Privateer, shot down over the Baltic Sea on April 18, 1950, are alive and in the Soviet prison camps."[27]

The clearest indication that some or all of the Privateer crew survived surfaced in 1956, when a State Department cable to the U.S.S.R. claimed that the U.S. government is

> compelled to believe that the Soviet Government has had and continues to have under detention crew members from the Privateer. . . . [M]embers of the crew of this United States aircraft were, and are, detained in Soviet detention places in the Far Eastern area of the Soviet Union. In particular, it [the U.S.] is informed, and believes, that in 1950 and in October, 1953 at least one American military aviation person, believed to be a member of the crew of the United States Navy Privateer, was held at camp no. 20 allegedly near Taishet, and Collective Farm no. 25, approximately 54 kilometers from Taishet, under sentence for alleged espionage. This American national was described as having suffered burns on the face and legs in the crash of his aircraft and using crutches or a cane. Reports have been received from

former prisoners of the Soviet Government at Vorkuta that in September 1950 as many as eight American nationals, believed to be members of the crew of the United States Navy Privateer to which reference is made, had been seen in the area of Vorkuta and specifically that one person who was interned at Vorkuta in September, 1950 stated that he was serving a twenty-five year espionage sentence and had been a member of a downed United States aircraft.[28]

In the late 1950s, Bob Reynolds was reportedly held in a Ministry of Internal Affairs psychiatric clinic in Sychevka, in the Smolensk region of the U.S.S.R. He told a Russian in the next cell that all the crew members had been isolated by the KGB, "which began at once working with him in order to win him over to the Soviet intelligence service." Reynolds refused to cooperate and was sent to "the special clinics at Sychevka."[29] This report appears to be corroborated by President Yeltsin's June 1992 letter admitting that U.S. aviators were held in psychiatric prisons during the 1950s.

But despite several U.S. requests, the Soviet Union never, including during the Gorbachev regime, accounted for the lost Baltic fliers. There is only one proven fatality from the shoot-down, the sixty-two-year-old father of Lieutenant Howard Seeschaf. "On Saturday morning, April 8, after reading the telegram from the Navy telling him his son was missing, the elder Seeschaf jumped five floors down the dumbwaiter shaft at his Bronx, New York, home. He died later in Fordham Hospital."[30]

But there would be casualties of other kinds as well. In the days after the shoot-down, Jane Reynolds's daughter would ask what happened to her father, and the mother could only say, "He's on a flight that took longer than usual. We'll hear from him soon." During Jane's sweat-soaked dreams, Bob Reynolds would appear and "take me in his arms and kiss me." But with the birth of her second daughter and the Navy's insistence that her husband was dead, Jane Reynolds continued her life. Her husband made her promise she would remarry and start a new life should something happen to him. "I never thought it was possible that he might have to make a life for himself in the Soviet Union. I hope he did."

The Cold War Heats Up

As surviving members of the Privateer crew met their fate in the U.S.S.R., the hottest action in the Cold War air conflict shifted to Asia. In June 1950, North Korea invaded the South. Officially, the war pitted South Korea and the U.S.-led United Nations forces against the North Koreans and, later, China. However, the Soviet Union, sharing a common border with North Korea, also played a key role in the war. Ethnic Koreans from the U.S.S.R. served in critical roles throughout the North Korean government. Thousands of Soviet troops advised communist units, manned anti-aircraft guns and flew combat missions against American aircraft.

While neither the U.S. nor Russia wanted a full-blown fight, the nations still exchanged military blows. In September 1950, Navy fighters downed a Soviet bomber off the Korean coast. The next month, two U.S. F-80s strafed a Soviet airfield near Vladivostok, just north of the Korean border.

Many Americans viewed the Korean War as the first step in a communist plan to attack Japan. For the Russians, Korea represented a massive projection of American military power near the Soviet Union's relatively weak Asian defenses. The key to that defense was a string of Russian-controlled islands called the Kuriles. Starting just above the northernmost Japanese-held island of Hokkaido, and continuing north to the Kamchatka Peninsula, this line of rocks seals off Russia's Sea of Okhotsk, protecting the coast of Soviet Asia from intruders. The Soviets had one problem, however; neither the United States nor Japan acknowledged Soviet ownership of the first four islands in the chain.

It was yet another dispute born of the Yalta Agreement. President Roosevelt had promised Stalin the Kurile Islands, plus the Japanese-occupied southern half of Sakhalin Island. The two leaders struck the deal at their second private meeting at Yalta on the 8th of February, 1945. The agreement was theoretically designed to reverse previous Japanese land grabs.

In reality, the Kuriles had not been stolen from the Russians they had been given away. "If the President had done his homework, or if any of us had been more familiar with Far Eastern history, the United States might not have given all the Kuriles to Stalin so easily," wrote diplomat Charles Bohlen, who was FDR's translator at the Yalta conference.[31]

Having bluffed their way into possession of the Kuriles, the Soviets completed their triumph by seizing the rest of what they wanted in the area in September 1945, moving into the Japanese Northern Territories. The Pentagon set out to profit from this diplomatic mistake. It came in the form of intelligence. Planners realized that aircraft launched from Japan could ferret almost the entire Soviet Asian coast.

American planes began to ferret Soviet Asia on a regular basis. In October 1947, the U.S.S.R. protested a violation of Soviet airspace over the Kurile Islands, the first of many complaints lodged in the 1950s. "It was in those years that American aircraft were repeatedly ordered to violate Soviet airspace in some cases getting shot down in order to provoke the Soviets to turn on their radars," making it possible for the electronic warfare specialists to gather the required data. By the 1960s, "the United States had mapped every significant radar site" in the Kuriles "and was on the alert for new facilities."[32]

On November 6, 1951, an American P2V operating under U.N. command in Korea was shot down over the Sea of Japan near the Soviet Union while allegedly on weather reconnaissance in connection with U.N. operations in Korea. The Soviets charged that the plane had violated its border and had opened fire on two Soviet fighters that had approached.[33] The plane had actually been on a shipping reconnaissance mission off the Soviet coast. The Soviets attacked the plane to prove that the same "severe Soviet air-defense policy" that resulted in the Privateer downing a year before now also applied to the Far East. A Rand Corporation study concluded that the incident had been a deliberate policy of the Soviet government and that the "Politburo wishes to convey the idea that the incident in question occurred as a result of policy."

According to a U.S. Air Force radar operator, the Soviets even allowed an Air Force amphibious plane to recover the dead from the plane, which had been downed right off Vladivostok Bay."

Despite clear evidence that the Soviet Union had deliberately downed an American plane and killed or captured the crewmen, the State Department decided to downplay the incident. The State Department did not want to have direct U.S. and Soviet dialogue over it since the shoot-down was actually a dispute between the United Nations and the U.S.S.R. The fate of the missing crewmen took a back-seat to diplomatic priorities. The State Department concluded:

> The American flyers were lost in performance of duty and, as such, are unfortunate casualties of the Korean War and, as much as we dislike it, there is little we can do to obtain redress from the circumstances that they were directly involved with Soviets in distinction to the indirect Soviet involvement which is causing general casualties in Korea. In the circumstances, I think it is probably more in

accord with realities of the situation if we take no further action in this case.[34]

After another American plane was shot down over Hungary and a $132,065 ransom paid for the return of the crew, worried Pentagon officials visited the State Department to press for a stronger American stand against the Soviet policy of attacking foreign aircraft. One Pentagon representative named Sullivan expressed concern about American inaction after the November 1951 downing of the Navy P2V, especially since the military was convinced that the plane had been shot down over international waters. "He emphasized again that it was very important that something be done to show the Soviets they cannot get away with it."[35]

The Navy's representative said, "It certainly would help our pilots to know that we would not sit idly by if anything happened to them." The aggressive stance adopted by the Navy put the State Department in the middle of an inter-service dispute, because the Air Force took the opposite approach. They feared that using returned airmen to publicly disprove Soviet claims about the location of shoot-downs would backfire, "if the US forces this case on the USSR the latter would retaliate in all future incidents by shooting the crews."[36] So the U.S. continued a restrained approach to the killing or capture of its reconnaissance air crews.

On the morning of June 13, 1952, a U.S. Air Force B-29 bomber modified for surveillance, took off on a classified mission to gather intelligence on Soviet shipping between the Sakhalin and Kurile Islands.[37] U.S. radar operators tracked the plane for more than three hours until it left their screens about 100 miles northwest of Hokkaido, cruising over the Sea of Japan 120 miles from the Soviet coast.

The next day search planes sighted at least one, and perhaps two, empty six-man life rafts floating about 300 miles off the southern tip of Hokkaido, 100 miles off the Soviet coast.[38] Another report said that a Soviet radio broadcast mentioned that an American survivor or survivors had been picked up in the area.[39]

On June 18, U.S. officials approached the Soviet government for help, noting the debris discovered off the Soviet coast, which included oxygen bottles and life preservers. "The presence of such items would indicate that there were survivors who may have been picked up by Soviet ships."

In the end, the Soviets claimed to have no knowledge about the crew. That was a lie. A Japanese repatriate from POW Camp 21 in Kharbarovsk reported that twelve or thirteen U.S. airmen were in this prison during the spring of 1953. He had heard from the Soviet prison guards that this was the crew of a military plane shot down by the Soviets.[40] An officer from this crew was later "observed in October, 1953 in a Soviet hospital north of Magadan. . . . This officer stated that he had been convicted, wrongfully, under item 6 of Article 58 of the Soviet penal code."[41]

Sergeant William Koski, who helped search for the missing B-29, was himself shot down the next month during a Korean War bombing run. Soon after arriving at a special POW camp in China, "the interrogation got around to Major Busch [from the lost B-29]. Continuously back to that subject, again and again. If he were dead at the bottom of the Sea of Japan, why all that interest? I am as convinced today as I was then that they had Busch . . . and maybe a few others of his crew."[42]

On October 7, 1952, the Soviets attacked another B-29 over Nemuro Bay. U.S. radar operators tracked two Soviet fighters heading toward the lumbering bomber. But it was too late for U.S. jets to come to the rescue. "They [the B-29 crew] were screaming 'Mayday' over the radio. The last transmission we heard was 'Let's get the hell out of here,'" recalled a radar operator who tracked the incident from Japan.

By the time U.S. fighters reached the scene, the plane had crashed, and Soviet patrol boats were leaving the crash site off the Russian-held Yuri Island.[43] The American government demanded to know the results of that search.[44] The U.S.S.R. admitted firing on the plane, but only after it had fired at Soviet fighters. The Soviets provided no information on the crew.

The next major incident was the attack that left Captain John Roche in the Sea of Japan in 1953. He had barely been picked up and dried off by the Navy before the Soviets grabbed the diplomatic offensive. A Soviet note delivered on July 30 claimed that the RB-50 had entered Russian airspace near Vladivostok and then attacked Soviet MiGs.

That evening, the U.S. response reached the American Embassy in Moscow. "It appears almost certain that Soviets now have in custody some survivors," said the telegram. "You are requested seek immediate appointment with Vyshinski or other available Foreign Ministry official and to convey to him" the U.S. position.

The next day, Charles Bohlen, now U.S. ambassador, met with Deputy Foreign Minister Andrei Gromyko to dispute the Soviet claims and demand an accounting of the missing American aviators. But the Soviets again took the initiative, presenting a protest over a recent attack by U.S. fighters on a Soviet IL-12 commercial plane over China, which the Soviets claimed had taken 21 lives.

When Bohlen brought the meeting back to the RB-50 incident, "Gromyko stated . . . there was no knowledge of the plane or its crew and repeated that statement contained in Soviet note that when last seen it was flying out to sea." A request for information on survivors also got nowhere: "Gromyko repeated he had nothing to add to his previous statement."

So the State Department ordered Bohlen to go over Gromyko's head and straight to the foreign minister of the U.S.S.R., V.M. Molotov:

Essential tactic in your exercise with Molotov would obviously be to treat Gromyko's position as representing only preliminary report from Soviet authorities in Far East and expressing hope that subsequent reports will be forthcoming regarding survivors. . . . Here you should refer to your conversation with Gromyko, implying you understand his negative report would be only a preliminary one and suggesting the possibility of later reports which might throw more light on the survivor question.[45]

But there was to be no help from Molotov. "I repeatedly requested him to have further investigation made. With equal persistence Molotov maintained his position that a thorough investigation had been made and that there was no basis for conducting a further search. . . . In view of position he took consistently that complete and thorough investigation had already been made and there were no grounds for further search, it is not likely we will receive any satisfaction from Soviet government on survivors," reported Bohlen on the meeting.[46]

And that basically ended American attempts to recover the men of the lost RB-50. The U.S. did, however, attempt to bill the Soviet Union for the shoot-down. On October 9, 1954, Ambassador Bohlen delivered a formal diplomatic claim to the U.S.S.R., charging the Russians $2,785,492.94 for the airplane and its crew. America

must conclude that these persons were either picked up alive by surface vessels of the Soviet Government in the area in which they hit the water, or that in due course, dead or alive, they were carried by prevailing currents to Soviet-held territory and into the Soviet Government's custody. . . . Those that were alive when they came into the custody of the Soviet Government, the United States Government finds and charges, suffered in addition injuries and anguish caused by their long detention by the Soviet Government, by the failure of the Soviet Government to inform the United States Government with respect to their whereabouts and their condition or to permit them to communicate with United States Government authorities.[47]

The Pentagon in 1955 noted "evidence based upon radar plots and intercepted voice messages, as well as upon the recovery of casualties, that a small number of Air Force crews whose missions involved flights over the Sea of Japan during the Korean War were shot down . . . some of whom are probably held by the Soviet Union."[48]

That same year, a returning Japanese POW reported seeing Warren Sanderson, a member of the RB-50 crew, in the Soviet's Inta POW Camp No. 7. (The details of the report appear better matched to the case of the crew of the Navy Privateer downed in 1950. But the Japanese POW did identify a picture of Sanderson.) Despite that evidence, the men were declared dead in 1955.

Two other sources, one a Soviet exile and the other a KGB officer, would later report that crewmen from the RB-50 had survived in Siberia until at least the 1970s, according to Paul Lindstrom, a Chicago-area reverend active in the POW/MIA issue.

Even the end of the Korean War brought no peace to the skies over Asia. America's U.N. representative, Henry Cabot Lodge Jr., got the message at a December 1954 lunch with Soviets from the U.N., including Under-Secretary I. Tchernychev. The cordial conversation, lubricated by two rounds of vodka, suddenly turned more serious. "He [Tchernychev] then said, with an entirely different expression on his face: 'Mr. Lodge, why do your airplanes constantly fly over the Soviet Union airspace and over Chinese territory? Why do they do that all the time?' I said I didn't know anything about that. . . .

"Distinguishing between the things that they really mean and the things they don't, I draw the conclusion from this that they are sincerely bothered by flights in and around their airspace. . ."[49]

That was proved again and again as the Soviets downed three more U.S. planes in 1954 and early 1955, killing one U.S. serviceman. On May 14, 1956, the Soviets protested repeated violations of their airspace, including one flight that penetrated 750 kilometers into the far north of the Soviet Union.

On September 10, 1956, another Air Force RB-50 and its sixteen crewmen disappeared over the Sea of Japan, with the U.S. government blaming the loss on Mother Nature. The United Press reported that an "Air Force spokesman discounted the idea that the RB-50 might have been shot down. The plane was tracking Typhoon Emma, which caused millions of dollars worth of damage in the Far East."[50]

But that was just a cover story. Recently declassified records show that the crew had planned to avoid the typhoon, which didn't even cross the mission's flight path until hours after the plane was due home. The RB-50's real mission had nothing to do with tracking weather. It was actually on an intelligence mission off the Russian coast. Because of the nature of the mission, radio silence was maintained following take-off. Radar tracked the plane as it flew between Japan and communist air space. The United Press reported that Japanese searchers found five or six empty life rafts believed to have come from the RB-50.[51]

On October 13, the U.S. Embassy in Moscow requested the assistance of the U.S.S.R. in obtaining whatever information they might have regarding the loss of the plane. One month later, the Soviets said that they had no knowledge of the fate of the plane or its crew. The crew was then declared dead.[52]

A Lull in the Cold War

It would be two years before the next known Cold War aircraft shoot-down. On June 29, 1958, an Air Force C-118 flew into Soviet airspace during a trip from Nicosia, Cyprus, to Teheran. Soviet fighters attacked the plane, and five crew members bailed out while the remaining four rode the plane in. Once on the ground, the crew blew up the plane with built-in explosives. The U.S.S.R. returned all nine fliers ten days later.[53]

The next group of Americans to land in that area of the Soviet Union wouldn't be so fortunate. On September 2, 1958, an EC-130 surveillance plane carrying 17 Americans violated Soviet airspace near Kinegi, Turkey. The plane was undoubtedly collecting intelligence, but questions remain about whether it deliberately entered Soviet airspace. The U.S. claimed that Soviet navigational beacons lured the C-130 across the line, and an Air Force review of the incident called the border crossing "inadvertent."[54] Evidence emerged, however, that the plane purposefully penetrated Soviet airspace, and two NSA defectors to Moscow publicly claimed the plane intentionally violated the border.[55]

As for the Soviets, they claimed to not know how the plane even crashed. But U.S. radio intercepts of Soviet fighters pilots provide the answer:

> 201, I am attacking the target . . . 218 . . . target speed is 300, I am going along with it. It is turning toward the fence . . . the target is burning . . . there's a hit . . . the target is burning, 582 . . . the target is banking. It is going toward the fence . . . open fire . . . 218, are you attacking? . . . Yes, yes . . . the target is burning . . . the tail assembly is falling off the target . . . 82, do you see me? I am in front of the target . . . look! Oh! . . . look at him, he will not get away, he is already falling, I will finish him off, boys, I will finish him off

on the run 62 . . . the target has lost control and is going down.[56]

On September 24, the Soviet Union returned six bodies, only four of which could be identified.

The Air Force could not determine their exact cause of death, but the condition of the remains, with carbon monoxide in their lungs, appeared "consistent with injuries experienced in aircraft accidents involving high speed impact preceded by fire."[57] The returned remains were "the torsos of those in the nose portion of the aircraft when it was hit by a rocket, causing an internal explosion and then fire."[58]

Those in the rear may have bailed out or been saved by Soviet soldiers "who arrived at the scene within minutes after the crash." The men in the rear of the plane would have included highly trained electronic intelligence experts, prized catches for Soviet military intelligence. The Soviets had no intention of revealing the status of the missing men.

Little more than a month after the shoot-down, Premier Nikita Khrushchev denounced the U.S. version of the incident, claiming that the EC-130 had been snooping on a new Soviet radar system. This time, however, U.S. officials showed an unprecedented desire to get the men back. They not only revealed the secret transcripts of the shoot-down, but also told the Soviets that America had "additional and very important information" on the incident.[59]

U.S. Ambassador Llewellyn E. Thompson pressed the case with Khrushchev, who again claimed ignorance about the cause of the crash and the fate of the missing crewmen. "Khrushchev impressed me as being embarrassed about C-130 case," he wrote. "Although there is slight possibility bodies were consumed in crash I think this unlikely. Probable Soviets have all or some of missing airmen but see no way out other than to stick to their story."[60]

In August 1959, Vice President Richard M. Nixon raised the issue with the Soviet leader and got nowhere. Concerned that Khrushchev had painted himself into a corner by publicly claiming he had no idea how the plane crashed or where the missing airmen were, the U.S. decided on one last tactic, a direct, personal and private approach from the president of the United States.

In October, the State Department relayed a message from Eisenhower to Khrushchev. "I know of Vice President Nixon's exchange of letters with you about this case, and I want to express my own hope that the appropriate Soviet services will again look into this question to see if there is further information which I can provide to the families of the missing airmen," Ike wrote. "I am encouraged to renew this personal appeal because of the fine and understanding attitude you took toward such human problems during our talks at Camp David." But Khrushchev stuck to the established line.[61]

The State Department concluded, "We believe it is now clear that the Soviet Government, barring a radical internal development or drastic change in our relations, will never concede that they have knowledge of the eleven men missing from this plane."[62]

One month after the shoot-down, the Soviet acting foreign secretary, Vasily Kuznetsov, told Ambassador Thompson that the "United States should look for these men." On the same day, the Soviet air attache in Washington, D.C., hinted that the missing airmen "might be walking about." The U.S. speculated that these disclosures meant that the Soviets were contemplating "dumping" the men or their remains on the Soviet-Turkish border. A report was also received indicating that the men had been seen alive on the ground, and the parents of Airman Robert H. Moore claimed to have information that the Soviets imprisoned their son in the Taishet labor camp,[63] where so many Americans have been sighted over the years.

The Moores' allegation gained credibility two years later, when a leading Soviet magazine reported that the missing Americans had parachuted from the plane before it crashed, only to be captured outside Yerevan. The article, by East German writer Wolfgang Schreir, created a sensation when it appeared in *Pravda* publishing's *Ogonek* magazine. The Soviet government denied the article was true, but it would never have been printed in a *Pravda* publication unless the government approved it. As the U.S. ambassador in Moscow concluded, the Soviets may have been sending a message that American air crews would become "unpersons," if captured flying over or near Soviet territory.

The Early 1960s

The next year, 1960, would see three major incidents, including the U-2 affair, when a U.S. pilot was captured after his spy plane was shot down. Exactly two months after the U-2 incident, Red Air Force pilot Vasily Polyakov won the Order of the Red Banner for downing a U.S. RB-47. The plane had been ferreting the massive radar complex along the Soviet's Kola Peninsula. Two days later, reporters in Austria asked the Soviet leader about the fate of the plane and its crew. "Chairman Khrushchev looked up blankly," and said, "I know absolutely nothing of the plane! And I wish you would stop bothering me with your damn planes!" He then laughed and reached for his drink.[64]

Two of the American aviators from the RB-47, Captains John McKone and Bruce Olmstead, were released in 1961. Khrushchev would later admit publicly that their release was delayed until after the 1960 presidential election in order not to help Nixon's chances of winning.[65]

All the high-tech electronics personnel in the rear of the plane had bailed out, but none returned. Prized intelligence assets that they were, any that survived joined the legion of American "unpersons" behind the Iron Curtain. Shortly after the U-2 shoot-down, the United States announced the termination of all spy flights over Russia. American satellites could perform the same function without the risk.

Looking Back

In 1973, 1976, 1978, and 1992, the State Department requested information on the Baltic fliers lost in 1950. After the 1978, approach the Soviets chided the United States, reminding the State Department that such things did "not serve the interests of a development of relations between our nations;" a not too subtle suggestion to abandon the aviators diplomatically as well as publicly.

It has been more than 30 years since the last known incident where an American was taken prisoner during a reconnaissance mission against the Soviet Union. In all those years, no one has better summed up the fate of America's lost POWs from the Cold War air campaign than the mother of a missing crewman from Captain Roche's plane when she wrote to President Eisenhower:

> It must be evident that these men just didn't disappear from the face of the earth someone knows something of their fate. . . . Believe me, I write from the fullness of my heart and not with bitterness or resentment. I love my son as you do yours. I only pray if he is dead, God will ease the pain and loss. But if he with his crew members are in a slave camp somewhere, God forbid our neglect of them.[66]

Chapter 15

Cold War on the Ground

*"About 40 years old, about 175 cm. tall; dark blond hair;
dislocated chin which slightly hindered him while talking;
very thin. Had been an officer in West Germany. While
on duty on zonal border had been kidnapped by Soviets
who threw a bag over his head, dragged him into their car
and drove him to East Germany, from whence sent to
Vorkuta [Soviet slave labor coal mine]."*

*—Americans Detained Under
Foreign Agency, U.S.S.R.
from declassified Army Intelligence
and Security Command file*

In 1954, Gregory Peck hinted at one of the Cold War's
darkest secrets in a Sidney Lumet movie called "Night
People." Peck played a tough American colonel in Germany trying to rescue GI Corporal Johnny Leatherby,
kidnapped by the Russians.

The Russians are willing to give Leatherby back in exchange for two Germans in U.S. hands. A trade "just like the Cubs and Phillies," Peck's character explains to the corporal's father, played by Broderick Crawford.

Peck gets Johnny back. But even Hollywood conceded that the endings weren't always happy in the real world. "Sometimes," Peck explains in the movie, "they [the Russians] dope them [U.S. soldiers] up and put them through a kind of kangaroo court. And sometimes you never hear anymore about them."

That nearly happened to Private Wilfred Cumish. When the company clerk at his Army intelligence unit in Vienna announced Cumish was being sent back to America for a "bad conduct" discharge, Cumish promptly went AWOL and got dead drunk. The binge would succeed in delaying his discharge for years. But, in this case at least, sooner would have been better for Cumish. His last memories from the day he got the bad news were of taking a room at the Gloria Hotel in the French zone of Vienna and going on a spree.

"On 3 or 4 March 1948, SUBJECT recovered from his state of intoxication sufficiently enough to realize he was not still in Vienna," Army intelligence reported. "I next remembered being arrested by the Austrian police in a small town . . . in the Soviet-occupied part of Austria," Cumish later testified. Still in uniform, he was put in the baggage car of a train. When he awoke from the trip, he was escorted to a Soviet police station. "The two policemen accompanying me were paid some money and I was turned over to a Soviet officer."[1]

The Soviets ripped the insignia and shoulder patch from his uniform and proceeded with the usual program of interrogation and torture. U.S. attempts to interview Cumish after April 1948 "were thwarted by the Russians who claimed they could not locate him, and indicated that they were interested in a woman connected with the case—a former Soviet kidnapping target—possibly in exchange for the alleged deserter." When the hostage deal collapsed, the Soviets convicted Cumish of espionage and sentenced him to fifteen years in the notorious Vladimir prison. Cumish would not return to U.S. control until September 1955. He was promptly given his bad conduct discharge and booted out of the Army.

Cumish was apparently the victim of the new stage of hostage politics that followed World War II. The Soviets, having failed to grab everyone they wanted in the hostage trading at the end of the war, turned to kidnapping, which also served as a handy method of collecting intelligence and scientific information. Staffers of a special Soviet intelligence section used Russian agents and foreign criminals to abduct Nazis, war criminals, anti-communist activists, Soviet defectors, scientists and intelligence agents. One American official even "aided the [Soviet security] organs by forcibly abducting Germans who lived in the U.S. secretly and who were on the Soviet arrest lists. To facilitate his 'work,' he used a U.S. Army jeep to transport victims to a Russian exchange point, where he sold them for cash. At his trial, he insisted that he was an entrepreneur, not an ideologue."[2]

During the October 22, 1945 "Operation Osvakim," battalions of Soviet troops blocked off whole areas of East Berlin as arrest squads swept down on their victims. By one estimate, it took the Russians only 24 hours to arrest 15,000 German scientists and technicians, who were told that they'd be returned after five years of forced labor for the Soviets.[3]

The Soviet kidnapping program targeted German scientists, according to Soviet defector Peter Deriabin. "German scientists were taken from Germany during the years of 1945-50 and forced to work for different Soviet military installations. And most of them were kept secretly from the world. But when their terms had expired, or when they wanted to do so [return home], they were not permitted to do so, because it was the feeling of the Government and of State Security that they could reveal some secrets of the scientific field, and they kept them against their wishes."[4]

Kidnapping of Americans

It is possible American scientists shared the same fate. In Stalinsk, a U.S. intelligence source "met an American engineer in 1948 whose name he could not recall . . . the engineer was engaged in building the Kubass Ministerstwo K Plant, a 9.4 mile long factory, which was apparently an artillery ballistics research center. . . . Other Americans were engaged in the project."[5]

But most Soviet abductions focused on more ordinary targets—just about anyone who got in the way of the Russian intelligence operations. "A favourite Soviet technique was the abduction of people wanted for routine questioning from one or the other of the Western Zones of Germany and Austria."[6] At first, MVD (Soviet intelligence) agents grabbed their victims during the day. After Western protests they turned to nighttime operations and disguises. Russian agents dressed as German police and, in at least one case, an American MP. They also contracted abductions out to gangsters, who were sometimes paid in cigarettes. "The Russians were relatively indiscriminate about who they grabbed or their nationality. Allied nationals who had happened to stray down the wrong street were just as likely to end up in an MVD cell as anyone else."[7]

That included Americans. A U.S. Counter Intelligence Corps agent was kidnapped while "guarding an American informant when a Russian snatch team attempted an abduction. This was cut short by the intervention of British Military Police, who arrested one of the Soviet agents along with the CIC agent and took them both off to an Austrian jail. Twenty minutes later a Red Army squad burst into the jail and took the CIC agent and the Soviet agent away by force. But the Soviet agent had left his papers behind and the next day these were traded for the CIC agent, who had been so badly beaten up that he had to be hospitalized."[8]

Many more Americans were kidnapped but never returned. These unlucky men appear to be among the more politically sensitive "soldiers of misfortune," perhaps because many of the servicemen were involved in espionage when captured. As a result, the Pentagon continues to censor the names of kidnapped Americans and the former Soviet prisoners who saw them.

One American captain, seen alive in 1950 at the Vorkuta coal mining complex, was arrested during World War II. "About 50 years of age; tall, slender, grayish blond hair. Said to have been seized by Soviets while traveling inside the USSR accompanying unknown type of lend-lease shipments during WWII. Sentenced to 15 years of forced labor."[9]

Most Americans were captured in the divided territories of Vienna and Berlin. The Soviets snatched an American military doctor in Berlin in May 1945. Years later the American, by then a long-time inmate in the Soviet labor system, told a fellow inmate that he had been born in Cuba, was a surgeon and had held the rank of lieutenant colonel in the U.S. armed forces. "He had performed a difficult brain operation on some . . . Russian . . . and that the Soviets had asked him to accept Russian citizenship," which he refused.

An Air Force lieutenant from New York was "arrested in East Berlin in 1948 or 1949 when he tore down a picture of Stalin while drunk. Participated in an uprising of POWs against the MVD guards on behalf of another prisoner and was thereupon sentenced to 25 years confinement and shipped to Asbest."[10] Perhaps it was this same officer reported in January 1952, a thirty-year-old American serviceman with short brown hair who had arrived at the Asbest Camp. He told a fellow prisoner that he had participated in a revolt against the authorities at his previous camp. The malnourished American "was a nervous wreck and refused medical treatment."

A Lieutenant Pfeiffer in the U.S. Air Force came under Soviet control "while driving a jeep." An "American officer who was intoxicated and got lost in the Soviet sector of Berlin," he was never heard from again. At Vorkuta Camp 9, a U.S. "source met a former U.S. CIC colonel who was known in the camp by his former German name, Fuerst von Brandenfels," who "claimed that he had been stationed in Berlin after World War II and had visited the Soviet Zone regularly with an East German pass for reasons unknown to source. Once he visited the 'Mexico' bar in East Berlin and got involved in a dispute. The bar was then checked by Soviet troops and, since Brandenfels was drunk, he showed his CIC credentials instead of his East German pass and was arrested." He was sentenced to twenty-five years "forced labor for espionage . . . and was transferred to Vorkuta where he was still stationed when source left in November 1951."[12]

At about the same time, in Vorkuta Camp 6, the Soviets held a Major Schwartz from the CIC. In his mid-fifties, Schwartz spoke English and some Russian. He said he had been arrested in Germany, probably turned in by a double agent.[13]

One report came in a letter addressed to the American Embassy in Germany. It began:

> Very honored Sir: As a German returnee from a Russian War Prison, I feel it my responsibility to inform you of the following . . . an American Colonel was held in custody at a Russian . . . prison . . . this colonel is supposed to have made an emergency landing . . . this colonel was sentenced to 25 years imprisonment for espionage and was enroute to Vorkuta . . . the Colonel urgently requested that American authorities be informed that his personal adjutant, a man in the rank of Major, worked hand in hand with the Russian Secret Service. Proof of this was brought out during the investigations. . . . I

believe that I remember the name of the Colonel to be Stevenson or something similar. Most respectful, Otto Hafner.

George MacKelly "was seen in a prison at Verkhni-Uralsk in November 1953. An Austrian who was in the adjoining cell communicated with MacKelly by knocking signs, and also twice saw him walking down the hall. MacKelly claimed he was a U.S. Army captain and had been stationed in Hanover, FrankfurtMain and Berlin. He was arrested by the Soviets in Berlin in 1950 and sentenced to 25 years by the court in Moscow." First Lieutenant Gaby, thirty-five years old, 5'8" tall, slender, black eyes, black hair combed back, told an Austrian he was a "member of an American Military Police unit stationed in Berlin, that he was kidnapped by the Soviets in 1948 while performing Officer of the Day duties and that he was sentenced to 25 years imprisonment."

In June 1953, a U.S. source saw an American officer in a Vorkuta convalescence camp. He was described as "About 40 years old, about 175 cm. tall; dark blond hair; dislocated chin which slightly hindered him while talking; very thin. Had been an officer in West Germany. While on duty on zonal border had been kidnapped by Soviets who threw a bag over his head, dragged him into their car and drove him to East Germany, from whence sent to Vorkuta."[14] A German POW in Vorkuta met a U.S. colonel with a name that sounded like "Latwek," during 1949. About forty-three years old, he had blond graying hair, was 5'10" and of Yugoslav origin, a first-generation American. He was arrested in the Soviet sector of Vienna in 1949 while wearing civilian clothes, pushed into a black sedan and driven to an unknown Viennese jail, convicted of espionage and given twenty-five years at hard labor.[15]

A U.S. Air Force officer was kidnapped in November 1950, in the Soviet sector of Vienna. The American was about thirty years old, blond hair, blue eyes, tall, limped badly and had to use crutches. He had either a burn or birthmark on the right side of his face. Treated well by the Soviets, he was considered to be one of the "prominent prisoners."

A young Austrian woman named Martha Oberegger went to the U.S. Embassy in Vienna in 1955 to report meeting "Frank." She had forgotten his last name, but he was a major in the U.S. Army and was still in uniform when she first saw him in a Soviet prison. The tall, slender and dark-haired twenty-six-year-old said he had recently married and had a baby. "Frank was apparently stationed in Trieste and while on a trip through Baden he was arrested, in September 1949." Frank was accused of espionage, had been sentenced to death and was to be executed in 48 hours. Eight days later, when she next saw him, he was taken away from the prison for a few hours. When he returned he was completely drunk. A short time later he was again removed and never seen again.

The Dangers of Sightseeing

Even sightseeing could be dangerous for American troops in Cold War Europe. "During the end of August 1947, three U.S. soldiers "were brought under escort to the MVD prison in Dresden. They were in uniform when they arrived. The Russians shaved their heads and replaced their uniforms with dirty German clothes." The prisoner who witnessed their arrival was able to get a look at the uniform insignias. One was a technical or master sergeant," thirty to thirty-four years of age, sturdy, about 5'9". The second was a 5'8" private, about twenty-seven years old. The last one was a stout private in his early thirties, about 5'7" tall.

The men had been on a trip to see the sights of Berlin. "The leader of the party was the sergeant who knew Berlin already and wanted to show some of the sights to the newly arrived soldiers. They were walking in the Soviet zone of Berlin when they were apprehended without cause."

In an ominously similar case three years later, a U.S. source saw an American officer and two enlisted men in full uniform arrive in early 1950 at the Soviet screening prison in Halle, East Germany. "They had been captured by Soviet troops when crossing the Bavarian zone border by mistake and East German radio announced that the Americans had asked for asylum." When the U.S. source later saw the three Americans, they had been convicted of espionage and sent to Vorkuta.

The steady loss of Americans finally provoked some action in Washington. In 1953, the State Department complained to the Pentagon about its poor record in recovering servicemen in Soviet and East Bloc hands. "Dept of State felt max effort not being made by mil auth overseas to determine whereabouts and seek recovery of individuals by direct contact with foreign officials or agencies concerned."[18]

Defections

Part of the problem may have been embarrassment. Not only was the military losing troops to Soviet kidnapping, it was also hemorrhaging a steady flow of defectors to the East. Not all Americans in the gulag were abducted by Soviet intelligence or Army units. By November 1966, at least 136 peacetime soldiers had defected to communism. While some had died and many others had returned to American control, 63 Americans were then still living in communist nations. At the height of the Cold War, there was even a "defectors colony" and special hotel for U.S. servicemen in Bautzen, East Germany.[19]

The motives for defection ranged from ideological conviction to alcoholism to prosaic domestic problems. Specialist 5 Thomas Badey went AWOL from his Berlin infantry unit in June 1963, later appearing in East Germany. "He defected because of mother-in-law problems. ... " Employed at an electrical plant, Badey was reported to have a fondness for drink and a strong dislike of East German TV.

Stephen Wechsler, on the other hand, was an intellectual who belonged to leftist groups while attending Harvard University. He defected to East Germany from a U.S. infantry unit in 1952. Wechsler later developed into a trusted member of East Germany's communist elite, according to Army intelligence records. Billy Mullis walked across the border from West to East Germany in 1959. Mullis "made communist anti-American speeches at meetings of his labor union, and once spoke in the Bautzen [East Germany] city hall before a large crowd. ... He has stated that he would never return to US control or the US until a socialist government is in power."

The more understandable motivations of Specialist 4 Leon Baker, a black GI, fall somewhere between ideological and personal. In November 1960, Baker defected to East Germany while on leave from his unit in the U.S. Baker was in love with a German woman and the "apparent reason for subject's defection was to enable him to marry the female West German citizen and cohabitate with her. ... Baker's fellow soldiers in Kentucky advised him that such would be impossible in Kentucky, and there are other indications that Baker felt resentment at what he considered racial prejudice."

So when Baker arrived in East Germany, he told an official "he was not interested in politics and just wanted a job." Baker soon learned that racism was not confined to capitalist countries. Baker got in a fight and quit his job because of racist remarks by East Germans. He later requested to return to U.S. control and began publicly referring to himself as a "full blooded capitalist American." By 1963, Baker's intelligence file ends. He had already been imprisoned twice for trying to escape to West Germany.

The full extent of U.S. defections and Soviet kidnapping is still buried in classified U.S. files. An American military intelligence agent who requested anonymity said the last well-known Soviet attempt at kidnapping a U.S. citizen in Berlin occurred during the late 1950s. But years later, Americans active against Soviet intelligence and/or briefed on sensitive U.S. projects still faced travel restrictions to minimize the risk of kidnapping. "There was no indication that they would [kidnap us], it was a precautionary measure," recalled the agent.

He noted, however, that Americans continued to disappear from Europe under murky circumstances. From the early 1970s to the late 1980s, an average of one American soldier per year vanished from units in Berlin. Most of them were categorized as "KWOLs," or knowledgeable (of classified information) AWOLs. They were dropped from the rolls as deserters. When asked if they could have been abducted, the intelligence agent replied, "I have no idea." The military services themselves, when questioned about the fate of KWOLs, claim to have no information.

Part V

Southeast Asia

Chapter 16

Indochina

"[T]he Soviets are willing to spend millions of dollars in bribery; they'll use sex, they'll use drugs, they'll use anything they can to get high-tech information."
— Jerry Mooney,
National Security Agency staffer

Mary and Stephen Matejov emerged from St. Raphael's Catholic Church in East Meadow, New York, on a cool day in March 1973. The funeral Mass for their son, Joe, an electronic warfare specialist shot down over Laos on February 5, 1973, had just concluded. They were nearly ready to get on with their lives. Then someone approached with a shocking message. "We have a message from one of Joe's friends [in Vietnam]," the stranger told the grieving parents. "Don't be surprised if Joe walks in the front door someday."

"What are you talking about?" the Matejovs replied.

The stranger responded, "We were told in the letter not to write back and ask questions. Not to bring the subject up in writing because the person who sent it could be in trouble for revealing information he shouldn't have revealed."

"That was the first indication we had that Joe was alive," Mrs. Matejov remembered. Since then, her family and the family of Peter Cressman, another crew member on the eight-man reconnaissance flight, have been trying to find out what happened to their sons. The Defense Intelligence Agency, which has the mission to identify and return any live POWs, claims "there is no evidence that any crew members survived the crash."

Matejov and Cressman worked for the NSA's Central Security Service (CSS), which ran electronic intelligence gathering flights over Southeast Asia. Their EC-47 lifted out of Ubon Airfield in Thailand about 11 p.m. on February 4, 1973. Two and one half hours later, the pilot radioed a forward air controller and reported receiving 38 mm anti-aircraft fire. After that, the plane dropped off the radar screen and crashed. On February 17, 1973, they were declared dead, eliminating an embarrassing obstacle to the impending Laotian peace agreement, which was signed the next day.

But in a letter to the Cressmans, the commander of the EC-47's air wing had admitted "a possibility that one or more crew members could have parachuted to safety." And on the day of the shoot-down, the NSA intercepted communist radio transmissions that stated: "Group is holding four pilots captive and the group is requesting orders concerning what to do with them." One month later, "a Lao provided U.S. intelligence with detailed descriptions of the four captives. The four were identified as Sgt. Peter Cressman, Sgt. Dale Brandenburg, Sgt. Joseph Matejov, and Sgt. Todd Melton."[1]

The first NSA staffer to expose what the government knew is Jerry Mooney. As an Air Force sergeant working for CSS, he tracked more than 300 POWs on the ground in Southeast Asia, of whom only 5 percent came home. But it wasn't until the late 1980s, after he left the service, that he started to disclose some of this confidential information. A member of the 6970th Support Group, Mooney had intercepted and analyzed North Vietnamese communications. Among them were orders to "shoot down the enemy and capture the pilot alive, and shoot down the enemy and execute the pilot."[3]

More importantly, he revealed, "North Vietnamese messages revealed an interest in selecting priority targets to include F-111 aircraft, airborne intelligence collectors, F-4 laser bomb-equipped aircraft and electronic support aircraft." The reason was to repay Vietnam's Soviet benefactors, who wanted access not only to American equipment but also the people who could use it— American POWs. Cressman, Matejov and the other members of the EC-47 crew would be a prized catch for Soviet military planners.

Despite what the government told the families, the men had been captured. "My section received, analyzed, evaluated and formally reported the shoot-down of the EC-47 aircraft in Laos," Mooney said. "Based upon the enemy message which we collected there were at least five to seven survivors who were identified as Americans and transported to North Vietnam.

"I personally wrote the message that these men had been captured alive. In secure phone conversations with the Defense Intelligence Agency we were in total agreement that these were the crew members of the downed EC-47Q."

According to Dr. Roger Shields, a member of the delegation to the Paris peace negotiations, the names of the four men were on the list of POWs American officials would give the Vietnamese, in expectation of their return. At the last minute, Bill Clements, secretary of defense, ordered the names removed from the list. "He said they were all dead," Shields revealed years later. "I told [Clements] we had no evidence of that and we couldn't say that." "You didn't hear me. You didn't hear what I said," Clements angrily shot back. "They're all dead."

Inconvenient Survivors

But they weren't dead. They were shot down after the United States and Vietnam signed the Paris Peace Accords and under that agreement theirs was an illegal flight. They were scratched from the list because they were an inconvenience that would have complicated Henry Kissinger's life. But they weren't dead. Most likely, they were going to the Soviet Union.

Given their actions in every previous conflict since 1945, there seemed little doubt the Soviets would abduct American POWs during Vietnam. By the end of the war, the Soviet Union had invested $3 billion in weapons and 3,000 troops, of whom 13 died, in the Vietnam War. And they wanted a return on their money.[2] As Mooney realized, "the Soviets are willing to spend millions of dollars in bribery; they'll use sex, they'll use drugs, they'll use anything they can to get high-tech information." Over the skies of Vietnam were intelligence assets, "high-tech pilots [who] came down in parachutes just like manna from Lenin, and fell into the hands of the allies of the Soviet Union."

To think that the Soviets would "not take advantage of that situation, a freebie, no expenditure of funds, no blackmail, no espionage, is absolutely ludicrous," Mooney believes. The analysts involved in tracking the POWs knew "from that principle EEI [essential elements of information] that our men would be taken advantage of, would be interrogated and taken on [to the U.S.S.R.] if proved fruitful. Once we knew that, we used our resources and we used our manpower to prove it. And we did."[3]

The First Vietnam POWs

The first American prisoners were apparently shipped from Indochina to the Soviet Union even before the first official U.S. combat troops arrived in the country. Pavel Ponomaryov, a former Soviet Air Force navigator who flew secret missions in Indochina, reported that in August 1961, his aircraft flew two American prisoners from Laos to North Vietnam, where they were delivered to a KGB official. Those two Americans did not return from the war.[4]

When the U.S. began flying sorties over North Vietnam in 1965, the Soviet government escalated its involvement, immediately dispatched military personnel and equipment,[5] and began to develop what would become the world's largest antiaircraft weaponry testing facility.

High-Tech Bounty

In the 1950s and 1960s, Soviet military equipment had performed poorly against the American-made equipment used by the Israeli military. Vietnam was the perfect opportunity to obtain a constant supply of American high-tech equipment and personnel, as well as being a laboratory in which to immediately test all the new ideas.

So the Soviet military established a "very secure area" near Ron Ron, North Vietnam. The Vietnamese called it "Ban," which means "friends." It was a heavily guarded complex that included two separate POW camps.[6] Through analysis, American intelligence established that the Soviets were looking for specific information that would make it possible to change radars for SAM missiles, computer input, targeting data; anything that would enable their equipment to perform better against their principal adversary, the United States. The information gleaned by the Ron Ron facility was exploitable "immediately and on a long term basis."[7]

Getting the equipment out of downed planes was one thing, but it's "what's in my head that makes that machine come alive," explained Terry Minarcin, another NSA staffer in Vietnam. By exploiting information inside selected POW brains, along with the information gained by inspecting and analyzing captured equipment, rapid upgrades were possible in the Soviet-Vietnamese defenses. It became a never-ending process. Increased Soviet competence mandated new American tactics and improved electronics systems, which in turn mandated a further improvement in Soviet capabilities, made possible by the inexhaustible supply of Americans parachuting into their waiting arms.

An American selected by the Soviets and exploited for intelligence purposes would not be allowed to return home. That had been Soviet policy since 1945. Besides, the information inside these high-tech brains was usable for a long time and it was hard to predict when the next supply of brain power would become available.

The U.S. government would not have to wait long for confirmation that the Soviets had established an interrogation center in North Vietnam for select captured Americans. In the fall of 1965, Larry Pistilli was working special, classified missions, the kind where you have "no ID, dog tags or other identification." Having completed a mission in South Vietnam, he was on his way back to base when he "saw a group of 9 Marines pinned down by Vietcong forces. Riding in I was able to make it to them while sustaining some injury. A single chopper came in to evac them but with all the wounded bodies and the VC walking in mortar rounds I waved the chopper off. A mortar round gave me a concussion and shrapnel wounds. When I came to I was roped up by the VC. Having no ID, dog tags or other identification, they took me to an interrogation camp between Dong Hoi and Ron Ron, North Vietnam,"[8] which is south of Vinh in the northern panhandle region.

English-speaking Soviet and Red Chinese interrogators ran the center. After a month of expert communist interrogation and torture, Pistilli escaped during an air strike, along with three other Americans. They commandeered "a French-made truck and drove it all out until we broke an axle," then continued south on foot until "the North Vietnamese finally caught up to us but lost in some frantic hand-to-hand combat."[9]

Continuing south they eventually "stumbled onto a South Vietnamese Ranger outfit that took us all back to an Army post." They were immediately separated and "sent for a classified debriefing." When asked to describe a "classified debriefing," he would only comment that the techniques used by the debriefers were similar to those used by the communists, only shorter in duration, to ensure that the person being questioned revealed all classified information that he had given to the enemy.[10] Three of the escapees had already received their marching orders. They had been selected by the Red Chinese and were preparing for the trip north when the escape occurred. Like the other American POWs who entered this interrogation center, Pistilli and his friends had a rather bleak future: "China, Soviet Union, or die."[11]

According to Mooney, the interrogation center in the panhandle was "a very special prison camp. We knew what types of personnel were being taken there, we knew the prison camp held Vietnamese, Soviet and probably East German interrogators. . . . We knew how they were moved on, over to Laos, which was more secure, up in the Sam Neua area. From there they disappeared into history, just like Korea and World War II."[12]

American aviators were also selected by the Soviets. "I do know that some Cubans and Russians interrogated some American prisoners and treated them badly," testified Bui Tin, former senior colonel in the North Vietnamese Army. During a Senate hearing, he said Russians interrogated B-52 crewmen in December 1972.[13]

While Le Thom, a Lao who later settled in London, was detained in Hanoi's Hoa Lo prison, there were two American prisoners in the next cell being interrogated by Russians. When he asked a guard what was happening, he was told that the Americans were being processed for departure to the Soviet Union. The guard said other U.S. POWs had shared the same fate.[14]

That was confirmed by a Red Army major who was told by a KGB officer that a U.S. POW was smuggled in 1967 through a "window" along the Sino-Soviet border used to move booty from Indochina to the U.S.S.R. "The American was kept alive to tell what he knew about electronic jamming measures on such U.S. aircraft as the RB-47 bombers and Phantom fighters," the major reported.[15] The American, by some accounts missing naval aviator Lieutenant Commander Kelly Patterson, had been sent to the Red Army air defense complex in Sary Sagan, Kazakhstan.

An American high-tech FB-111 was shot down just north of the demilitarized zone on November 7, 1972, probably by a SAM-7 "airburst that caused a vacuum which in turn caused a flameout. . . . [T]he aircraft crashed almost intact," said Minarcin, the NSA analyst, and within 100 hours it was in transit to the Soviet Union. The air crew, Majors Robert Morrissey and Robert A. Brown, were also sent to the U.S.S.R. at that time, according to the former NSA staffers. "Once in the Soviet Union, the hulk of the FB-111 would be stripped bare and completely analyzed. The Soviets would have the added bonus of exploiting the air crew to compliment the analysis of the FB-111 and vice versa."[16]

Mike Bosiljevac was also the kind of high-tech guy the Soviets were looking for. An electric countermeasures (ECM) expert, Bosiljevac "had also gone through an Atomic Energy Commission fellowship to get a master's degree in radiation shielding." Flying an F-105, his plane was hit by a SAM missile over North Vietnam on September 29, 1972, only three months before American participation in combat ended. Bosiljevac and his partner, Lieutenant Colonel James O'Neill, punched out.[17] Other pilots in the area "watched their parachutes, had radio contact with them, and knew exactly where they were. It was one o'clock in the afternoon and Red Crown [the electronic countermeasures aircraft] had contact with them on the ground." Two days later, CBS News broadcast a picture of O'Neill taken in Hanoi.

O'Neill was released five months later during Operation Homecoming in the spring of 1973. "The biggest shock of his life," Bosiljevac's wife said he told her, "worse than being shot down, was to look around the airport in Hanoi ... to give Mike the 'thumbs up' signal. And Mike wasn't there." A Vietnamese prison guard had told O'Neill that Bosiljevac was "alive and well and uninjured." He also cryptically said, "and luckier than you."[18] A few months before Bosiljevac went down he was on leave in Hawaii with his wife, Kay. "The Vietnamese are using Soviet intelligence," he told her. "They know everything about me."[19] He was one of the pilots Mooney spoke of as being specifically targeted, and as he prophetically stated, the NSA would "assume they were gone forever." The Vietnamese had even told Bosiljevac of the birth of their son over Radio Hanoi before the Red Cross did.[20]

Six months after the last POW returned, she went to Southeast Asia. In Thailand, "an American who was attached to MACTHAI [Military Assistance Command, Thailand] took me aside and said, 'I want to talk to you.'" They walked away from the building and he told her, "I found Mike's name on a list with thirty-six others. It was a 'possibles' list." Mike could have been moved to a third country, neither Vietnam nor China, he said. It was a list of technicians.[21]

After the War

In 1976, she flew to Paris and spoke with Mark Pratt, first secretary for Indochina affairs at the American Embassy. "He took me upstairs and closed the door." There, he told her they were "having difficulties making inquiries through the French, because in the past, Henry Kissinger would not allow any activity to go on anywhere without being personally involved."[22] When she told him what the MACTHAI official had said about Mike being in a third country, "his response was, 'It's more likely Russia than China.'"[23] That was diplomatic understatement. After the fall of 1967, Minarcin said, the Soviet Union had the exclusive use of "select" captured Americans, except for a few captured in extreme North Vietnam, near the China border.[24]

For several years, she kept up her hopes. ". . .the packages I continued to send Mike," his wife said, "were always precisely returned to me on our son's birthday. And letters would be returned without photos that I had enclosed, on Mike's birthday. The last one I received, in 1981, came back with an East German postmark . . . on my son's birthday."[22]

Bosiljevac's body was returned from Vietnam in 1982, bearing evidence that he had survived at least several years in captivity and been autopsied in a manner not used by the Vietnamese. According to a Vietnamese defector in 1992, Vietnam "leased" some U.S. pilots to the Soviets. Perhaps Mike Bosiljevac was just such a encyclopedia on loan.

Through the efforts of NSA analysts, the United States government knew that 65 Americans had disappeared after being taken to the Soviets' interrogation center in North Vietnam. By analysis, another 180 to 90 disappeared, eight to 15 into Red China and the rest to the Soviet Union.

But this was not a secret confined to the top levels of the American and Soviet governments. Khamou Boussarath was the chief of security for the noncommunist Laotian government during the war. As such, he had gathered enough information to conclude that "some American air crew specialists were moved to the Soviet Union where the Russians used the POWs to glean information about electronic warfare capabilities of U.S. aircraft."[25]

"The Russians wanted the technology . . . about American airplanes," Boussarath said. They "were having trouble in the Mideast. [Russian] MiGs were all the time getting shot down by American-built planes flown by Israel." They wanted to know why.

After the war, the Soviets continued to exploit the information that continued to be on tap in the surviving American brains held in Vietnam and transported to the U.S.S.R. The SA-6 anti-aircraft missile system fielded by the Soviets after the war would not have been possible without exploiting captured Americans, according to Minarcin. The radio frequency changes and electronic warfare upgrades the Soviets were able to install in this new missile system "had to come out of POW brains."[26]

Even the Soviet space program apparently received a badly needed boost from Americans shipped to the Soviet Union, according to Minarcin. Major (promoted to colonel while MIA) Robert Brown, shot down on November 7, 1972, was an electrical engineer who worked on the Gemini space program's electrical circuitry for command loops and life support. *Aviation Week* and *Space Technology* reported that by 1974 the Soviet Soyuz/Salyut "were now at the Gemini level." The July 15, 1974, issue "attributed the upgrade to enhanced circuitry design in the command loops and in life support," both areas of Colonel Brown's expertise.

According to Minarcin, a linguist who listened in on communist radio signals, after the war the Vietnamese maintained a series of special camps for American as well as British, Canadian and Australian prisoners. Starting at Vinh, the camps stretched through Quan Lang, Bai Thoung, Hoa Lac, Ninh Binh and Thanh Hoa.

Other sources indicate that American POWs were kept in Indochina after the war, with access provided to the Soviets. Former KGB general Oleg Kalugin said his subordinates interrogated U.S. prisoners in Vietnam years after the war.

According to a DIA "Stony Beach" report, American POW Patrick Martin Fallon (USAF) was allegedly debriefed by 12 Russian officers from September 17, 1983, until October 13, 1983, at the commissary building of the old USAID compound in Vientiane. He had been brought from captivity somewhere in Sam Neaui.

Throughout the postwar years, U.S. intelligence reportedly tracked Americans in a number of Indochinese camps. "We knew Cressman and Matejov were alive because there were no deaths" at the camps in which they were most likely held between 1973 and 1978, Minarcin claimed. He believes Cressman, Matejov and 26 other Americans, including special operations troops, were shipped to the Soviet Union between December 1977 and January 1978 because American intelligence was intercepting radio signals concerning flights from the special POW camps to Hanoi. After that, Soviet IL-62 transports piloted by KGB personnel transported the American POWs from Gai Lam International Airport, Hanoi, on a flight path that took them over the Himalayas and on to the Soviet Union. On the last flight, U.S. intelligence picked up a conversation: "There are no more SIGINT [signals intelligence] specialists in country." Cressman and Matejov were SIGINT specialists.

Minarcin heard from another source that, upon landing, the American POWs were hustled onto planes or the Trans-Siberian Railroad for a ride to Sokol on the Poloustrov Tajmir Peninsula. There, the high-tech specialists could be put to good use. Heavily guarded by the KGB, Sokol was the forward deployment base for the Soviet strategic bomber force.

Officially, the Pentagon says there is "no evidence" that any U.S. POWs ever went from Indochina to the Soviet Union. However, the Bush administration does concede that the Soviet Union had a system for moving U.S. deserters from Asia to the U.S.S.R. Up to 25 U.S. deserters went from South Vietnam to Japan to the U.S.S.R., then Sweden.[27] "Beheiren," the Japanese/Vietnam Peace Committee backed by KGB agents, helped move deserters to and through Japan. Once in the U.S.S.R., they were handled by the Soviet Afro-Asian Solidarity Committee (under the Communist Party's International Division).[28]

Now the Russians admit that four American deserters made the trip in 1969.[29] But both the U.S. and Vietnam deny that any U.S. POWs went from Hanoi to Moscow. And Vietnam even adds that no deserters ever made the trip from North Vietnam to Moscow. But the U.S. and Vietnamese claims are contradicted by the case of Jon M. Sweeney, a Marine enlisted man who traveled from North Vietnam to Beijing to Moscow at a time the Pentagon now admits he was a POW.

Sweeney, captured in February 1969, eventually pretended to be a collaborator. During his travels, he escaped an armed Vietnamese guard and turned himself in to U.S. officials at the Stockholm embassy on August 31, 1970.

The Marine was later found innocent of charges that he was a traitor, and, responding to an FOIA request from the authors, the U.S. Marine Corps confirmed that "Mr. Jon M. Sweeney was a prisoner of war" during the time he traveled from Hanoi to Moscow. The Pentagon has refused to release details about the duration and details of Sweeney's time in China and the Soviet Union.

The fate of other American prisoners taken to the Soviet Union is still unclear. A former Soviet political prisoner tells the story of an American who had defected from

Hungary. He married an American woman, had a child and became a U.S. aviator. "Then he was sent to fight to Vietnam, was captured there, deported to the Soviet Union and from there sent to Hungary to go under trial."

The former prisoner said a Soviet military officer also told him in the early 1980s about two American pilots living in Novosibirsk. "They were forced to marry and were constantly guarded to prevent them from leaving."

Those men were not alone. According to a still-classified 1982 CIA report, 200-300 U.S. POWs were transported from Indochina to the Soviet Union during the Vietnam War.

Part VI

The Cover-Up

Chapter 17

Cover-Up in
the Cold War Years

Lehrer: *"A lot of people are wondering why in the world the government of the United States hasn't been raising hell [publicly] about this for the last 15 years or so, or even before that."*

Secretary of State Baker: *"Well, it may have been that the decision was made that if we were going to do any good, particularly with the U.S.-Soviet relationship being what it was, it might have been better to do it privately than try to do it publicly."*

—"MacNeil/Lehrer Newshour," June 18, 1992

"A further complicating factor in the [POW] situation is that to continue to carry this personnel in a 'missing' status is costing over one million dollars annually. It may become necessary at some future date to drop them from our records as 'missing and presumed dead.' "

—Assistant Secretary of the Army Hugh Milton II, in a 1954
memo to his superiors

Some Americans believe that a small group in the U.S. government has engaged in a complicated long-term conspiracy to write off our nation's POWs. We disagree. We believe the truth is even more awful. It was political expediency and indifference–not conspiracy—that shaped the government's cover-up of U.S. prisoners in the Soviet Union.

Presidents Truman and Eisenhower were aware that the Soviet Union held American POWs. For example, in early 1955, President Eisenhower was personally briefed on evidence that hundreds, perhaps thousands, of American prisoners had been shipped from Korea to Siberia. On several occasions, their administrations even asked the Soviets to return American servicemen from World War II, Korea and the Cold War. (However, Eisenhower ordered his staff to write off the American soldiers sent from Korea to Siberia, as is described in more detail later in this Chapter.)

The Soviets responded by denying they held any Americans. The U.S. government knew that was a lie, but rather than hammer away on an embarrassing problem, it filed away the evidence in classified vaults while downplaying and sometimes denying the truth in public.

"Sure top Truman and Eisenhower administration officials knew," POW/MIA advocate Congressman John Miller (R-Seattle) has concluded. "But that doesn't mean that every succeeding bureaucrat knew."

Over the years, evidence of the tragedy sank deeper and deeper into the bureaucratic recesses, buried under mounds of deceptive letters and press releases, until most officials—and perhaps even presidents—didn't know the true scope of the problem. In later years, especially during the Reagan and Bush administrations, those officials confronted with the evidence simply denied or downplayed it, taking refuge behind the previous form letters and denials and leaving the pursuit of the truth to someone else down the line.

Contrary to the claims of America's leaders, U.S. POWs in the Soviet Union were never the "highest national priority." Rather, they were an inconvenience to be ignored when possible and denied when expedient. In this way, the cover-up of POWs in the Soviet Union took on a life of its own, sentencing many Americans to lifetime terms in communist captivity.

There were times when the West actively deceived its people about American POWs and the ugly issues tied to their loss. After World War II, both George Orwell and Alexander Solzhenitsyn noted the success of Western governments in suppressing the awful truth about forced repatriation. "These facts, known to many journalists on the spot, went almost unmentioned in the British [and American] press. . . . " Orwell wrote.[1]

"It is surprising that in the West, where political secrets cannot be kept long, since they inevitably come out in print or are disclosed, the secret of this particular act of betrayal [forcible repatriation] has been very well and carefully kept by the British and American governments. This is truly the last secret, or one of the last, of the Second World War," wrote Solzhenitsyn.[2]

But as the reader has learned, forcible repatriation was indeed not the last great secret of the war. Rather, it was a link in the bloody hostage crisis chain that dragged so many Western POWs into the gulag.

As the war in Europe wound down in 1945, a political decision was made to abandon thousands of American and British prisoners. Documents were manufactured in late May and released on June 1, 1945, creating a revised history to cover the loss. FDR, Henry Wallace, Harry Hopkins, Harry Dexter White, Alger Hiss and other left-wing officials created an unprecedented moral, political and diplomatic disaster through their pandering to Joseph Stalin. The victims of this disaster were the abandoned

POWs, forcibly repatriated Russians, the Constitution and the American people—who would thereafter be saddled with a bureaucracy that learned how to survive and even thrive by lying to the electorate, creating a false history and using disinformation to perpetuate the lie.

The revised history created an almost impenetrable bureaucratic wall that many would assail but none would penetrate for nearly five decades. The *Wisconsin State Journal* exposed the truth on December 1, 1946, when it revealed that 20,000 American soldiers were still held by the Soviet Union more than a year after the end of the war. That was the only Cold War journalistic effort yet unearthed that seriously challenged the accepted historical myth, and it died in a fog of disbelief and government denials.

Ida Mae Reitz Stichnoth, America's first POW activist, knew the *Wisconsin State Journal* report was true. Her son, Edward Lawrence Reitz, was shot down over Rumania in 1943 and listed as an MIA. As detailed in Chapter 11, she eventually learned that her son had been taken to the gulag.

But the U.S. bureaucracy kept pace with her efforts to reveal the truth, running a disinformation program to discredit her and create doubt in the minds of congressmen, senators and journalists prone to take an interest in her story.

After years of battling such a cynical bureaucracy, Ida Mae Reitz Stichnoth could take no more. She lost her mind, wandering the streets of Berlin in search of her son. More mothers would face that kind of shattering grief starting in 1950, when war broke out in Korea.

American intelligence began tracking the movement of American and South Korean POWs to Siberia during the first year of the war. Meantime, U.S. forces began capturing large numbers of communist Chinese and North Korean troops, many of whom turned out to be anti-communists forced into the Red armies.

The communists soon demanded the forced repatriation of all their troops in return for all American POWs. The hostage politics of 1945 had returned to haunt U.S. officials. Once again, a U.S.-Soviet hostage crisis loomed. Americans were abandoned in 1945 because of FDR's agreement with Stalin to forcibly return anti-communists; more Americans would have to be abandoned at the end of the Korean War in order to reverse the policy.

When the Chinese and North Koreans began demanding forcible repatriation of prisoners from their side, the president's Psychological Strategy Board developed a top secret analysis of the problem, sending it to the secretary of state, secretary of defense and the Joint Chiefs of Staff. According to the study:

> Our treatment of Soviet and satellite expatriates has an unfortunate history, as you will recall. As a result of an agreement at Yalta, the United States in the years immediately after World War II assisted the Soviet Union in the repatriation of various categories of Soviet bloc persons—chiefly prisoners of war, escapees, and displaced persons. The result of our cooperation was that more than four million Soviet citizens were returned to the Soviet Union and that thousands were executed or punished in other ways without regard to the conditions which caused their displacement from Soviet controlled territory. In addition, persons escaping from the Soviet area after World War II were forcibly returned to Soviet control as a matter of U.S. policy up until well into 1948. This treatment of Soviet expatriates became well known to the populations within the Soviet area and, as has been well documented, became the cause of widespread despair. It practically stopped the flow of defectors, and it would make it very difficult to wage effective psychological warfare against the Red Army in event of war.[3]

Almost seven years after the fact, the government was still struggling with the disastrous consequences of FDR's actions at Yalta, a policy that Truman had allowed to extend into 1948. But that policy was now changing as Truman administration officials grappled with the POW issue.

"At first, no one expected the POW question to present such difficulty. Our objective had been to get all our POWs back," recalled U. Alexis Johnson, then-deputy assistant secretary of state for Far Eastern affairs.[4]

But Johnson's boss, Secretary of State Dean Acheson, soon let it be known that there were more important factors than the return of American prisoners. "On question of nonforceable return there is both political and mil interest by Sovs. There will be grave consequences on defectors and Sov army if principle [of forcible repatriation] is established," Acheson wrote in a top secret 1952 cable.[5]

The Pentagon, along with many members of the public, disagreed with the diplomats. The military supported forcing even anti-communist prisoners back to China and North Korea. The generals argued that it was the only way to guarantee the return of American in communist captivity. "[T]he Joint Chiefs felt deeply that simple loyalty to our men, plus the morale of our fighting troops, dictated that our overriding concern should be securing the quick and safe return of our soldiers, even if that required us to return to our enemies—for likely reincorporation into their armies—all the POWs we had," recalled Johnson.

But President Truman himself overruled the generals in February 1952. Secretary of State John Foster Dulles later explained the U.S. insistence on voluntary repatriation during a September 1953 speech:

> Let me explain why this principle is so important: the Soviet leaders fear that, if they were to launch a

major war of aggression, many of their soldiers and airmen would seize the opportunity to desert or allow themselves readily to be made prisoners. Such desertions are occurring even now. Therefore, Soviet leaders hoped that the Korean Armistice would establish a principle which would discourage future defections and thus make their Armies more dependable. They demanded in Korea that any who deserted or who were made prisoners, and who espoused the cause of freedom, must be forcibly returned to where they could be punished for their defection. In Europe, after the end of World War II, many who were claimed by the Soviets were forcibly returned, except as some elected suicide as a preferable fate. The Communists wanted the Korean Armistice to elevate that practice into generally accepted international law. We refused.[6]

Of course, Dulles did not publicly disclose the policy's cost—abandoning American POWs in communist hands. In a classified report, U.S. planners had concluded that over the long run, demanding voluntary repatriation would save "more American lives than are involved in the exchange of prisoners problem."[7]

It therefore came as no surprise that when the Korean War POW prisoner exchange ended in early September, many American prisoners did not return. The U.N. commander in chief, General Mark Clark, recognized that he had abandoned many of his troops. "I was in a quandary. The question to me was, 'How do you get these people back without pointing a gun at the Communists?' When you have no gun threatening the Reds, there is no way to demand and enforce compliance from them."[8]

The U.S. did not even attempt to recover Americans taken to Siberia. The Eisenhower administration could not publicly reveal the Soviet role because of the then-secret "Fig Leaf" policy, a White House directive to avoid "confronting the USSR directly" over its major involvement in the Korean War.[9]

American negotiators did press the Chinese and North Koreans to return missing U.S. servicemen. But the U.S. position was hampered by incredibly sloppy staff work on the POW issue. Before June 1951, during the peak loss of Americans, Army intelligence had failed even to maintain a list of U.S. POWs identified in communist radio broadcasts and press releases.

Discrepancies

Once the Pentagon compiled such lists, officials missed many prisoners and miscategorized others. For example, Joseph Hammond, who was captured December 1, 1950, came to know during his years of imprisonment two Americans who were not repatriated: Keith Godwin (unknown rank or service) and Ed Downey, "First Marine Corps." Those men are not on official U.S. lists of unaccounted for prisoners. Air Force Sergeant William Kennedy was seen in Camp Eight but neither repatriated nor listed.[16] Technical Sergeant Langtry, a Marine from VMO-6, was shot down in June 1952 and captured. His name was lost, or withheld, from Pentagon lists.

Corporal Sunnie Lee marched north into captivity with Lieutenant Phillip E. Teague. Teague came home but Lee was listed A-1, killed in action, in the final accounting. Captain Joseph Errigo spent months in a prison camp, but was not listed as captured. Instead, Errigo was categorized as A-2, died of wounds.

More discrepancies appeared in June 1992, when the Russians released a list of Americans who had been captured during the Korean War. The list included a number of men the Pentagon had claimed were killed in action. In addition, 11 Americans the communists captured but never returned were not listed at all on official U.S. casualty lists.

In 1956, an Army intelligence memo summed up the situation: "no real effort has been made toward the collection of information of an intelligence nature regarding Prisoners of War and missing personnel."[10]

The real effort seemed to have been directed at writing off the missing men, and the POW issue, as quickly as possible. The reasons ranged from political to financial. For example, in January 1954, Assistant Secretary of the Army Hugh Milton II warned his superiors that "to continue to carry this personnel in a 'missing' status is costing over one million dollars annually. It may become necessary at some future date to drop them from our records as 'missing and presumed dead.'"

The missing Americans were also costing the administration political capital. In January 1954, the same month as the bean-counters were planning to drop the missing Americans, Ike's POW Working Group nervously discussed a recent congressional attack on administration POW policy and noted: "there is a rumor that the mothers of the missing GIs may organize and bring pressure to bear on the White House and Congress."[11]

Senator Joseph McCarthy and other conservatives had begun to champion the plight of the lost Americans, and the White House apparently feared the explosive nature of the POW issue, especially during a time when superpower tensions were already dangerously high.

On February 3, 1954, a new Army television film on Korean War atrocities made the headlines of the *Washington Post*. The newspaper focused on "Gen. [Mark] Clark's statement concerning communist withholding of allied POWs," an acknowledgment that this activity was indeed taking place. At White House direction, the Pentagon immediately censored Clark's comments from the film, because "including the sequence, on a nation-wide basis would clearly embarrass the Administration."[12]

Downplaying the POW Issue

By early 1954, the Eisenhower administration was actively downplaying the POW issue. During a meeting of top officials in early February, "Discussion pointed out the necessity of gearing any PW effort to a program of political action and also of avoiding a situation where we might raise the hopes of the public and subsequently have to disappoint them."[13]

The Eisenhower administration also wanted to avoid revealing that the principle of voluntary repatriation was still more important than the freedom of American prisoners. The trade-off had come into sharp focus when U.S. negotiators demanded a name-by-name communist accounting of missing Americans last known to have been in North Korean or Chinese hands.

"The Communists have countered the request . . . by demanding that the United Nations Command account for more than 98,000 Chinese and Koreans," White House planners noted. "The United Nations Command does not intend to give the Communists a full accounting of missing Communist prisoners because this would involve identifying all prisoners who had chosen not to return to Communism and could result in Communist retaliation against their families in Communist China and in North Korea."[14]

Since the U.S. was refusing to give an accounting of communist prisoners, the Chinese and North Koreans had a perfect excuse to avoid returning all their American captives. The Pentagon even knew that the Chinese were secretly holding U.S. aviators as "political prisoners."

Fighting Homefolk

The truth had to be hidden because the POW issue was politically explosive. In February 1954, the relatives of missing Americans, banded together in a group called

"Fighting Homefolks of Fighting Men," protested outside the United Nations. The next month, they took their protest to the White House. Soon POW/MIA mothers began returning their sons' medals—ranging from Purple Hearts to the Medal of Honor—to President Eisenhower. "Our sons want your loyalty, not your medals," the mothers wrote.

Eisenhower Knew

Some Eisenhower administration officials were still loyal, working to win the return of lost Americans. In 1954, the State Department publicly requested that the Soviet Union return American POWs from Korea. Moscow replied: "There are not and have not been any such persons in the Soviet Union."

But the White House knew the Soviets were lying, and ordered Philip Corso, then an intelligence adviser to President Eisenhower, to prepare a study on the subject. "It [the request] came from the president through C.D. Jackson [Eisenhower's chief national security aide]. I was supposed to answer the question about missing POWs from Korea," Corso remembered.

The colonel was a logical choice for the project, having worked for military intelligence during Korean War assignments in Korea and Japan. "I knew about that [POWs going to Russia] before. But I needed confirmation that would stand alone. I wanted a living returnee witness in the United States," Corso recalled.

In early 1955, Corso called the CIA and ordered the agency to deliver Soviet defector Yuri Rastvorov to offices directly across from the White House. Two agency operatives soon arrived with Rastvorov, who appeared extremely nervous about his appointment, no doubt recalling the unfortunate fate of many Soviets who were suddenly summoned to the Kremlin.

But Corso treated Rastvorov gently, learning the defector could confirm at least one trainload of 400 U.S. POWs going to the Soviet Union. "He was certain of one shipment. And I knew of other shipments," said Corso.

Within days, Corso and Jackson marched into Eisenhower's office bearing their typewritten report. It was brief and to the point, as Ike liked his reports. "The conclusion was that Korean War POWs by the hundreds, perhaps thousands, had been sent to the Soviet Union," Corso reported to the president.

The aide surmised the Soviets might use the U.S. prisoners for intelligence purposes, extracting biographical details from them for use as cover stories for KGB agents. Corso said it was unlikely that the men would survive and that the Soviets would ever admit imprisoning them. In short, they were, in effect, dead men.

Corso recommended that the fate of the men be hidden from the American people. According to the colonel, Eisenhower "knew about these things. He was pretty tough." Ike never batted an eye when advised to write off the hundreds, perhaps thousands, of U.S. POWs in the Soviet Union.

"He said, 'I think you're right. I accept your recommendation. . . . Thank you, colonel, you did a fine job.' " According to Corso, "the report [about U.S. POWs in the U.S.S.R.] could never be made public and it never was."

Apparently, some officers in the Pentagon were less willing than the White House to abandon American prisoners. By June 1955, the Joint Chiefs of Staff had drawn up plans for a "sea and air blockade of the China Coast" or U.S.-supported attacks on the People's Republic by Taiwanese troops.[15]

But President Eisenhower had ordered that "all peaceful means" of retrieving the POWs be tried before any military action. Cooler heads noted that such provocative military moves had not been used even at the height of the

Korean War. And the Pentagon also conceded that America's allies were "reluctant" to use force.

The Pentagon concluded:

> The problem becomes almost a philosophical one. If we are "at war," cold, hot or otherwise, casualties and losses must be expected and perhaps we must learn to live with this sort of thing. If we are in for fifty years of peripheral "fire fights" we may be forced to adopt a rather cynical attitude on this [POWs] for the political reasons.[16]

After the "cynical attitude" policy was adopted in 1955, American POWs in the Soviet Union (and North Korea and China, then essentially under Soviet control in the POW area) were written off.

By 1955, Eisenhower and his top advisers knew the Soviets had imprisoned American POWs from World War II, Korea and the Cold War. Yet most such information was hidden from the American people and Congress (and some Eisenhower Administration POW records are still classified by order of President Bush and the Pentagon).

Yet such information was never shared with the American people or Congress (and those two reports are still classified as of this writing). In fact, just months after the defector's report was filed, a U.S. senator asked the administration in August 1955 about Korean War U.S. POWs in the U.S.S.R. Assistant Secretary of State Thurston Morton responded that: "To the Department's knowledge there are no United States soldiers in the category of prisoners-of-war being held in the Soviet Union."[17]

The U.S. government even actively suppressed the truth about missing Americans. In that same month that the senator was being deceived by the State Department, air-man Steve Kiba and his air crew returned from China where, as "political prisoners," they had been illegally detained for two years after the war. He reporting seeing one of his fellow crewmen, First Lieutenant Paul E. Van Voorhis, on several occasions in a Chinese prison. But Van Voorhis had not been returned.

Kiba was ordered not to discuss his sightings. And the United States publicly accepted the Chinese claim that Van Voorhis had been killed in his plane's crash. (Decades later, Boris Yeltsin's government confirmed that Van Voorhis and other POWs whose survival was denied by the Chinese had indeed been captured alive.)

The Pentagon did not want to admit a problem it could not solve. On September 16, 1955, Marine General G.B. Erskine, assistant to the secretary of defense, wrote to Walter Robertson at the Department of State, reminding him to keep quiet about American prisoners in the U.S.S.R.:

> There is also evidence based upon radar plots and intercepted voice messages, as well as upon the recovery of casualties, that a small number of Air Force crews . . . are probably held by the Soviet Union. . . . Your attention is again invited to the undesirability of providing any information through any source which might lead the next of kin of these armed forces personnel discussed herein to assume or believe that these personnel might still be alive and held unless the communists are prepared at some point to document such information.[18]

Just as with the lost WWII POWs, whose fate was linked to the anti-communist Russians then engaged in classified guerrilla warfare against the Soviet Union, the fate of the Cold War aviators had to be downplayed in order to maintain the secrecy of their missions. With rare exceptions, unless the communists unilaterally took the first step and admitted they held a specific American, the government would act as if the individual were dead, regardless of information to the contrary. On the few occasions that America did ask the Soviets for information—requests one family member called "powder puff letters"—Moscow's denials were not contested.

Perhaps that could have been justified by an administration fearful of triggering a nuclear confrontation. But even in secret diplomacy, the United States government would soon drop the prisoners as a serious bilateral issue with the Soviets.

So the family members decided to press the Eisenhower administration in court. On January 14, 1957, the strong-featured, charismatic Rita Van Wees stood before the judge of the U.S. District court for the District of Columbia. Representing dozens of other mothers, Van Wees announced that she was suing the president because he had "abandoned members of the Armed Forces under his command as Commander in Chief by leaving them in the hands of the enemy in Korea."

But Assistant U.S. Attorney E. Riley Casey immediately moved to dismiss the case, saying the court had no jurisdiction and that the mothers had failed "to state a precise claim under which relief can be granted."

Matthew McGuire, the sympathetic federal judge, turned to Van Wees. "Do you know what that means, 'no jurisdiction?' "

"I have an idea of what it means," Van Wees responded.

"What is your idea?" asked the judge.

"According to what I have heard, the Court does have jurisdiction," she insisted.

"Let's see if you and I understand each other as to what is meant by jurisdiction," the judge patiently continued, asking: "What do you mean by jurisdiction?"

"I imagine, as Commander in Chief of the Armed forces, he is responsible . . ."

"No, no," interrupted Judge McGuire, explaining: "Mr. Casey [the government attorney] says you are suing the United States here and that his Court has no jurisdiction."

"May I ask who would have [jurisdiction]?" Van Wees responded.

"That is another question," said the judge. "No jurisdiction means that the Court has the right, actually and literally, of saying nothing in the matter. And I think that is true in these circumstances. I will be very glad to hear you, though. Suppose you tell me what you think."

"I think our sons certainly rate a hearing after they have been as loyal to this country as they have been; and they have all been presumed dead with no proof whatsoever. . . . And besides, we [the mothers] shouldn't have to fight with anybody. This is the responsibility of the Commander and Chief."

But it was not a responsibility the commander in chief would fulfill. Rita Van Wees's lawsuit was tossed out of court. And the Eisenhower administration, rather than see its foreign policy challenged, actively deceived the public and Congress about the survival of American POWs.

In May 1957, Stephen S. Jackson, deputy assistant secretary of defense, testified to the House Foreign Affairs Committee that ". . . the impression is still current among some segments of the American people that the United States Government believes that a large group of American military personnel are still alive and held in Asian countries by Communist captors. . . . we do not have any further positive information or intelligence from any source that such is the case."[19]

Yet at that very time, according to then-secret Air Force intelligence records: "through information collected from repatriated U.S. and U.N. prisoners of war, Japanese repatriates, foreign refugees, and numerous intelligence reports, a strong possibility emerged that a large number of personnel listed as 'missing in action' may still be alive and interned in Communist prison camps."[20]

By 1959, a White Russian anti-communist activist based in Greece had told Van Wees that many U.S. and British POWs from Korea were still imprisoned in the Soviet

Union. Later, he would add that her son, "Dutch" himself, was alive and working as a tractor driver. None of this evidence impressed the U.S. government, which in any event already knew the truth.

One of Van Wees's frequent pleas to the White House brought a 1959 response. Edwin Martin, State Department director for Chinese affairs, wrote: "You state that 'there is so much evidence that a great number of Americans are now in the Siberian slave camps.' I am aware that there continue to be rumors and unsubstantiated reports to this effect. However, I must emphasize that the United States Government at this time cannot identify any American military missing from the Korean hostilities as being alive and still held in prison in Communist China, North Korea, or the Soviet Union."[21]

On Labor Day, September 5, 1960, a Polish refugee walked into the U.S. embassy in Brussels, Belgium. There he told duty officer James White a remarkable story. Earlier that year, the Pole had been released after seven and a half years of captivity in Soviet prison Camp No. 307, near the town of Bulun. In that camp, the refugee had met two American prisoners.[22]

The Americans had both been captured in Korea during 1951. One was an infantry lieutenant, about thirty-eight years old. His birthday was April 12 or 13. He had two sisters and was from Buffalo. The second American POW was an airborne sergeant of Polish extraction from Chicago.

"The health of both men is poor as a result of working in the phosphorous mine associated with the camp," White reported, adding that the refugee "said the chemical attacks the head and liver. He showed me how is own head is constantly scaling."

White said the Polish man had not come to the embassy for money. Rather, the man simply wanted to pass on a message from his friends. "These men, who think their families believe them dead, asked [the refugee] to inform the Embassy ... that they were prisoners in the USSR," the diplomat wrote.

It is likely that those men spent the rest of their lives as slaves in the Soviet Union, for there is no evidence the U.S. government ever followed up on the report. Indeed, the record was classified and locked away in a State Department safe for thirty years, until the co-authors forced it out of the Bush administration under the Freedom of Information Act. But while the truth about U.S. POWs would start escaping during the Reagan-Bush era, the U.S. government would continue doing its best to avoid dealing with the inconvenient reality that Americans had been abandoned in the Soviet Union.

Chapter 18

Cover-Up in the Reagan-Bush Years

"The resolution of this issue is one of the highest national priority [sic] in this administration. . . . May God be with you and aid us in ending your many years of suffering."
—letter from President Reagan
to Rita Van Wees,
whose Korean War MIA son
was reported alive in Russia,
December 1982

"I think we're going to end up with absolutely zero . . . my gut feeling is that there's nobody alive under Russian control."
—Malcolm Toon,
Bush POW emissary to Russia,
June 25, 1992

In 1986, two events were occurring that would help destroy the U.S. government's half-century cover-up of U.S. POWs in the Soviet Union. In Moscow, Mikhail Gorbachev had begun unleashing political and economic forces that would eventually sweep out the communist party. And in the United States, a tough former police investigator named Jim Sanders, retired and with plenty of time on his hands, became interested in the POW issue.

Sanders, a co-author of this book, had seen articles by Bill Paul, a *Wall Street Journal* reporter who covered the POW issue throughout the 1980s. When Sanders called Paul offering to help with research on Indochina POWs, the reporter made another suggestion.

Paul revealed that in 1982, a Soviet source had told him that 10,000 American and British POWs from World War II were alive in the Soviet Union. The source even showed Paul a recent picture of a reunion of "The Big Red One," the storied U.S. First Infantry Division of World War II. This reunion had occurred in Siberia.

The *Wall Street Journal* had checked with historians, but no one could explain how so many Allied prisoners could have gotten into the gulag. If Paul's source was correct, a massive cover-up had occurred in 1945. And if that were so, it would provide a logical foundation to an otherwise illogical premise: that the United States abandoned prisoners of war after Vietnam and Korea.

So in June 1986, Paul recommended that Sanders, who had a strong interest in history, check the National Archives for records on WWII U.S. POWs in the Soviet Union. It was there, in the dusty boxes of the archives, that Sanders learned that American POWs "liberated" by the Red Army had disappeared in 1945. It was also apparent that the official military history of WWII POWs was essentially fictional.

Sanders figured that if those initial findings were accurate, some former POWs who had been under Red Army control must have known what happened. He turned to the American Ex-Prisoners of War organization, which provided the names of more than 1,000 former POWs from camps liberated by Soviets.

With help from Texas Christian University graduate student Patricia Wadley, the retired cop listened to the stories of more than a hundred graying ex-POWs. Collectively, the accounts told the story of the hostage politics on the Western front in 1945, the murder of American and British POWs attempting to escape from Soviet forces, and the forcible repatriation and killing of thousands of anticommunist Russians sacrificed for the return of other American and British soldiers.

At the same time, another, very different kind of researcher was digging into the Soviet POW connection. In the summer of 1987, former CBS executive Ted Landreth was unveiling his Vietnam POW documentary "We Can Keep You Forever," co-produced with the BBC. The program included testimony from former National Security Agency worker Jerry Mooney, who asserted that some American POWs had been shipped to the Soviet Union.

Unlike Sanders, who as a cop had solved murder and kidnapping mysteries but lacked journalistic experience, Landreth's Harvard education and years at CBS gave him impeccable establishment credentials. But his show, the most definitive yet on the POW issue, still ran into problems. "Stations which had agreed to buy the documentary were suddenly not talking to the distributor," Landreth recalled. He soon learned why.

The management of one station reported getting a call from the White House. "If you put that British program on the air, you can forget about coming around the White House for the rest of the Reagan administration," the management was told.

That station and many others declined to air the documentary. "This was pretty stunning, as you can imagine," Landreth recalled.

Jim Sanders was about to experience the same stunned feeling. His research almost completed, Sanders and reporter Bill Paul began preparing articles for publication. On August 13, 1987, the *Wall Street Journal* published the first serious report since the 1940s on World War II U.S. POWs in the Soviet. Three months later, the *Washington Times* published a second article written by Sanders.

Immediately, the ongoing Pentagon debunking of Indochina POW stories was expanded to meet this current threat. Colonel Howard Hill, a former Vietnam prisoner and then Pentagon spokesman for POW-related issues, was dispatched to the annual convention of the American Ex-Prisoners of War. There he told the organization's executive director, Chuck Williams, and anyone else who would listen that the newspaper articles were based on "faulty analysis" and completely untrue.[1] Hill managed to persuade the ex-POWs to drop plans for reprinting the Wall Street Journal story.

Understandably perturbed by the Pentagon's assault on his research, Sanders asked Hill for proof the articles were faulty. The colonel's answer was remarkable: He was a "military brat," and while growing up on various bases he had heard many things considered top secret, but never anything about World War II POWs being shipped to the gulag. Then, as a POW in North Vietnam, he had exchanged top secret information with other U.S. prisoners as a way to pass the time. No one swapping stories with him at the Hanoi Hilton ever told him about U.S. POWs in the Soviet Union. Finally, Hill declared that he had searched the National Archives and found nothing to support Sander's research.

But Sanders soon learned that the colonel's brief trip to the National Archives was not of a scholarly nature. Shortly before the ex-POW convention, Hill had visited Room 13W of the archive's Military Reference Section. In uniform, the colonel had demanded that the Military Reference Section stop leaking World War II documents related to prisoners of war kept by the Soviet Union,[2] according to Richard Boylan and John Taylor, Military Reference employees.

In the meantime, congressmen and senators began receiving letters from constituents outraged by the revelations in the newspaper articles. They were assured that the Department of Defense had begun a thorough investigation of the WWII POW issue. But on January 25, 1988, Congressman Jeffords of Vermont revealed to a constituent that "no report was ever initiated."[3]

The Department of Defense had no intention of actually getting to the bottom of the World War II POW tragedy. Instead, on February 6, 1988, a meeting was held at the Pentagon and a decision was made to "neutralize" not only the World War II POW issue, but the personal credibility of co-author Sanders as well.[4]

The initial effort to "neutralize" the issue was soon discovered by Sanders, who had been warned by an inside source about the Pentagon decision. Several documents had suddenly been inserted into the Military Mission to Moscow files, Box 24[5], at the National Archives. The records could not have been accidentally put in the wrong box because they were inserted into the middle of several hundred pages bound together with a metal holder.

The act of insertion was certainly deliberate. The next question to be answered was whether the records were connected to an alleged Defense Department program to "neutralize" the issue. Sanders contacted National Archives supervisor Richard Boylan just outside the Main Reading Room and told him of the discovery. Boylan said the Military Mission to Moscow files had received considerable attention since the newspaper articles began to appear, and if Sanders's allegation was true, the inserted documents could have been placed there by anyone. He refused to inspect the documents sitting on a desk less than twenty-five feet away, turned and walked away.

At virtually the same time, Dr. Carl D. Jackson, deputy assistant secretary of defense, prepared a speech on POWs for presentation to the American Legion in Washington, D.C. The February 29, 1988, lecture was the government's opening public salvo to "neutralize" the issue. Jackson's comments were of such a venomous nature that there could be no change in direction at a later date:

> While discussing the MIAs of World War II, it is instructive to note that conspiracy theories abound here also. For example, there have been recent allegations that the Soviet Union kidnapped nearly 16,000 [sic] American soldiers liberated from Nazi POW camps in Poland.... However, even a cursory review of available information fails to substantiate the proposition that American service members by the thousands were kidnapped by the Soviets. In every instance, we must check the veracity of every story even though we realize, on the basis of historical experience, that most of them will turn out to be rumors at best, and even intentional falsehoods in some cases....

But the falsehoods were all Jackson's. Not one word of his speech, as it related to World War II, was based on fact. He was merely following established policy, just as Colonel Hill had a few months earlier. For the Pentagon's POW policy makers, political considerations, not fact, established policy. And therefore, policy had to become fact. According to the Reagan administration, no American POWs were kept by the Soviet Union after World War II, Korea or Vietnam.

Despite the Pentagon's disinformation efforts, pressure continued growing for a better U.S. government response to Sanders's research. On April 22, 1988, Rear Admiral E.B. Baker, from the office of the assistant secretary of defense for international security affairs, wrote to the commander of the U.S. Army Center of Military History, Brigadier General William A. Stofft. Baker asked for Stofft's organization to undertake an historical analysis of the World War II allegations.

Finally, the Pentagon had decided to do some actual research on Sanders's revelations. But Baker, from the same office that had earlier decided to "neutralize" Sanders's information, made it clear that this research was not to be objective. In his order to the military historians, the admiral emphasized that: "Prominent within the [Sanders] accounts is the charge that U.S. officials were aware of these alleged occurrences and took no corrective action. This aspect is being portrayed as proof of a pattern of U.S. Government abandonment of American POWs. Thus far, a generalized response (attached) has been used to address queries on this subject. However, a stronger, definitive statement will be necessary in order to satisfy public and congressional questions generated by these or similar articles."

The guidance provided by Baker left little doubt as to the direction Army historians were expected to take: "The assertions raised in the articles are surprising. Initial review of available information does not substantiate any proposition that American servicemen are being held captive in the Soviet Union, China or North Korea. Also, we find it very difficult to believe that American officials would allow American servicemen to be treated as poorly as suggested in the articles. . . ."[6] With such instructions from his superiors, General Stofft and his historians could have no doubt as to the conclusions they were expected to reach.

Five weeks later, after the Army Center for Military History had expended only 100 hours reviewing a small portion of the records, Stofft wrote back to Baker, admitting that "a thorough effort would probably consume the full time of a historian for a period of six months to a full year. The Center's ongoing commitments in a time of constrained resources preclude such an effort." He also told Baker that the 100 hours of research had proven "inconclusive." (Actually, a source inside the Army Center of Military History said the Army's limited research had already uncovered evidence that about 5,000 POWs were lost to the gulag.)

Cunliffe's Report

So the Army, perhaps hoping to duck out of the Pentagon's plan to "neutralize" the issue, tossed the archival hot potato to William H. Cunliffe, director of the Special Archives Division of the National Archives, who agreed to prepare a short study related to American POWs liberated by Soviet forces.

On July 8, 1988, Cunliffe forwarded to the Army Center of Military History a report that not only reflected sloppy methodology, but also indicated that thousands of Americans had never returned from the Soviet Union. For obvious reasons, the Pentagon kept the report hidden until Sanders forced it out under the Freedom of Information Act.

The report listed 108 POW camps containing American POWs "presumably liberated by the Russians." The National Archives analyzed individual punch cards made for each POW when the Red Cross confirmed that he was a prisoner. This method of tabulation, based on the initial location of each POW, was flawed, since U.S. prisoners were often moved from camp to camp before being "liberated" by the Soviets.

Despite that, Cunliffe concluded that "at least 36,852" American POWs came under Soviet control. Yet in 1947, the official RAMPs report, which the Pentagon then regarded as authoritative, stated that only 28,662 Americans returned from Soviet control. So Cunliffe's own study indicated that 8,190 Americans were not returned by Stalin.

The number of returnees, using the National Archive's methodology, suggests that an even larger number of POWs disappeared behind Soviet lines. For instance, Cunliffe's study indicated that Stalag 4G had 520 returnees, while records show the camp held 7,076 Americans; Stalag 3A lists only 1,115 returnees but held 4,894 Americans; Stalag 2D had 6,894 American enlisted men shortly before the Red Army overran it, but only 258 are listed as returning; Stalag 2B held 7,087 Americans, but only 5,782 returned; 2,395 POWs returned from Stalag 2A out of a population of 3,700; and of 2,100 Americans at Stalag 3C, only 1,420 returned.

No wonder the center wouldn't release Cunliffe's report—the government's own incomplete research showed that 20,261 Americans never returned from Soviet control.

Cunliffe's response to that problem was to ignore it and bravely soldier on in lock step with the established and growing disinformation effort. He concluded: "it appears that at least [sic] 36,852 POWs were routinely transferred to us by the Russians in the closing days of the war."[7]

When Sanders's requests under the Freedom of Information Act threatened to expose this study's errors, the Army came up with a new ploy. On July 22, 1988, Stofft, the military historian, suggested to Baker "that an appropriate response to allegations that the Soviets retained US ex-POWs would be to ask those making the allegations to identify the individuals allegedly retained."

It was an obvious attempt to place researchers and journalists on the defensive, but Sanders accepted the challenge, offering to produce up to 2,000 names from documents already analyzed and an additional but unspecified number from documents yet to be read. The government beat a hasty retreat, refusing to accept the names.[8]

But Cunliffe would soon get another chance to repudiate Sanders's research. Boylan, the archivist in charge months before when Sanders discovered that new records had been inserted in the archives, finally forwarded copies of those "new" documents to Cunliffe.

On September 2, 1988, Cunliffe began using the inserted documents to neutralize the World War II POW issue. The archivist wrote that he had begun the research "prompted by an article by James Saunders [sic], who cited a message in late May 1945 from Marshall to Eisenhower stating that 15,597 US POWs were held by Marshall Tolbukin [sic], 3rd Ukranian [sic] Army." Cunliffe said that the newly discovered documents showed those 15,597 men were really Soviets, not Americans.

Actually, despite the "new" documents, the historical record shows those men were indeed Americans (see Chapter 8). But the Sanders article had actually stated that the Pentagon knew by May 19 that Stalin was holding 25,000 Americans hostage. It later referenced the 15,597 POWs being held in Austria. The article's conclusion that more than 20,000 U.S. POWs had been abandoned in Europe was not based on the report discussing 15,597 men reported in Austria. But the government focused on that second report, because the new documents appeared to disprove it.

Cunliffe, displaying a true gift for making up history as circumstances dictated, went on his report to pontificate on the method used to return Allied POWs. "The usual handling of such cases was not to pass these POWs back to us across the link-up of USSR and Allied lines in Europe. Generally, the POWs were passed eastward and out through Odessa and the Black Sea," he wrote.

In fact, only 10 percent (2,858) of the American and 22 percent (4,331) of the British POWs were exchanged in this manner. Here was a government official, an employee of the National Archives, who twice demonstrated in writing that he was an incompetent historian or a willing creator of historical fiction—or at the very least unable to shed some light on the truth. He focused exclusively on the "new" documents, incorrectly alleging that they were "the source for Saunders' [sic] assertion."[9]

Someone in government had gone to a lot of trouble to find the World War II disinformation files, long classified, and insert them in the open files as part of a government plan of action to neutralize the issue. And they would be used, because the disinformation warriors had no better course of action.

In October 1988, the minority leader of the U.S. House of Representatives, Bob Michel, endorsed the Pentagon's disinformation in a letter to a Illinois newspaper: "First, the allegation that 20,000 American POWs from World War II were shipped to labor camps by the Soviets and never returned is absolutely false. Apparently, a historical document alleging such an occurrence does exist. However, several later documents reportedly exist correcting that erroneous belief. Authors of stories about this matter apparently did not pursue their archival research far enough."

His constituents later sent Michel information proving that the Pentagon was not telling the truth. But the minority leader was apparently too busy to pursue the truth and continued to spout the Pentagon line.

Still trying to uncover the full truth, Sanders in 1989 contacted Colonel Joseph A. Schlatter, head of the Defense Intelligence Agency's Special Office for POW/MIA Affairs. Sanders asked Schlatter about the "comprehensive report" on WWII POWs that the DIA had promised. The colonel responded by saying the Pentagon needed no new study. "The written study has been done," said Schlatter. "It was done in 1940 whatever, and it's the RAMPs study, and you have a copy of that."

Sanders countered, "Then you are basically standing on the RAMPs report?" It was then that Schlatter revealed the new, key government disinformation statement that would become the Bush administration's policy on the subject.

"Well, I'm not only standing on the RAMPs report," the colonel said, "I'm standing also on the fact that the Soviet Union has been the central focus of all U.S. intelligence operations for at least 50 years of this century, and I find it amazing that I can get exhaustive details out of Soviet prison systems and I find not a single shred of evidence showing American soldiers after World War II in that prison system."

It is not clear whether Schlatter simply was not entrusted with a high enough security clearance to see the evidence, or if he was simply lying, although historical precedent strongly suggests the latter. However, during his travels around the country, in uniform as the Pentagon's top POW/MIA expert, Schlatter continued to declare there was not "a single shred of evidence" that any U.S. POW from World War II had been held in the Soviet Union.

The Air War

Soon the DIA was forced to defend another flank. In November 1989, co-author Sauter presented a series on Seattle's KIRO-TV (CBS) concerning the abandonment of U.S. POWs from the Korean War.

Entitled "Secret Prisoners," the stories produced a major response. At the Sowles home outside Seattle, the TV stories hit like an artillery barrage. Sergeant Willy Sowles was an MIA from Korea, and his son Bill had spent years trying to learn the fate of a father he had barely known. Bill Sowles, a bookish-looking man with the intensity of a street fighter, immediately took the KIRO information to his congressman, Seattle Republican John Miller.

"When he laid out his claim to me I was surprised but skeptical," recalled the congressman. But Miller was soon converted by the stonewalling of the Pentagon: "They certainly were not very forthcoming about the evidence. I remember feeling very frustrated."

Sowles also wrote to President Bush. On February 23, 1990, Army Colonel M.A. Hohertz responded. "As much as he would like to, President Bush cannot personally respond to every communication he receives; therefore, I have been asked to assist you. In the following letter I will attempt to clarify some of the issues you have raised."

The letter went on to combine provable lies with more subtle disinformation. For example, Hohertz informed Sowles: "There is no evidence that 389 (or any other number) Americans were held in captivity and not released at the end of [Korean] hostilities." That statement contradicted even the Pentagon's official policy. According to a 1990 statement from the Defense Intelligence Agency: "there are 389 Americans that we know were held by the North Koreans at one time and are still unaccounted for."

Hohertz also claimed that Colonel Delk Simpson's report of American POWs being shipped to Siberia aboard trains really referred to "French colonial troops," once again repeating proven falsehoods about that report.

Perhaps the most cynical response by Hohertz was his questioning of videotaped statements by former aviator Steve Kiba, who reported seeing his fellow crew member, unrepatriated POW Paul Van Voorhis, in Chinese hands.

"Although he [Kiba] could not give a positive identification, he thought it was Van Voorhies [sic]," claimed Hohertz. That was disinformation. The truth, which was then secret, later came out when records were declassified at the National Archives.

Contrary to that letter sent on behalf of President Bush, Kiba, immediately after his release from China, had indeed reported seeing First Lieutenant Paul E. Van Voorhis on at least four occasions between July 20 and 29th, 1953.

According to the declassified document: "Source [Kiba] stated that if this man was not Lt. Van Voorhis, he was Lt. Van Voorhis's twin brother."

So the Pentagon, speaking for Bush, had twisted Kiba's words to raise doubts about his identification. In truth, the

Pentagon had been worried about Kiba's explosive testimony for years.

"Now when I came home and reported this to the Air Force intelligence and to the CIA and to the State Department, they all told me to forget about it . . . that I didn't see them [Van Voorhis and other unreturned Americans] and that I should never talk about it," Kiba remembered.

An outraged Sowles wrote back to Colonel Hoherz, noting among other points that "Mr. Kiba represents his statements to be true and 'would be willing to swear to it.' Would you, Colonel Hoherz, be willing to do the same?" For obvious reasons, neither Hoherz nor President Bush ever wrote back.

(The Pentagon's plan to discredit Kiba and bury even the memory of Van Voorhis might well have succeeded but for one unforeseen occurrence: the collapse of the Soviet Union. In June 1992, Russia revealed that Soviet interrogators had questioned Van Voorhis. This proved the aviator, and other U.S. POWs, had been imprisoned alive by the Chinese and knowingly abandoned by their own government.)

Despite such premeditated dissembling by the Pentagon, co-author Sauter, a former Army officer, still found it hard to believe the Bush administration would knowingly write off U.S. prisoners. In April 1990, he took the evidence to Washington, D.C., asking State Department spokesman Richard Boucher why, given the new Gorbachev era and "glasnost," America was not trying again to recover prisoners that U.S. government documents showed were never returned from the U.S.S.R.

"I'm not familiar with the previous documents, particularly any classified ones," responded Boucher with Orwellian elan. "We do not believe that there are any U.S. POWs in the Soviet Union, [so] we have not raised it." The only outburst of honesty at Foggy Bottom that spring came from a State Department historian who, for obvious reasons, requested anonymity. American POWs in

Siberia, he admitted, "just sort of became a non-issue, I'm afraid."

Rather than reviving the issue and asking the Soviets about the lost Americans, the U.S. government decided, as it had with Sanders, to kill the messenger's reputation.

In mid-1990, Sauter learned of a Pentagon letter responding to his reports, which was surprising since Pentagon officials had refused repeated requests to appear on camera to address KIRO's stories.

Written by Lieutenant General Allen K. Ono, U.S. Army deputy chief of staff for personnel, the letter was apparently being sent to influential Americans who had expressed concern about the KIRO-TV reports:

> Unfortunately, considerable misinformation periodically surfaces concerning Americans from the Korean War and World War II still being held in Communist prisons. The latest media coverage was an investigative report by KIRO/CBS News of Seattle, Washington. . . . The Special Office for Prisoners of War and Missing in Action, the Defense Intelligence Agency, and the U.S. Army Center for Military History have looked into the many allegations that continue to arise. Please allow me to share some of the information these agencies have presented to help clarify the issue.

Ono attempted to make his case by attacking the 1954 report of GIs from Korea being shipped to Siberia aboard trains. The general wrote: "The source did not have enough knowledge of English to identify the language but was convinced that the prisoners were American because many of them were black." That was provably false. The source had also identified the prisoners as American because they were in "American uniforms," specifically "Army field service jacket M1943" with, in some cases,

U.S. "Air Force non-commissioned officer sleeve insignia of Staff Sergeant rank."[10]

Ono claimed that the prisoners were really French-colonial troops being shipped home from the war in Indochina. The Pentagon later said the communists called the French troops "Third World brothers."

Even though numerous other U.S. intelligence reports corroborate that the blacks on the train were American, not African, the authors did pursue Ono's allegation. The French Embassy denied that it had been their troops on the train. And after months of effort, the Pentagon finally released its single shred of evidence that those men were Africans, not Americans. The evidence was a 1950s report that French Foreign Legionnaires had been shipped from Asia through Russia.

But for obvious reasons, Ono had never quoted that report in its entirety. The reason: the legionnaires going through Russia had been German. And even U.S. military intelligence knew there were no black "Third World brothers" among the often Nazi Germans in France's post-World War II Foreign Legion.

Ono's letter never mentioned the many other U.S. reports, some still classified, showing that Americans had indeed been shipped from Korea to the Soviet Union. Indeed, the general lied about them, saying: "[T]he Soviet Union has been the central focus of U.S. and allied intelligence for almost 50 years. Similarly, one must conclude that this scrutiny would have revealed at least a hint of American POWs in the Soviet Union or China if they had been taken there. As in the case of Korea, no such evidence has ever surfaced."[11]

In response, Sauter called Ono's office at the Pentagon. The general refused to speak to Sauter, who informed Ono's aide that someone was writing letters on the general's stationary that included provably false and legally actionable misstatements. As far as the authors know, the letters stopped.

But the disinformation continued. On June 28, 1990, the DIA took its debunking campaign before a larger and more important audience–the U.S. Congress. During hearings before the House Subcommittee on Asian and Pacific Affairs, the DIA's deputy director testified on the POW/MIA issue. While willing to discuss Indochina, Rear Admiral Ronald Marryott, in full uniform, avoided speaking about the Soviet Union either to the congressional representatives or a waiting television crew.

Instead, he submitted written testimony stating "there are no intelligence indicators that U.S. personnel from the Korean conflict were not returned to U.S. control at the end of the war." As the reader has discovered, that statement was a provable falsehood.

But Marryott continued. "Likewise, the Soviet Union has been the central focus of U.S. and Allied intelligence activities for most of this century, and China has been watched for almost 50 years. I believe this scrutiny would have likewise revealed at least a hint of American prisoners held in either country had they been taken there. Again, no such evidence has ever surfaced," the admiral told Congress.

Yet on that same day, a DIA letter later released admitted the agency knew of information that American POWs had been held in the Soviet Union and was "attempting to obtain after action reports from the agencies that originated many of the live-sighting reports referred to in KIRO broadcasts."

Luckily, the DIA's blatantly deceitful testimony did not go unnoticed. In the summer of 1990, co-author R. Cort Kirkwood joined the fray from his position on the *Washington Times* editorial page. On July 18, an editorial entitled "No Such Evidence" appeared, detailing the duplicitous testimony by Marryott.

As DIA POW/MIA chief Colonel Millard Peck recalled, the editorial spurred furious action and interest. Amid the furor, Peck circulated evidence of Soviet POWs to his superiors, and "Everyone turned out to see [a screening of the KIRO] tape," said Peck. The colonel even invited co-author Sauter to the Pentagon, where Peck asked for help, admitting that the DIA—because it was created in the 1960s—did not even possess many of the 1950s POW documents found by the authors in the National Archives and classified records of Army and Air Force intelligence. Peck's efforts soon resulted in an apparent victory—tentative approval was given for four new employees to research Korean War and American prisoners.

Congressmen Miller and Dan Quayle

By now Congressman Miller was convinced that American POWs had been abandoned in the Soviet Union. "I thought it was bureaucratic inertia—but a pretty advanced case. My inquiries quickly shifted from trying to find evidence to pushing the White House and State Department to raise the issue with the Soviets."

Miller gained a new ally in September 1990, when Vice President Dan Quayle arrived in Seattle. Sauter, on camera, handed the Vice President a set of documents that "list by name American POWs in the Soviet Union. Your national security adviser, Dr. [Carnes] Lord, has seen these documents. The Pentagon knows about them—hundreds of American POWs in the Soviet Union. Yet your administration, publicly, has done nothing to secure their release. What is the policy of the Bush administration in terms of the U.S. prisoners of war in the Soviet Union?"

The vice president responded: "Well, I am not aware of any prisoners of war in the Soviet Union. But I'll be glad to take the documents, and we'll try to get you an answer, and if there are prisoners [in the U.S.S.R.], I'm sure President Bush would take it up with President Gorbachev immediately."

"The vice president took it seriously," recalled Quayle spokesman David Beckwith. But Quayle staffers immediately ran into Pentagon disinformation. To their credit, when told by the military that there was "no evidence" of U.S. POWs in the Soviet Union, Quayle's people chose to believe their own eyes and the hundreds of documents provided them by Sauter and POW/MIA family members.

Despite the new pressure from Quayle's office, Pentagon officials continued to drag their feet. By January 1991, Colonel Peck had grown disgusted with the DIA and was pessimistic that anything would ever be done for the Soviet prisoners. Earlier promises by the highest level of the DIA for additional analysts to study U.S. POWs in Russia had been retracted. "We do what we are told," he wearily told Sauter at the time. "I have had no impact on policy."[12]

But while the Pentagon continued its cover-up, the State Department, nudged by Quayle and Miller, began a shift in policy—a shift probably arising from two factors. First, some State Department officials actually felt it was wrong to write off American POWs. Congressman Miller credited Secretary of State James Baker and his chief aide, Deputy Secretary Lawrence Eagleburger. "He [Eagleburger] was not aware of the issue when I first called him," according to Miller, who said the State Department began aggressively pursuing the issue as soon as top leaders learned the truth.

A second, less altruistic factor, was probably also at play. Defense Secretary Richard Cheney and National Security Adviser Brent Scowcroft had both served in critical White House positions during the abandonment of U.S. POWs from Southeast Asia. Scowcroft had been President Nixon's military aide and then the national security adviser in the Ford administration. Cheney had been Ford's chief of staff. (George Bush served in that era as director of the CIA.)

Revealing the truth about the American prisoners in Russia would probably re-ignite the issue of POW/MIAs in Vietnam, raising tough questions for Scowcroft and Cheney, the latter a clear rival to Baker in his ambition to succeed President Bush.

But Baker, smart enough to see the inevitable revelation of the truth and with no fingerprints on the Vietnam POW mess, would be a hero if he helped resolve the Soviet POW issue. With one policy change, Baker could do the right thing while helping his own political prospects and harming Cheney's.

When asked whether Secretary Baker pushed the POW issue for political or humanitarian reasons, one State Department insider responded: "Both." The insider said the Baker team ultimately took action "probably because we haven't been involved with it [the POW issue] until recently. So we don't have anything to cover up."

So in early 1991, Assistant Secretary of State Janet Mullins wrote Congressman Miller, admitting the State Department had information on Americans imprisoned by the Soviet Union. "When the Department became convinced that certain of these reports were credible, it aggressively undertook to confront Soviet officials and demand the release of those U.S. citizens. In some of these cases, American citizens were freed. In others, the Soviet Government denied knowledge of their existence."[13]

Despite the State Department confession, the White House and Pentagon continued their cover up. In early 1991, Scowcroft blocked the release of a secret 36-year-old White House document requested more than a year before by co-author Sauter. Entitled "US POWs in USSR," the report detailed evidence from Uri Rastvorov, a Soviet intelligence defector, who had confirmed that U.S. POWs were shipped from Korea to Siberia.

On White House stationary, Scowcroft had ordered the National Archives not to release the document, declaring the report, years older than Sauter, was still "SECRET and should be properly secured."[14]

That record is just one of many POW records, some dating back to 1946, that the Bush administration has hidden or censored, often in flagrant violation of the spirit and letter of the Freedom of Information Act. For example, in August 1989, the Defense Intelligence Agency stated, in a formal response to a Sauter FOIA request, that the "DIA holds no records on those missing or captured during the Korean conflict." However, it was later revealed that the DIA possessed a March 1988 memo entitled "Alleged Sightings of American POWs in North Korea from 1975 to 1982," a report that discussed possible "American prisoners from the Korean war."

According to a 1962 document, obtained under the Freedom of Information Act, "the Department of State has a list of United States citizens imprisoned in Communist countries.... [The list] is classified and is not available for distribution.... As you can well imagine, this is a matter of considerable sensitivity." The State Department still refuses to release that decades-old list.

During the 1950s, at the same time the U.S. government was denying to Congress that any Korean War POWs were alive, a secret Air Force project called "Project American" concluded that "a large number of the personnel listed as 'missing in action' may still be alive and interned in Communist prison camps." For reasons never revealed, that project was suddenly stopped in 1959, despite attempts to expand it. And now the Pentagon says it has "lost" the "Project American" files.

The Bush administration has also cynically applied legal exemptions to the FOIA. Earlier chapters mentioned the story of two American POWs, dying from their years of slave labor in a Soviet phosphorous mine, who got word of their existence out with a Polish refugee. The detailed report on those Korean War prisoners, from 1960, was classified for decades until the authors dragged it out of a State Department safe through the Freedom of Information Act.

It's likely that those men died as Soviet slaves. But even at this writing, there is no way to learn their fate. While the U.S. government claims that all American POWs from Korea were dead by the mid-1950s, and that none ever went to the Soviet Union, the State Department refuses to release the names of the two prisoners in the report. The U.S. government says it would be a "violation of their privacy" for the American people to know that they had been abandoned in Siberia.

Such policies, along with gross errors in the handling of the Indochina POW issue, wore away at Colonel Mike Peck, the decorated Green Beret veteran of Vietnam assigned as chief of the DIA's POW/MIA office. In March 1991, word leaked to the press that Peck had resigned his job. In a five-page resignation letter, Peck revealed that the office was devoted to busy-work, not a resolution of the POW scandal. "The sad fact, however, is that this is being controlled and a cover-up may be in progress. The entire charade does not appear to be an honest effort, and may never have been. . . . That national leaders continue to address the prisoner of war and missing in action issue as the 'highest national priority' is a travesty," he said in his letter.

Peck's departure ushered in an era of new attention to the POW/MIA issue. At the end of May 1991, the Republican staff of the Senate Foreign Relations Committee released "An Examination of U.S. Policy Toward POW/MIAs." The report supports the findings of this book.

Then on the 11th of July, Sauter was admitted to a packed press conference in the State Department's Diplomatic Lobby. Secretary Baker and Soviet Foreign Minister Alexander Bessmertnykh were meeting to hammer out an arms agreement before the July summit. But Sauter had another issue to cover.

Shouting questions with the other reporters, Sauter suddenly caught the attention of Baker. "Mr. Secretary, will you also be discussing the American POWs in the U.S.S.R.? The Senate says that over 20,000 have been taken since 1945. On 9 April, you asked for them back. Have you gotten an answer from the foreign minister? Do you expect one?"

"We will touch upon that subject very briefly," said the secretary, to laughter from some members of the national media, which had long ignored the topic and still treated it as a joke. Not surprisingly, the major networks and newspapers never made any mention of the secretary's POW remark.

The U.S. media, including *Time,* the *New York Times,* the *New Republic,* "Nightline," "60 Minutes" and the "CBS Evening News" (which had funded much of co-author Sauter's research and then refused to air the information) had all known of the story in this book but never revealed it to the American people.

The authors' experience was matched by that of documentary producer Ted Landreth and former *Time* writer Ed Tivnan, who had been gathering evidence on the shipment of Vietnam POWs to the Soviet Union. The PBS show "Frontline" and the *New York Times* had originally financially supported their research. But "Frontline" soon dropped out, and when the story was ready in the late summer of 1991, the *New York Times* killed it.

The newspaper's top executives, according to Landreth, said they believed the story but felt it should be covered by a staff writer, rather than a free-lancer. But the former CBS staffer felt there were other factors at play.

"The *New York Times* had never, never done any original reporting on the POW issue. In effect, it was a matter of the *Times* having to say: 'Whoops, here's a story that we completely and totally missed.' "

The *Times* preferred to lose the story—even have it never appear in print and allow the official cover-up to continue—rather than have its own staff shown up by two free-lancers, Landreth concluded.

The *Los Angeles Times* proved more daring and published an article in October 1991. But U.S. TV networks still refused to touch the topic. Landreth was able to get the story aired only in Australia.

"At [most] fault [in the POW scandal] is the media, not the government," Landreth concluded. "The media simply let us down on this one."

At a minimum, the national media made it easy for the Bush administration to dodge the issue. During the July 1991 superpower summit, President Bush, reacting to congressional pressure, finally passed a note to President Gorbachev mentioning U.S. POWs taken to the Soviet Union. But when the president got home, he downplayed the topic.

"Did you ask the Soviets about any prisoners they might have from past wars?" a reporter asked the president during a Rose Garden press conference.

"Yes," Bush replied, "We raised that with the Soviets. They've maintained before and I would expect maintain again that they know of no American prisoners."

The president then backed earlier statements by "General Scowcroft" dismissing evidence of live U.S. POWs in Indochina.

The remark stunned POW/MIA family members, who took it as a clear signal to the Soviets that the Bush administration was not eager for the truth.*

More eager was the Senate, which in August 1991 created a special committee to investigate the POW issue. The secretary of state also continued his efforts. In October, Baker raised the issue with the new director of the KGB and with President Yeltsin.

During the fall of 1991, KIRO, the *Los Angeles Times,* the *Washington Times* and the Moscow newspaper *Commersant* broke stories concerning the shipment of U.S. POWs from Vietnam to the Soviet Union, including the possibility that Navy Lieutenant Commander Kelly Patterson had been sent to Soviet Kazakhstan during 1967. Senate hearings soon produced evidence concerning the Soviet interrogation of U.S. POWs in Vietnam—even years after they were supposed to have been returned.

Shortly before Christmas 1991, co-author Sauter journeyed to Moscow, hoping to find opportunity in the chaos of the Soviet Union's last days. Early signs were positive. A Soviet customs official singled Sauter out from the crowd of Russians arriving on the Aeroflot flight, directing the co-author to a lonely booth. There the official grimly inspected Sauter's visa, turning it this way and that as if detecting subtle improprieties.

Just as Sauter thought he was about to be ejected from the country, the inspector cast a blood-shot eye on the co-author's baggage, looked up and asked: "You have cigarettes?" Sauter, a non-smoker, did indeed have some Marlboros, having been forewarned by previous travelers to Moscow. It took just one pack to clear customs. And as Sauter roared into town in a gypsy cab, the entrepreneurial driver leaning out of the car at full speed to wipe away slush while loudly cursing the vehicle's inoperative windshield wipers, the co-author began to think it possible the truth could now emerge.

But some of the old Soviet Union remained. Sauter's first translator, a Russian journalist, quit after three hours, saying the co-author was dealing in a "gray area," did not have proper papers and could face problems because of his persistent questioning of the security organizations.

Suddenly, the prospects appeared as dim as the snowy Moscow days. But then, within days, Sauter was saved by a number of Russian human rights activists and journalists, all strangers but immediate allies in the hunt for U.S. POWs. Through them, he was literally taken by the arm and deposited in the office of Vyacheslav Bakhmin, head of the Russian Foreign Ministry Department of Global Problems and Humanitarian Cooperation.

Although it was well into the evening on that day, bureaucrats still scurried through the halls of the downtown office building, many lugging bundles and boxes. Bakhmin, a balding man with professorial looks and an easy grin, explained that these people were Yeltsin's foreign ministry. And the very next day they would be moving into the Soviet Foreign Ministry's offices, where they would physically and figuratively displace Gorbachev's bureaucrats as the U.S.S.R. became the Commonwealth of Independent States.

Bakhmin knew nothing about American POWs, but he knew a lot about the Soviet prison system, having served several years for revealing the psychiatric abuses of Russian dissidents. Shaken by the POW story, he suggested establishing a joint U.S./Russian commission to uncover the truth about U.S. prisoners.

Bakhmin asked for a list of American POWs held by the Soviet Union after World War II, Korea, the Cold War and Vietnam. Sauter immediately began work on a Russian language list of POW names from this book's research.

Days after meeting with Bakhmin, Sauter received a phone call at his hotel—from the "new" version of the KGB, specifically the domestic branch then called the Ministry of Security and Internal Affairs, or MSIA. Their representative said his agency had been ordered to check its records for files on American prisoners. The KGB man revealed that he already had one list with the names of about 50 Americans, but he vaguely indicated that his agency was not satisfied with that document. He asked if Sauter could produce a better list—a list of real POWs.

On the 2nd of January 1992, Sauter presented the MSIA with the list of 121 Americans, along with a request for information on U.S. servicemen seen in specific Soviet prisons but never identified by name. The information, translated into Russian and accompanied by pictures of several missing Americans, was also given to the Foreign Ministry and Ministry of Defense.

As for that faulty list of 50 to which the MSIA had referred, Sauter learned that the U.S. media was reporting that the State Department had recently presented Moscow with its own list of Korean and World War II prisoners taken by the Soviets. "The list was 'the best cases' about missing servicemen and ones the Russian authorities may be able to resolve," a U.S. official had announced in Washington.[15]

So Sauter, in a meeting at the U.S. Embassy, asked to see the list, which the embassy officer in charge of the POW issue proudly brought forth as proof of the new U.S. determination to recover its lost prisoners. The list, given to the Russians in early December, started with a firm but polite request for information, noting that: "Below is a list of the individuals about whom we have inquired previously but never received a convincing response."

But Sauter, taking a break from Moscow's cold in the cheerful embassy cafeteria, nearly choked on his Dr Pepper as he read the list. The first name was Wilfred C. Cumish, who had been returned by the Soviets in the 1950s. The second name was Sidney Ray Sparks—the Georgia boy who also came home in the 1950s. The third name on the list was Major Wirt Thompson, a WWII POW. They got that one right.

The fourth and fifth names were Colonel Cerny and First Lieutenant Cushman, names the authors had researched but could never link to real U.S. servicemen. It is possible they were Germans looking for a way out of Siberia. The sixth name on the list was William Baumeister. While the authors believe it possible he was imprisoned in the U.S.S.R., during the late 1950s the Pentagon informed Baumeister's family that his remains had been found in Burma and that it was impossible for him to have been held in the Soviet Union. The remaining names were of missing Cold War aviators.

Contrary to stories then being leaked to the national press by the Bush administration, there were no POWs on the official list from Korea or Vietnam. And, of the first six people whose return the United States government was demanding, only one could be said with certainty to be an American imprisoned but never returned by the Soviets. This was the official, U.S. government handling of what President Bush called his "highest national priority."

The diplomat at the Moscow Embassy, a cordial but overworked man who apparently had more pressing duties than his part-time POW assignment, appeared sincerely surprised when told of the problems with the official list. He wondered how Sauter knew that Cumish and Sparks had been returned. Sauter replied that the authors had talked with Sparks and had read the report Cumish dictated upon returning to U.S. custody. In addition, the return of both men had been reported in American newspapers.

Privately, the State Department was deeply embarrassed, blaming the Pentagon for unforgivable sloppiness. Department of Defense spokesperson Captain Susan Strednansky would only say that there were no Vietnam POWs on the list because "we don't have any information on U.S. prisoners from Vietnam going to the Soviet Union." She declined to discuss the other names on the list.[16]

It took Sidney Ray Sparks, speaking from his home in Georgia, to sum up the boondoggle. "I'm right here. I wonder why they're looking for me over there? I called the Department of Defense. . . . They said they'd get back to me. They haven't called yet."[17]

Once again, the Bush administration had sent a clear message. How could the Russians believe the POW issue was the "highest national priority," if the administration could not even produce an accurate list of missing Americans?

And the Moscow Embassy continued to send distressing signals about the true priority it gave to missing Americans. After leaving Moscow, co-author Sauter learned that a Russian journalist had received letters for Sauter containing information on U.S. POWs in Russia.

The journalist didn't have Sauter's address, so he took the letters to the U.S. Embassy. There a functionary promised to take care of the information.

After months had passed, Sauter asked the State Department what had happened to the letters. A spokesman said they had been mailed to Sauter. Worried that the letters had been lost, Sauter asked what information they contained. The State Department said it didn't know, because the officials in its Moscow Embassy had been "too busy" to check the information for potential leads.

As of this writing, they have still not surfaced. Russians have told the authors that over the years, other letters concerning U.S. POWs have been sent to the U.S. Embassy in Moscow. They too disappeared into a bureaucratic black hole.

Later in 1992, the Ark Project, a tiny but dedicated nonprofit group of Americans and Russians formed to search for U.S. POWs in the former Soviet Union, discovered a mentally ill American defector, ex-NSA official Victor Hamilton, hidden in a psychiatric prison outside Moscow.

The discovery brought threats to the project's associate director, Boris Yuzhin, a former KGB agent sent to the Gulag for helping the FBI break up a Soviet intelligence operation against American citizens on the West Coast. Human-rights activist Susan Mesinai, the project's only other full-time employee, frantically called the U.S. Embassy in Moscow for help in repatriating Hamilton. Her repeated phone calls were not returned.

Back in the U.S., the Pentagon, reacting to continuing media and congressional pressure, in January 1992 appointed Alan C. Ptak as the first deputy secretary of defense for POW/MIA affairs. The former CIA official promptly informed POW/MIA family members that he was committed to accounting for U.S. POWs taken to the Soviet Union.

But questions about the Pentagon's motives continued to arise. A Rand Corporation expert, commissioned by the military to produce a study on Korean War POWs, had earlier approached the authors. He asked them to identify still-secret files on U.S. POWs in the Soviet Union, promising to have the documents declassified and sent to the authors. He also pledged that his report to the Pentagon would be made public in June 1992. When that date arrived, the Pentagon refused to release the report. And the Rand Corporation, with close links to U.S. intelligence, has never sent to authors the promised documents.

In the spring of 1992, co-author Sauter covered a U.S. Air Force transport flight of food and other relief supplies from the state of Washington to Khabarovsk, the capital of Russian Asia. The Pentagon announced that this was the first visit of U.S. military personnel to the city in recent history. However, as the reader has discovered, that city was reportedly a staging point for the shipment of Korean War POWs to Siberia. More recently, a group of American aviators, probably survivors of the June 13, 1952, shoot down of the RB-29 over the Sea of Japan, were reported at Khabarovsk POW Camp 21.

Since some of those men were reported alive into the late 1950s, and at least one American was alleged to have been buried in the city, Sauter took along information on the missing Americans, along with pictures.

But when the Air Force captain commanding the flight learned about the information, he urged Sauter not to raise the issue with the Russians, saying it might prompt them to refuse the U.S. aid. The Air Force officer recommended that Sauter be "a good diplomat for America" and not ask about the potentially embarrassing missing Americans.

Co-author Sauter's view of his responsibilities as an American were somewhat different, and he did raise the issue, diplomatically and in passing, with Russian charity workers and journalists in Khabarovsk. As with the Russians in Moscow, the Khabarovsk residents were extremely sympathetic and vowed to help find lost Americans.

Yeltsin and Bush

Russian cooperation on the POW issue was also improving on a governmental level. The Senate Select Committee on POWs and the State Department had been negotiating with the Russians to form the joint POW commission earlier discussed by co-author Sauter and the Russian Foreign Ministry. By February 1992, despite all the mixed messages and foul-ups, the Yeltsin government seemed willing to pursue the fate of lost Americans in the former Soviet Union.

The U.S. government soon announced the formation of the joint commission, conspicuously refusing the requests of POW/MIA relatives that they be allowed to serve in the organization. While the administration did bow to intense public pressure to name Representative John Miller to the panel, it designated Malcolm Toon to head the U.S. delegation. As a former ambassador to the Soviet Union, Toon was being asked to uncover facts that presumably would show that he had sat in the Moscow Embassy, never really pressing the POW issue, while American servicemen languished in Siberia.

Russia's chief delegate, Dmitri Volkogonov, had a similar conflict of interest. While serving as a Red Army historian during the Gorbachev regime, Volkogonov had issued a false report on U.S. POWs in the Soviet Union. The March 1990 report, sent by a Soviet military attache to a U.S. POW activist, reported that: "Mr. Volkogonov says that his extensive archive research has not produced any evidence regarding to internment of American POWs in Siberia."[18]

Yet while the joint commission appeared predisposed to a total whitewash, it produced a surprise in the spring of 1992, releasing a statement acknowledging that Soviet regimes, including Gorbachev's, had lied about the presence of U.S. prisoners in the Soviet Union. It also told Congressman Miller's office that the GRU, or military intelligence, was refusing to open its POW files, which presumably held information on many Americans captured by Soviet military units.

The GRU cover-up may explain the next development, a June 1992 letter from Yeltsin to the U.S. Senate, which contained two glaring omissions. First, Yeltsin claimed the Red Army "liberated" only about 23,000 U.S. POWs after World War II. As the reader has seen in earlier chapters, the actual number was about twice that (of whom more than 20,000 were kept by the Red Army). In addition, the Russian president claimed: "The documents contain no information about holding US POWs [from Korea] on the USSR territory." In reality, up to 2,000 American POWs from Korea were held in the Soviet Union.

Yet at the same time, President Yeltsin did tell the truth about American prisoners from two other conflicts, in the process delivering a mighty blow to the U.S. cover-up in the days leading up to the mid-June Yeltsin/Bush summit.

First, in his letter to the Senate, the Russian president admitted what every Soviet leader from Stalin to Gorbachev had denied, that as of Aug. 1, 1953, at least 12 Americans, perhaps aviators shot down during the Cold War, were alive in Soviet gulag.

Then Yeltsin revealed that U.S. POWs from Vietnam had ended up in the Soviet Union. "Our archives have shown this to be true. Some of them were transferred to the territory of the former U.S.S.R. and were kept in labor camps. We don't have complete data and can only surmise that some of them may still be alive," Yeltsin told NBC during his flight to the U.S. for the summit meeting with President Bush.

The revelations sent the Bush administration scrambling. The President's men, no longer able to claim that "no evidence" existed of U.S. POWs in the Soviet Union, were forced to come up with a new line. Within days, two themes emerged from the White House. First, the administration claimed it had never known about U.S. prisoners held by the Soviets. And second, President Bush emphasized that he would do everything possible to determine whether living American POWs were in the former-Soviet Union.

Since almost all of the information in this book came from U.S. files, and since many of the documents were literally handed to Vice President Quayle and mailed to President Bush, it would have appeared difficult for the administration to claim it had no idea any Americans were ever held in the Soviet Union. But the administration, confident of its ability to control the uninterested national media, decided to go with the big lie.

President Bush started by claiming that he had never, either in the White House or at the CIA, heard that the Soviets had imprisoned Cold War U.S. aviators. Then, on June 16, 1992, Bush officials held a "background" briefing for the White House press corps by two of the administration's top Russian experts. One was an assistant secretary of state whose office had received, and acknowledged, much of the information in this book. The other briefer was a high National Security Council official, who reported to Brent Scowcroft.

Both men blatantly misled the media, and American people, concerning U.S. knowledge of American POWs in Russia. In the White House transcript of the briefing, the men are identified only as "senior Administration officials."

Reporter: "Senator Smith ... said ... our intelligence agencies have known about this [POWs in the Soviet Union] for years and years and have simply classified this information."

Senior Bush administration official: "I don't know to what you're referring in terms of U.S. intelligence information on

POWs/MIAs in Russia or the countries of the former Soviet Union because I've never seen anything on the subject. So I'm totally unaware of what he's talking about."

Reporter: "So you're basically denying this assertion [by Senator Smith]?"

Official: "I am. I am."

Once the White House had convinced the media that Yeltsin's revelations came as a total surprise, it made a conspicuous point of promising an immediate search for U.S. POWs in Russia. President Bush wisely ignored the issue of what the government knew about Americans kept in the U.S.S.R. after WWII, Korea, and the Cold War. Instead, he focused only on living Americans from Vietnam, vowing that: "If anyone's alive, that person—those people—will be found."[19]

Malcolm Toon, co-chairman of the U.S.-Russian POW commission, was immediately dispatched to Moscow. After just five days of work in Russia, Toon, who had read a manuscript of this book before leaving, repudiated Yeltsin's statement that Vietnam POWs had been sent to Russia and that they or other Americans might still be alive.

"I think we're going to end up with absolutely zero. . . . my gut feeling is that there's nobody alive under Russian control," he declared in June 1992.*

The major media jumped on Toon's remarks, saying they cast "further doubt" about reports of U.S. POWs in Russia, reports the media called "vague." The *Los Angeles Times* declared that attempts by the joint commission to find an imprisoned Korean War POW were a "wild goose chase."[20]

Such furious establishment attempts to downplay the topic of U.S. POWs in the Soviet Union came as no surprise to one State Department source, who said the search for lost American servicemen was clouded by a hidden agenda among some Bush officials.

"The most explosive issue is not the POWs but the agency [CIA]," said the source in June 1992. The CIA not only had known about U.S. POWs in the Soviet Union, but had also lost many of its own people there. The agency had never revealed the truth about those Americans. And the CIA might never allow the whole truth out because that would mean having "to acknowledge the fact that they and our whole government have been deceiving or lying for a long time," the diplomat concluded.

Indeed, as this book went to press, the CIA continued to withhold many of its files on U.S. POWs in the Soviet Union. In July 1992 Ambassador Toon, the President's personal emissary to Russia on the "highest national priority," admitted that the CIA and Pentagon had not given him all their information on U.S. POWs in the Soviet Union.

In theory, Toon's enforced ignorance, shared by many other U.S. POW/MIA officials, would by itself have crippled efforts to account for the lost Americans. But then, as one U.S. official put it, Toon had already rang the "death knell" for American prisoners in the former Soviet Union by declaring in Moscow that he expected to find no live Americans under Russian control.

Russian hardliners had correctly interpreted Toon's statement as a signal that it was safe to continue business as usual. In June 1992, a former Soviet prisoner reported that an American aviator from Korea had been held in labor camp PL-350/5, 900 miles northeast or Moscow, as late as 1989. The Russians immediately produced officials who categorically denied the man had ever been imprisoned. But then American POW/MIA investigators in Moscow, a ridiculously understaffed but dedicated band of three men, found a second Soviet inmate who corroborated the story, even revealing that the American had taught him the song "Happy Birthday to You." Based on the evidence, U.S. experts later concluded that the mysterious prisoner, with the Russian name David Marken, was most likely an American POW held for almost 40 years in the Soviet gulag. But as of this writing, Russian officials have been unwilling or unable to find and free him.

And there's certainly no real pressure on Russia from the Bush Administration, which has joined Russian prison officials and torturers in denying the existence of Korean War POWs in the former Soviet Union. In late July 1992 the Pentagon's chief spokesman, Pete Williams, declared that there was "no evidence" that any American POWs had been shipped from Korea to the Soviet Union—an outright and official U.S. lie (see Chapter 12) strongly implying that the Russians were expected to produce no embarrassing information to the contrary.

But there wasn't much danger of that, co-author Sauter learned during an August 1992 trip to Moscow. Russian intelligence agencies, essentially ignoring orders of President Yelstin to tell the truth, were not about to open their POW files, exposing sensitive intelligence operations and incriminating their officers in war crimes such as gruesome medical experimentation.

The new KGB was more subtle. While publicly cooperating, it secretly destroyed POW records. A private Russian POW/MIA investigator said that intelligence agents said that his throat would be slit if he persisted in his search. A Red Army officer, now retired, explained to Sauter that even powerful former officials were afraid to come forward. Yeltsin could be gone tomorrow, he said, but the KGB is forever.

It is doubtful that the U.S., Russian, Chinese, North Korean, Vietnamese and Laotian governments will ever tell the full truth about the "soldiers of misfortune." The heroism of many of those men will be fully known only to God. But now, at least, some of the truth has escaped, even if most of the men never will.

PROBLEMS OF OUR RELATIONS WITH THE RUSSIANS

I.

It appears that a large number of Russians are in the German Army, most of them probably by compulsion. These may come into our hands in various ways and may be subject to claims by the Russian government that we should turn them over to them. That is already happening about some prisoners of war.

1. As to these prisoners of war, my own view is that they should be asked whether they are willing to return to their own government and, if they are, they should of course be returned; if not, I think we should decline to send them. My reasons are:

    a. That we owe a responsibility for them under the Geneva Protocol because they are prisoners of war whom we have taken and it would not be consonant with those responsibilities to return them when we have reason to believe they will be executed or otherwise punished.

    b. The Russians have already threatened to refuse to turn over to us American prisoners of war whom they may get possession of in German internment camps. The Russian government has claimed that this is a parallel situation with the other. Of course it is not and the Russians have no earthly basis for withholding them from us. I do not believe that we should allow such a claim to interfere with our judgment in not giving up the Russians.

2. Another similar issue with the Russian government may arise when we take over our portion of Germany and when the Russians take over their portion of Germany. There will probably be Russians apprehended in the German Army in both places, and the Russians may seize the Russians in eastern Germany and execute them as traitors or otherwise punish them.

1. This document was found in Secretary of War Henry Stimson's safe after World War II. In the document, he acknowledges that as of fall 1944 the Soviet Union had already threatened to hold American POWs hostage. The British were given the same warning.

SECRETARY WDGS

SUBJECT: Disposal of Members of Pro-Axis Para Military and Collaborationist
Organizations (CCS 576/8)

CAdC recommends, with regard to General Eisenhower's request (pages 5-6)
for authority to turn over to their respective national authorities French, Belgian,
Dutch and Luxembourg nationals captured while serving with Axis military and collaborationist organizations, that:

a. In order to maintain consistent policy on this question with regard to
all Allies, final action be deferred on this request until decision has been
reached in current negotiations with U.S.S.R. with regard to disposition to be
made of Soviet nationals captured while serving with Axis.

b. That upon conclusion of Soviet negotiations, directive in consonance
therewith be issued to General Eisenhower with regard to French, Belgian, Dutch
and Luxembourg nationals.

Proposed message for General Eisenhower, advising of above action, is set forth on
page 4.

On 9 August 1944 CCS instructed General Eisenhower (FACS 53) not to turn over
to Allied Governments any of their nationals captured while serving or collaborat-
ing with Germans, except by arrangements between governments concerned, or unless
such nationals had been found suitable for incorporation in their national forces
or for formation into units for labor purposes. This decision applied to persons
entitled to treatment as prisoners of war, as well as to civilians who had col-
laborated with Axis. On 6 October 1944, upon General Eisenhower's recommendation,
CCS relaxed this directive (FACS 94) to allow French, Belgian and Netherlands
nationals, not entitled to prisoner of war status, to be turned over to their
respective national authorities. In substance, therefore, General Eisenhower's
latest message (pages 5-6, SCAF 191) recommends that he be authorized to turn over
captured personnel entitled to prisoner of war status.

At present tri-partite conference, negotiations are being conducted with
U.S.S.R. as to disposition to be made of Soviet nationals liberated by Allies.
CAdC concludes that, in order that consistent policies may be adopted with regard
to all liberated Allied nationals, decision on General Eisenhower's recommendation
be deferred until Soviet negotiations are complete. This procedure is believed to
be desirable for there are number of thorny political questions involved in Soviet
negotiations, which when decided will furnish guidance in formulating policy to be
applied to nationals of other Allied governments. For instance, question is presented in Russian negotiations of whether U.S. will agree to turn over Russians
captured while serving in German armed forces who resist return to Soviet control,
claiming protection of Geneva Convention. (State Department at present does not
intend to agree to return of these individuals.)

Although SCAF 191 (pages 5-6) was repeated to conference, JCS in Washington
has received instructions that action on this message be taken in Washington.

Action recommended by OPD:
Approve recommendations contained in CCS 576/8 (par. 10, page 3).

Coordination:
Mr. McCloy (Maj Sommers) no comment;
G-1 (Gen Berry); ASF (Maj Cone);
AAF Advisory Council (Maj Owin).   T. D. R.

SECRET

STRATEGY & POLICY #11

2. One of the questions on the table at the Yalta Conference in
February 1945 was the issue of forcible repatriation of anti-communist Soviets captured while in German uniform and claiming
protection under the Geneva Convention. The United States and
Britain later agreed at Yalta to forcibly repatriate them, except
those held in the United States. They were brutally forced back to
the Soviet Union. The U.S. and Britain classified these troops as
"Surrendered Enemy Personnel," rather than prisoners of war, to
evade the Geneva Convention.

MEMORANDUM FOR THE ASSISTANT SECRETARY, WDGS:

Subject: Disposition of Russian Nationals Captured with German Military and Para Military Units (CCS 657/2).

CAdC recommends dispatch of message (page 2) to General Eisenhower (in reply to SCAF 110) regarding disposition to be made of Russian nationals falling into hands of 12th U.S. Army Group. This message authorises him to turn them over to 6th U.S. Army Group, 21st Army Group, or to U.K. to be handled "in accordance with already established procedures."

In SCAF 110 General Eisenhower states that at present following dispositions are being made of captured Russian nationals by 21st, 6th and 12th Army Groups, respectively:

21st Army Group - Segregated and evacuated to U.K. where they are formed into Russian units preparatory to repatriation.

6th Army Group - Segregated and evacuated to North Africa where turned over to British for repatriation to Russia.

12th Army Group - Passed to Communications Zone, segregated and held pending further instructions.

General Eisenhower points out that different treatment accorded Russians by 12th Army Group may result in adverse Soviet reaction and he requests authority to implement fully "requirements of the Soviet Government in respect of their nationals."

Until recently, U.S. and British policy has been to turn over to Soviet authorities for repatriation all Russian nationals desiring to go back. Soviet Government has now demanded return of all its nationals, whether they volunteer or not. British Government has agreed to this. In JCS 1141, now also before JCS for consideration, it is recommended that JCS advise State Department that, from military point of view, U.S. should also adopt policy agreed to by British.

Action recommended by OPD:

Approve recommendation contained in CCS 657/2 (para. 4, page 1).

Coordination:

Mr. McCloy (Col. Cutter)
G-1 (Col. Barry)
ASF (Major Hamlin)

F. N. R.

SECRET

STRATEGY & POLICY FILE COPY

3. *General Eisenhower, pointing out that the Soviet Union was likely to retaliate if its demands were not met, requested authority to return Soviet nationals, against their will if necessary.*

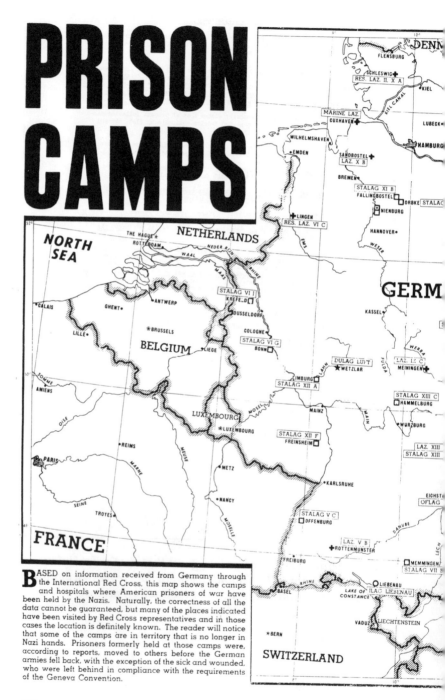

PRISON CAMPS

BASED on information received from Germany through the International Red Cross, this map shows the camps and hospitals where American prisoners of war have been held by the Nazis. Naturally, the correctness of all the data cannot be guaranteed, but many of the places indicated have been visited by Red Cross representatives and in those cases the location is definitely known. The reader will notice that some of the camps are in territory that is no longer in Nazi hands. Prisoners formerly held at those camps were, according to reports, moved to others before the German armies fell back, with the exception of the sick and wounded, who were left behind in compliance with the requirements of the Geneva Convention.

EHR-KREIS	British	U.S.	Russian
I	68	-	50891
II	3361	25771	47940
III	3212	10158	42089
IV	44536	7653	68454
V	2677	494	19489
VI	149	265	194404
VII	12870	6580	16615
III	62238	8751	98272
IX	6401	6539	26044
X	4247	155	44901
XI	21100	585	38076
XII	2608	2187	41257
II	7713	1764	38810
II	2983	4204	26520
II	10940	123	14060
XX	14480	14	14269
XI	9	1611	2304
ALS	199592	76854	784395

RE	British	U.S.	Russian
F SHAEF	49783	17750	399712
IAN	135886	54777	344103
RIAN	13923	4327	40580
S	199592	76854	784395

4. *According to German documentation, as of March 24, 1945, six weeks before the end of World War II, there were 199,592 "registered" British and Commonwealth POWs, known by rank and serial number. Only 168,746 returned. The top table is by "Wehr Kreis," or war zone and the lower table is by area: Germany, Russia and Austria.*

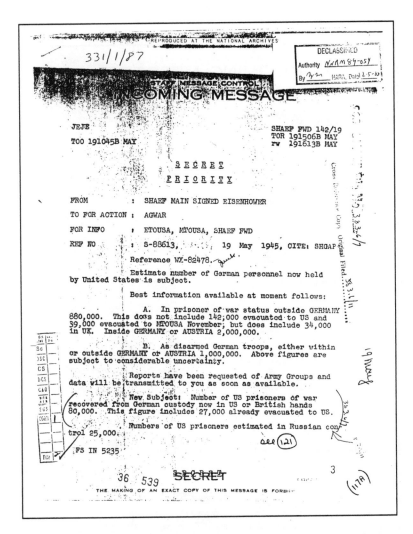

REPRODUCED AT THE NATIONAL ARCHIVES

331/1/87

DECLASSIFIED
Authority NNAM 89-054
By 2 22 NARA, Date 2-5-22

STAFF MESSAGE CONTROL
INCOMING MESSAGE

JEJB
T00 191045B MAY

SHAEF FWD 142/19
TOR 191506B MAY
rw 191613B MAY

S E C R E T
P R I O R I T Y

FROM : SHAEF MAIN SIGNED EISENHOWER

TO FOR ACTION : AGWAR

FOR INFO : ETOUSA, MTOUSA, SHAEF FWD

REF NO : S-88613, 19 May 1945, CITE: SHGAP

Reference WX-82478.

Estimate number of German personnel now held by United States is subject.

Best information available at moment follows:

A. In prisoner of war status outside GERMANY 880,000. This does not include 142,000 evacuated to US and 39,000 evacuated to MTOUSA November; but does include 34,000 in UK. Inside GERMANY or AUSTRIA 2,000,000.

B. As disarmed German troops, either within or outside GERMANY or AUSTRIA 1,000,000. Above figures are subject to considerable uncertainty.

Reports have been requested of Army Groups and data will be transmitted to you as soon as available.

New Subject: Number of US prisoners of war recovered from German custody now in US or British hands 80,000. This figure includes 27,000 already evacuated to US.

Numbers of US prisoners estimated in Russian control 25,000.

FS IN 5235

36 539 SECRET

THE MAKING OF AN EXACT COPY OF THIS MESSAGE IS FORBID

5. *During the height of the hostage crisis, General Eisenhower sent this memo to AGWAR, stating that 25,000 American POWs were still under Soviet control. According to this document, 105,000 American POWs should have been returned (actually there were 99,000 confirmed American POWs held by Germany and 8-9,000 MIAs were also recovered, according to a hand-written note believed to have been penned by George Marshall; which means that 107,000 or more should have been returned). The government claimed 92,000 returned, but that number is inflated—actually only about 85,000 returned.*

STAFF MESSAGE CONTROL

INCOMING MESSAGE

WAR

TOO 211849Z MAY

SHAEF 241/21
TOR 212210B MAY
1jb 212336B MAY

~~S E C R E T~~

~~P R I O R I T Y~~

FROM   :   AGWAR FROM MARSHALL

TO   :   SHAEF MAIN FOR EISENHOWER

REF NO   :   W-85496, 21 MAY, 1945.

DECLASSIFIED
Authority NND 760210
By CMA NARA Date 7/5/90

 Concerned over report your S-88613 that 25,000
US prisoners still in Russian hands.

 Request completest details and when transfer to
US control expected.

S-88613 is SMC OUT 1986B, 21/5/45, G-1

ACTION   :   G-1

INFORMATION :   SGS
                 G-2
                 G-3
                 G-4
                 G-5
                 SUSPENSE
                 AG RECORDS

*Interim reply
sent to AGWAR
22 May, stating
full report
will follow.*

SMC IN 6839   22 May 45   0055B   SL/1p   REF NO: W-85496

15 0023   ~~SECRET~~   FILE No. 383.6/10

COPY NO.

THE MAKING OF AN EXACT COPY OF THIS MESSAGE IS FORBIDDEN

THE MAKING OF AN EXACT COPY OF THIS MESSAGE IS FORBIDDEN

6. General Marshall expresses his concern about of 25,000 U.S. POWs in Russian hands to General Eisenhower on May 21, 1945. A handwritten note states that a "full report will follow." The "full report" has never been declassified.

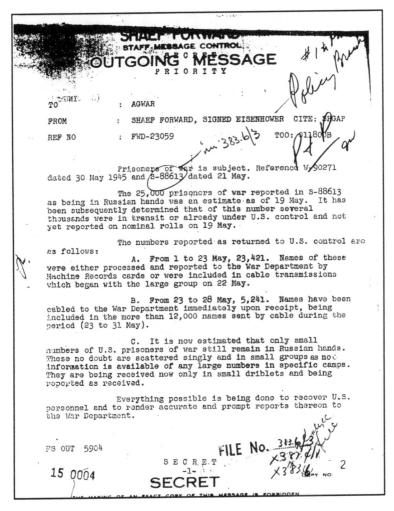

SHAEF FORWARD
STAFF MESSAGE CONTROL
OUTGOING MESSAGE
PRIORITY

TO : AGWAR

FROM : SHAEF FORWARD, SIGNED EISENHOWER CITE: SHGAP

REF NO : FWD-23059 TOO: 011800B

Prisoners of war is subject. Reference W-90271 dated 30 May 1945 and S-88613 dated 21 May.

The 25,000 prisoners of war reported in S-88613 as being in Russian hands was an estimate as of 19 May. It has been subsequently determined that of this number several thousands were in transit or already under U.S. control and not yet reported on nominal rolls on 19 May.

The numbers reported as returned to U.S. control are as follows:

A. From 1 to 23 May, 23,421. Names of these were either processed and reported to the War Department by Machine Records cards or were included in cable transmissions which began with the large group on 22 May.

B. From 23 to 28 May, 5,241. Names have been cabled to the War Department immediately upon receipt, being included in the more than 12,000 names sent by cable during the period (23 to 31 May).

C. It is now estimated that only small numbers of U.S. prisoners of war still remain in Russian hands. These no doubt are scattered singly and in small groups as no information is available of any large numbers in specific camps. They are being received now only in small driblets and being reported as received.

Everything possible is being done to recover U.S. personnel and to render accurate and prompt reports thereon to the War Department.

FS OUT 5904

FILE No. 383.6/3

15 0004

SECRET
-1-
SECRET

THE MAKING OF AN EXACT COPY OF THIS MESSAGE IS FORBIDDEN.

7. The document signed by General Eisenhower and released June 1, 1945, explains away the loss of 23,500 Americans to the Soviet gulag. Notice the handwritten note in the upper right: "#1 to PW Policy Branch." This was the first disinformation document and is the Department of Defense's main line of defense in the current attempt to cover-up the indefensible actions of the American government.

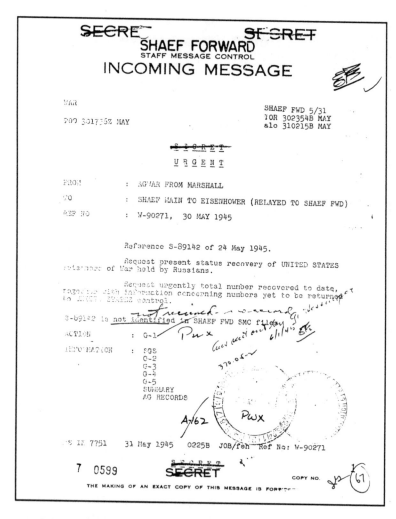

8. General Marshall sent to General Eisenhower this secret and urgent message dated May 30, 1945 requesting present status recovery of United States prisoners of war held by the Russians. The answer to this message has never been declassified.

Displaced Persons, Allied ex PW and German PW   30 May 1945

IV. Allied ex PW remaining in Shaef Sphere.

Accurate figures are not obtainable in many cases as the transfer to and from the Russian Sphere has commenced.

Figures obtainable:

US/Br	8,000
Poles	50,000 •
Russian	400,000
Yugo Slavs	50,000 •
Italians	50,000 •

V. Displaced Persons:

1. SHAEF Area

Nationality	On hand in Germany	Repatriated
French	200,000	882,000
Belgian	70,000	147,000
Dutch	56,000	120,000
Russians	1,284,000	160,000
Poles	654,000	)
Yugo Slavs	56,000	)
Czechs	31,000	) - under
Greeks	7,000	) discussion
Italians	242,000	)
Other Allied	106,000	)
Other ex enemy	85,000	)
Approximate Total	3,055,000	

Repatriation of Western Nationals is proceeding rapidly and these figures are the latest obtainable but are already out of date.

No figures of Displaced persons hospitalized in Germany are available.

2. Russian Sphere.

	PW	DP
Belgian	50,000	115,000
Dutch	4,000	140,000
British	20,000	
U.S.	20,000	
French	250,000	850,000
Approx. Total	1,145,000	

• No information as to repatriation obtainable, subject under discussion.

2   1005   - 2 -

9. Two days after the United States said that repatriation across Soviet lines ended, this memo for General Kenner was written by Lt. Colonel K. H. Clark, RAMC.

SU█ █GION GOEPPINGEN
COUNTER INTELLIGENCE CORPS REGION I

File Nr. I-G- 820

APO 154
FIELD OFFICE ULM/D
4 August 1947

MEMORANDUM TO THE OFFICER IN CHARGE

Subject: American and Allied soldiers held in Siberia

RE : Project 154032

1. **Reason for Investigation.**

Reference is made to Orientation and Guidance Report #2 dated 30 April 1947 re: Project 154032.

A casual informant, HOFMANN, Hans Joachim, recently released German Prisoner of War from Russia contacted CIC ULM (I49/x63) thru the local American Red Cross on 2 August 1947 to give information about American and Allied personnel held as prisoners in SIBERIA, USSR.

(b) (6) & (b) (7) (c)

2. **Results of Investigative Activity.**

a. Informant HOFMANN was released from the Dachau Prisoner of War Processing Center on or about 17 July 1947. The informant did not contact American authorities there, but German officials in DACHAU told informant to contact UNRRA in ULM. The informant did this and was referred to the American Red Cross Club in ULM.

b. The informant gave this agent three (3) pictures of American soldiers attached hereto as exhibit A, B, and C.

c. The informant claims to have talked with the soldier shown on the picture marked exhibit "A" whose name is BOEHM, Viktor ████████ emigrated to the United States of America in 1928, lived in ████████ According to the informant BOEHM served in the Army of the United States, was taken prisoner by the Germans and then taken over by the Russians on or about 5 May 1945 in OELMUETZ, Silisia, Germany and transported to SIBERIA on 17 July 1945 to the NOROSIBIRSK Camp 311 near KRASNOE, Siberia where BOEHM is presently working in a tank factory. The informant worked with BOEHM who speaks German. BOEHM gave HOFMANN the attached pictures.

d. The informant claims there are two hundred (200) American soldiers working in this plant and about nine hundred (900) Allied soldiers, mostly English and French soldiers.

REGRADED UNCLASSIFIED
ON 2 0 SEP 1991
BY CDR US/█████COM F01/PO

10. Pentagon has said there is "no evidence that Americans were kept by Soviets since World War II." This document is one of the dozens that show otherwise.

HEADQUARTERS
COMBINED COMMAND FOR RECONNAISSANCE ACTIVITY KOREA
8242nd Army Unit
APO 301

JCO 350.05
10 August 1953
8007th

CCRAK SPECIFIC REQUEST
Number 66-53

SUBJECT: UN PW Camps in Manchuria and China

TO: See Distribution

DECLASSIFIED
Authority *NND763054*
By *AC* NARA Date *5/14/12*

1. BACKGROUND:

a. A compilation of reports indicate that during the past two years several PsW have been transferred from PW Camps in North Korea to points in Manchuria, China and Siberia. These points include MUKDEN (4130N-12315E), HARBIN (4645N-12645E), ANTUNG (XE194437), FENCH'ENG (4028N-12405E), CHIAMUSSO (46/49-130/21), MIENSIEN (2418N-11613E), PIEPING (3950N-11715E), SHANGHAI (3120N-12128E), CHUNGKING (2930N-10630E), TIENTSIN (3920N-11715E), CANTON (2430N-11315E). More recent reports, however, have been scarce and incomplete. Many PsW transferred have been technicians and factory workers. Other PsW transferred have had a knowledge of Cantonese and are reportedly used for propananda purposes.

b. Figures show that the total number of MIA plus known captured less those to be US repatriated leaves a balance of over 8000 unaccounted for.

2. SPECIFIC REQUEST:

a. Are there now or have there been indications of US PsW being moved from PW Camps in North Korea across the Yalu into Manchuria through the following routes: SINUIJU (XD1840), MANP'OJIN (BA7358), HOERYONG (XB6398). If so, how many, what routes of travel are used; how are they being moved and where is the destination?

b. Are there indications of increased small boat traffic in the ports of SINUIJU, ANJU, CHINNAMPO, and SONGJIN capable of handling groups of personnel? If so, where are they located, what types of craft, how many, and what is the cargo?

c. Are there indications of PW Camps in or around the cities mentioned in paragraph 1, above? If so, what nationality of PsW are being held, and how many?

3. SPECIAL INSTRUCTIONS:

a. This is a continuing requirement and will remain in effect until cancelled by this headquarters.

b. This is a priority II intelligence requirement within the meaning of Intelligence Directive No. 1, USAFFE, dated 1 March 1953.

c. Information will be forwarded as obtained.

d. All replies to this SRI will be identified by CCRAK Control Symbol: CCRAK SRI Number 66-53.

BY COMMAND OF BRIGADIER GENERAL STUART:

M. L. Evans

DISTRIBUTION:
D-E-F-G-K

M. L. EVANS
WOJG USA
Adjutant

11. American "technicians and factory workers" were shipped from North Korea to the U.S.S.R. and China.

12. Two US POWs from Korea were still alive in 1960 after almost a decade of slave labor in the Soviet Union. To this day, the State Department has refused to release their names, saying it would be an "invasion of their privacy."

AIR POUCH   CONFIDENTIAL   Confidential File

FOREIGN SERVICE DESPATCH

FEB 24 1954

Political Adviser, Headquarters, Desp # 45
US Army, Europe, Heidelberg

TO   THE DEPARTMENT OF STATE, WASHINGTON.   February 18, 1954

REF   Mydesp #43 dated February 2, 1954, subject same as below

SUBJECT: Report of Americans Imprisoned in USSR

    The following information has been received by the Headquarters from
H.Q., British Intelligence Organization, WAHNERHEIDE, British Army of the
Rhine 19. It concerns the possible detention of five alleged American citizens in the USSR none of whose names appear in the Department's telegram
to Moscow 497 or Moscow's telegram to Department 944:

    1. Source, Augustin SPRIEKER, a German returnee from the USSR, who
appeared to be quite intelligent and alert; cooperative and made a favorable
impression. Report quoted - "In May, 1950, while in custody (Untersuchung-
schaft) in the prison in HALLE known as "Zuchthaus Rote Ochse," source discovered that the next cell contained two alleged Americans with whom he
communicated by means of tapping on the wall, using the "numerical code,"
i.e. one tap for letter 'A' and so on up to twenty-six taps for letter 'Z'.
He remembered the following details which his neighbors spelled out to him:
H. Clause MOORE, 95 Krafft St. NEWARK, Delaware -- Captain Andrew
MAISANO. No other details obtained. Source further gathered by the same
means that they had been arrested while visiting a girl or girls in
MAGDEBURG. Date of arrest or other details of their previous history not
known. Source never saw these two men, and could, therefore, give no des-
criptions. After two or three days, the Russian guard personnel became
aware of Source's tapping activities, and he was removed from the cell."
(BAOR Ref BITFG/32-2/3 (C)')

    2. Source, Dr. Anton PETZOLD, a German civilian returnee from the USSR,
who appeared to be intelligent and cooperative. Report concerns a Major
William THOMPSON (U.S. AIR FORCE). Report quoted - "THOMPSON told source
that after a forced landing in 1944 he was arrested by the Russians and
subsequently sentenced to 25 years' imprisonment for alleged espionage.
From 1944 to 1948 he had been incarcerated in the BUDENSKAYA prison in
Moscow and had then been transferred to TAYSHET camp (compound 026). The
only other information source could give concerning THOMPSON was that he
once mentioned that his home had been in San Antonio, Texas. Description:
Age about 38, height 1.85 meters, slim build, thin features, fair hair, blue
eyes." (BAOR Ref: BIT/32 - 2/3 (A)")

Confidential File

HPFales/gfm
WJO+Donoghue REPORTER   CONFIDENTIAL

This copy has been designated
the RECORD COPY. It must be
returned to DC/R for filing.

INFORMATION COPY
Retain in divisional files or destroy in accordance with security regulations

611.61251/2-1854

13. The family of William Thompson was never told he was alive.

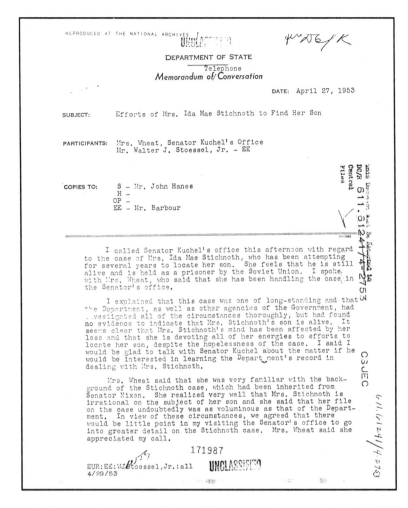

DEPARTMENT OF STATE

Telephone
Memorandum of Conversation

DATE: April 27, 1953

SUBJECT: Efforts of Mrs. Ida Mae Stichnoth to Find Her Son

PARTICIPANTS: Mrs. Wheat, Senator Kuchel's Office
Mr. Walter J. Stoessel, Jr. - EE

COPIES TO:
S - Mr. John Hanes
H -
OP -
EE - Mr. Barbour

I called Senator Kuchel's office this afternoon with regard to the case of Mrs. Ida Mae Stichnoth, who has been attempting for several years to locate her son. She feels that he is still alive and is held as a prisoner by the Soviet Union. I spoke with Mrs. Wheat, who said that she has been handling the case in the Senator's office.

I explained that this case was one of long-standing and that the Department, as well as other agencies of the Government, had investigated all of the circumstances thoroughly, but had found no evidence to indicate that Mrs. Stichnoth's son is alive. It seems clear that Mrs. Stichnoth's mind has been affected by her loss and that she is devoting all of her energies to efforts to locate her son, despite the hopelessness of the case. I said I would be glad to talk with Senator Kuchel about the matter if he would be interested in learning the Department's record in dealing with Mrs. Stichnoth.

Mrs. Wheat said that she was very familiar with the background of the Stichnoth case, which had been inherited from Senator Nixon. She realized very well that Mrs. Stichnoth is irrational on the subject of her son and she said that her file on the case undoubtedly was as voluminous as that of the Department. In view of these circumstances, we agreed that there would be little point in my visiting the Senator's office to go into greater detail on the Stichnoth case. Mrs. Wheat said she appreciated my call.

171987

EUR:EE:WJStoessel,Jr.:all
4/29/53

UNCLASSIFIED

14. Sergeant Lawrence Edward Reitz's mother was the first POW activist. Between 1947 and 1960 she conclusively proved that her son had been captured by the Germans, "liberated" by the Red Army and shipped to Siberia. She was even able to track him in the slave labor system through 1956. The U.S. government initiated a disinformation program, lying to Congress and the press. In 1956 she began to crack under the strain. The government, to its everlasting shame, used that information to destroy her.

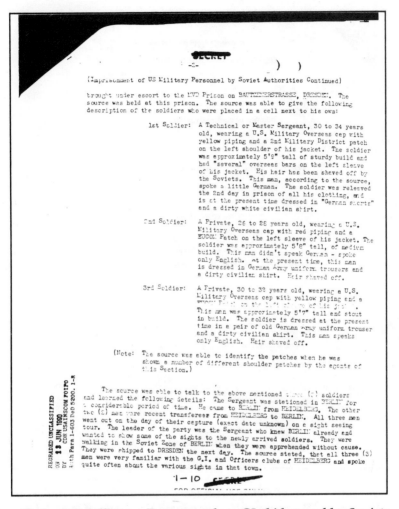

~~SECRET~~

-2-   )   )

(Imprisonment of US Military Personnel by Soviet Authorities Continued)

brought under escort to the MVD Prison on BAUTZINERSTRASSE, DRESDEN. The source was held at this prison. The source was able to give the following description of the soldiers who were placed in a cell next to his own:

1st Soldier: A Technical or Master Sergeant, 30 to 34 years old, wearing a U.S. Military Overseas cap with yellow piping and a 2nd Military District patch on the left shoulder of his jacket. The soldier was approximately 5'9" tall of sturdy build and had "several" overseas bars on the left sleeve of his jacket. His hair has been shaved off by the Soviets. This man, according to the source, spoke a little German. The soldier was relieved the 2nd day in prison of all his clothing, and is at the present time dressed in "German shorts" and a dirty white civilian shirt.

2nd Soldier: A Private, 26 to 28 years old, wearing a U.S. Military Overseas cap with red piping and a EUCOM Patch on the left sleeve of his jacket. The soldier was approximately 5'8" tall, of medium build. This man didn't speak German - spoke only English. At the present time, this man is dressed in German Army uniform trousers and a dirty civilian shirt. Hair shaved off.

3rd Soldier: A Private, 30 to 32 years old, wearing a U.S. Military Overseas cap with yellow piping and a ~~EUCOM Patch~~ on the left sleeve of his jacket. This man was approximately 5'7" tall and stout in build. The soldier is dressed at the present time in a pair of old German army uniform trouser and a dirty civilian shirt. This man speaks only English. Hair shaved off.

(Note: The source was able to identify the patches when he was shown a number of different shoulder patches by the agents of this Section.)

The source was able to talk to the above mentioned three (3) soldiers and learned the following details: The Sergeant was stationed in BERLIN for a considerable period of time. He came to BERLIN from HEIDELBERG. The other two (2) men were recent transferees from HEIDELBERG to BERLIN. All three men went out on the day of their capture (exact date unknown) on a sight seeing tour. The leader of the party was the Sergeant who knew BERLIN already and wanted to show some of the sights to the newly arrived soldiers. They were walking in the Soviet Zone of BERLIN when they were apprehended without cause. They were shipped to DRESDEN the next day. The source stated, that all three (3) men were very familiar with the G.I. and Officers clubs of HEIDELBERG and spoke quite often about the various sights in that town.

1-10   ~~SECRET~~

FOR OFFICIAL USE ONLY

15. Army Intelligence Report on three GIs kidnapped by Soviets while sightseeing in Berlin. The Army has not released the names of these soldiers and other kidnap victims seen in Soviet custody.

CONFIDENTIAL

DEFENSE ADVISORY COMMITTEE ON PRISONERS OF WAR

CPOW/3 D-1
17 June 1955

STUDY GROUP III

RECOVERY OF UNREPATRIATED PRISONERS OF WAR

Problem A - Assess Efforts to Recover Unrepatriated Military
Personnel.

B - Study Possible Alternate or Additional Courses
of Action

C - Consider the Import of Pending Senate Approval to
Ratification of the Geneva Conventions of 1949

Document Presented By

Office of Special Operations

Office of the Secretary of Defense

8 June 1955

This document contains information affecting the national
defense of the United States within the meaning of the
Espionage Laws, Title 18, U.S.C., Sections 793 and 794. The
transmission or the revelation of its contents in any manner
to an unauthorized person is prohibited by law.

1 8 JUN 1990

:CLASSIFIED ON:
IWNGRADE TO
SECRET ON: ----------------
NFIDENTIAL ON: ---------------- REVIEW ON 17 Jun 1985
DIRECTOR, FREEDOM OF INFORMATION
1ECURITY REVIEW, OASD (PA)

18 MAR 1985

0470195

CONFIDENTIAL

16. *Cover page of Defense Advisory Committee on Prisoners of
War report "Recovery of Unrepatriated Prisoners of War," dated
June 17, 1955*

CPOW/3 D-1

range of possible additional efforts to recover personnel now in custody of foreign powers. On the one hand, we are bound at present by the President's "peaceful means" decree. The military courses of action apparently cannot be taken unilaterally, and we are possessed of some rather "reluctant" allies in this respect. The problem becomes almost a philosophical one. If we are "at war," cold, hot or otherwise, casualties and losses must be expected and perhaps we must learn to live with this type of thing. If we are in for fifty years of peripheral "fire fights" we may be forced/to adopt a rather cynical attitude on this for political reasons. If such is the case, then we, in the military, must follow a course of action something like General Erskine outlined which would (1) instill in the soldier a much more effective "don't get captured" attitude, and (2) we should also push to get the military commander more discretionary authority to retaliate, fast and hard against these- Communist tactics.

7. Reference 1 (d) (3):

The war plans currently developed and their annexes dealing with recovery of military personnel are not available to me. As you know from your discussions with Mr. Godel, they have many interagency ramifications. I would suggest that you make this item a subject for further development with Mr. Godel. He can open doors and make contacts for you on this subject which would give you as accurate a picture as is to be had.

JAMES J. KELLEHER
Office of Special Operations

17. Fifth page of Defense Advisory Committee on Prisoners of War document dated June 17, 1955. Note that the document states that "losses must be expected . . . we may be forced to adopt a rather cynical attitude on this [POWs] for political reasons." Also note that the Pentagon letter proposes instilling in soldiers a "don't get captured" attitude.

UNITED STATES GOVERNMENT

memorandum

DATE: 12 FEB 1991

REPLY TO
ATTN OF: POW-MIA   U-0173/POW-MIA

SUBJECT: Request for Relief

TO: DR

1. PURPOSE: I, hereby, request to resign my position as the Chief of the Special Office for Prisoners of War and Missing in Action (POW-MIA).

2. BACKGROUND:

a. Motivation. My initial acceptance of this posting was based upon two primary motives; first, I had heard that the job was highly contentious and extremely frustrating, that no one would volunteer for it because of its complex political nature. This of course, made it appear challeng...

3. CURRENT IMPRESSIONS, BASED ON MY EXPERIENCE:

a. Highest National Priority. That National leaders continue to address the prisoner of war and missing in action issue as the "highest national priority" is a travesty. From my vantage point, I observed that the principal government players were interested primarily in conducting a "damage limitation exercise", and appeared to knowingly and deliberately generate an endless succession of manufactured crises and "busy work". Progress consisted in frenetic activity, with little substance and no real results.

...its re... ...ds never had a chance. We, all, were subject to control. I particularly salute the personnel in the POW-MIA Office for their long suffering, which I regrettably was unable to change. I feel that the Agency and the Office are being used as the "fall guys" or "patsies" to cover the tracks of others.

5. RECOMMENDATIONS:

a. One Final Vietnam Casualty. So ends the war and my last grand crusade, like it actually did end,.I guess. However, as they say in the Legion, "je ne regrette rien..." For all of the above, I respectfully request to be relieved of my duties as Chief of the Special Office for Prisoners of War and Missing in Action.

b. A Farewell to Arms. So as to avoid the annoyance of being shipped off to some remote corner, out of sight and out of the way, in my own "bamboo cage" of silence somewhere, I further request that the Defense Intelligence Agency, which I have attempted to serve loyally and with honor, assist me in being retired immediately from active military service.

MILLARD A. PECK
Colonel, Infantry
USA

18. Colonel Millard A. Peck was the head of the DIA's POW/MIA office. Traditionally, the person holding that position is responsible for the Department of Defense's POW disinformation program. Peck, a Vietnam War hero, resigned in 1991 rather than deceive the American people.

Endnotes

Preface

1. Department of Defense: "Response to unfounded allegations that the U.S. government abandoned POWs in World War II and Korea." (current)
2. The Defense Advisory Committee on Prisoners of War, June 17, 1955.

Chapter One

1. All information related to former POWs, including that which is in quotes, was obtained by interview or letter from the named individual.
2. Details of uniform from Stalag 3A newspaper, May 3, 1945, collection of D.C. Wimberly.
3. National Archives, RG 332, released under the Freedom of Information Act, no entry number or box assigned. Previously located in the Military Mission to Moscow files, but removed shortly after the first newspaper accounts on the subject appeared.
4. *Ibid.*
5. *Ibid.*
6. *Ibid.*
7. *Ibid.*
8. Five-page letter, dated August 15, 1945, from Australian Norman Dodgson to Sidney Miller.
9. *Ibid.*
10. *Ibid.*
11. *Ibid.*
12. *Ibid.*
13. NA, RG 331 entry 7, box 51, "Official History."
14. Americans returned "...months and years..." after the war. The Russians have now admitted this. Col. Gen. Dmitri Volkogonov, now Russian chairman of the joint U.S.-Russian POW commission, admitted that three World War American POWs were released "several years" after the war. January 30, 1992, *New York Times,* p. A6, "Russian Offers Americans Access to K.G.B. Files."
15. NA, RG 59, has extensive information on Reitz in the decimal files.
16. NA, RG 331, entry 7, box 51.

Chapter Two

1. NA, RG 165, entry 421, box 473.
2. NA, RG 165, entry 421, box 473, secret memo for Hull.
3. NA, RG 165, entry 421, box 473, memo for the assistant secretary, WDGS, Nov. 2, 1944.
4. Eric Larrabee, "Commander in Chief" (New York, 1987), p. 16. The JCS, formerly the Joint Army-Navy Board, in 1942 had been "transformed from an interdepartmental consulting group into a potential source and instrument of national strategy, lifted above the departmental level and joined in a special link to the President alone."
5. NA, RG 165, box 473, JCS 1141.
6. *Ibid.*
7. *Ibid.*

8. Henry L. Stimson and Anthony Eden both indicated that the Soviets had made the return of U.S. and British POWs contingent on the return of "all" Soviet citizens demanded by Stalin. Both references are footnoted elsewhere.

9. Alex Masterton was interviewed in 1988 and 1990. All information and quotes related to Masterton came from those interviews, unless otherwise noted.

10. NA, RG 165, entry 421, box 473, SPMGO (27. 383.6, January 2, 1945)

11. NA, RG 165, entry 421, box 473.

12. NA, RG 331, AFHQ microfilm R-185-E.

13. Ibid.

14. NA, RG 107, entry 74A, box 12, p. 1.

15. *Ibid.*

16. *Ibid.*

17. NA, RG 84, Moscow Embassy, box 78, message 866.

18. NA RG 59, records of the Central European Division, 1944-45, box 1.

19. *Ibid.*

20. Just as the Soviet threat to hold hostages emerged in the fall of 1944, the Morgenthau Plan appeared in the White House. It first took shape at a meeting of the cabinet Committee on Germany, September 2, 1944. Harry Hopkins, FDR's personal representative, met with John McCloy, from the War Department, Freeman Matthews and H.W. Riddleberger of the State Department, and Harry Dexter White from Treasury. White was one of Henry Morgenthau Jr.'s most influential advisers and heavily influenced the Germanophobic Morgenthau Plan.

History would later reveal that the two most influential members of this committee were communist agents, Hopkins and White. According to the notes from the meeting, White "produced the Treasury plan for Germany and gave a lengthy interpretation of this plan which, in its general tenor, was more extreme than the memorandum itself."

White outlined a transfer of territory that closely paralleled the demands Stalin would make at Yalta five months later. "Poland would receive East Prussia and Upper Silesia," giving them sufficient German land to compensate for the loss of eastern Poland, which Stalin would once again annex. No one questioned the morality of agreeing to give him something originally obtained when he was an ally of the Nazis. France would receive the Saar and additional western territory. "The remainder of the Reich would be divided into two independent states."

Germany would, for all intents and purposes, lose its sovereignty, and Europe would lose the only remaining barrier to Soviet expansion to the Atlantic. On September 6, FDR met with Stimson, Hull and Morgenthau, who outlined his plan in detail. The four men discussed it at great length. Stimson and Hull presented a counter-proposal for rebuilding Germany as a democracy, but Roosevelt did not decide which plan to support.

Three days later, Morgenthau and Stimson once again met with FDR, each presenting additional written arguments for their respective plans. By this time, FDR had collected several sets of memos and reports outlining the opposing plans and had logged many hours of dialogue. Within forty-eight hours, he came down in favor of the plan that would open Western Europe to Stalin and against the plan the British desperately needed if a noncommunist, democratic, Western Europe was to rise from the ashes of World War II.

Roosevelt then went to Canada to meet with Winston Churchill at the Quebec conference, September 11-16, 1944, and summoned Morgenthau to join him. Churchill opposed the Morgenthau plan when it was first presented. He inquired "with annoyance whether he had been brought over to Quebec to discuss such a scheme as that and stating that it would mean 'England would be chained to a dead body.' "

FDR, however, withheld the promise of an additional $6.5 billion in aid until Churchill agreed to publicly support the plan. Unlike the Americans, the British never allowed the plan to be implemented in their zone of occupation. U.S. execution of the plan was also limited after it leaked to the press, causing strong opposition.

21. David Irving, "The War Between the Generals" (New York, 1981), p. 327. The United States Joint Strategic Survey Committee "and their fellow planners in the S. & P. section of the Joint Chiefs urged policy decisions that seemed designed to force Britain to commit its dwindling resources to operations like the frontal assault on the Continent," certain to maximize its already substantial casualties. (p. 413).

22. *Ibid.*, p. 412. Soviet Foreign Minister V.M. Molotov had confronted British Foreign Secretary Anthony Eden during a meeting in Moscow in October 1944, with a proposal for the same conditional agreement, to return all British POWs only if an agreement was reached to return all Soviet citizens.

Chapter Three

1. NA, RG 84, Moscow Embassy, telegram #18, from SECSTATE to AMEMBAS-SY, Moscow, January 3, 1945, signed Stettinius.

2. NA, RG 165, entry 421, box 473, January 21, 1945, Top Secret memo from U.S. Military Mission to Moscow to War Department, MX 22423, p. 4.

3. *Ibid.*, p. 3.

4. NA, RG 84, Moscow Embassy, box 78, #766, from SECSTATE to AMEMBAS-SY, Moscow, March 31, 1945.

5. NA, RG 165, entry 421, box 473.

6. *Ibid.*

7. *Ibid.*

8. NA, RG 165, entry 421, box 473.

9. *Ibid.*

10. General Vlasov had been one of Stalin's favorite generals prior to his capture. Within months he had turned against Stalin and had recruited thousands of Soviet POWs, held by the Germans, to the anti-communist cause. His presence in western Europe, with armed divisions under his command, was a significant threat to Stalin's post war plans. The United States turned Vlasov over to the U.S.S.R. on May 12, 1945. Play acting was used to make it appear that Vlasov was taken by the Soviets through the use of force, from his American captors.

11. NA, RG 84, Moscow Embassy, memorandum of conversation, Crimea conference, 711.4, February 9, 1945.

12. See appendix.

13. NA, RG 84, Moscow Embassy, box 78, letter to Joseph Grew from Andrei Gromyko, February 27, 1945, p. 3.

14. NA, RG 84, Moscow Embassy, box 78, SECSTATE to AMEMBASSY, Moscow, #766, March 31, 1945, p. 2.

15. *Ibid.*

16. NA, RG 165, entry 421, box 473, #1520, March 3, 1945.

17. Winston Churchill, *Triumph and Tragedy* (Boston, 1953), pp. 352-363.

18. Robert Rhodes James, *Anthony Eden* (London, 1986), p. 290.

19. John Costello, *Mask of Treachery* (New York, 1988), p. 437.

20. William Stevenson, *Intrepid's Last Case* (New York, 1983), p. 193.

21. David Irving, *The War Between the Generals* (New York, 1981), p. 412.

22. *Op. cit.,* Costello, p. 438.

23. Peter Wright, *Spy Catcher* (New York, 1987), p. 182.

Chapter Four

1. Letters from former POWs Tasco Wilson and Howard Mintle.

2. POW letter.

3. NA, RG 334, box 22, Unnecessary Delay in Identification & Repatriation of American Officers Escaped From German Control.

4. NA, RG 334, box 22.

5. NA, RG 334, box 57, EES/18645/1/22.

6. NA, RG 334, box 22.

7. NA, RG 334, box 22, memo from Crockett to Hampton.

8. NA, RG 334, box 22, memo #055070, February 23, 1945.

9. NA, RG 334, box 22, The Lublin Trip, p. 1.

10. *Ibid.,* p. 2.

11. *Ibid.*

12. *Ibid.*

13. *Ibid.*

14. *Ibid.*

15. *Ibid.*

16. *Ibid.*

17. NA, CPM Branch, MIS-X, box 636, Final Historical Report.

18. NA, RG 334, box 22, The Lublin Trip, p. 5.

19. NA, RG 334, box 24, March 24, 1945, memo.

20. Op. cit., The Lublin Trip, p.6.

21. NA, RG 334, box 22, Meeting at OVS, p. 1.

22. *Ibid., p. 2.*

23. NA, RG 334, box 24, Evacuation of Liberated American Prisoners of War, p. 1.

24. *Ibid.*

25. *Ibid.,* p. 2.

26. *Ibid.,* p. 4.

27. NA, RG 334, box 24, Liberated Prisoners of War, p. 1.

28. *Ibid.*

29. *Ibid.,* p. 2.

30. *Ibid.*

31. Message M-23174, March 12, 1945.

32. *Ibid.,* p. 2.

33. Telegram 738, March 14, 1945, from Harriman to Secretary of State, p. 3.

34. *Ibid.*

35. Op. cit., The Lublin Trip.

36. *Ibid.,* p. 8.

37. Memo 866, March 16, 1945, from Archibald Clarke Kerr, p. 1.

38. *Ibid.,* p. 9.

39. *Ibid.,* p. 10.

40. ONA, RG 165, box 164, #2971.

41. NA, RG 331, box 22.

42. *Ibid.,* pp. 16-18.

43. NA, RG 331, 383.6x370.05-2-3, Tab E-Annex 1, p. 1.

44. *Ibid.*

45. *Ibid.*

46. Department of State telegram ASB-1304, April 13, 1945, 740.00114 EW/4-1345, signed Kirk, p. 1.

47. *Ibid.*

48. *Ibid.*, p. 2.

49. NA, CPR Branch, MIS-X, box 636, Final Historical Report.

Chapter Five

1. Department of State telegram #514, February 23, 1945, 740.00114EW/2-1245, signed Kirk.

2. NA, RG 334, box 22.

3. Statement of former Stalag 2B POW Edmund T. D'Arcy-Clarke.

4. *Ibid.*

5. *Ibid.*

6. *Ibid.*

7. *Ibid.*

8. *Ibid.*, NA, RG 334, box 22, The Lublin Trip, p. 7.

Chapter Six

1. NA, RG 59, box 3553, incoming message #1426, April 30, 1945, p. 1.

2. *Ibid.*, pp. 1-2.

3. Christopher Simpson, "Blowback" (New York, 1988), p. 8.

4. NA, RG 331, SGS, box 88, S-87705, May 11, 1945.

5. Reinhard Gehlen, "The Service" (New York, 1972), pp. 90-91.

6. NA RG 331, G-1, box 21, "Repatriation of Russian and Allied Personnel."

7. *Ibid.*

8. NA, RG 331, G-1, box 21.

9. ONA, RG 331, AFHQ microfilm, R-152-H, AG383.7/114 D-O, Repatriation to Russia, confidential memo, Subj.: Disposition of Soviet Citizens, Section Two, states: "By the terms of a recent agreement reached between the Governments of the U.S. and Soviet Union. . . . May 31, 1945.

10. *Ibid.*

11. NA, RG 331, G-1, box 21, memo from General R.W. Barker to Eisenhower, May 23, 1945, p. 4.

12. NA, RG 331, entry 6, box 24.

13. NA, RG 331, G-1, box 21, telegram #449.

14. Statement of former 4B POW Ted Perkins.

15. *Ibid.*

Chapter Seven

1. AFHQ V Corps sitreps and war diary; 8th Army war diary; W0170/4241; W0170/4/83; WO 170/4184, 536, as referenced in the High Court Justice, Queens Branch Division, plaintiff Toby Low (Baron Aldington v Nigel Watts and Count Nikolai Tolstoy Miloslavsky, defendants, February 24, 1988), p. 33.

2. Nikolai Tolstoy, "Stalin's Secret War" (New York, 1981), p. 298.

3. W017c/4241.

4. *The Sunday Times*, October 2, 1988.

5. NA, RG 331, reel R-16-L, top secret message WX-72239, May 14, 1945.

6. COS 501, May 14, 1945, from 8th Army to V Corps.

7. Top secret British cipher telegram FX-76939, May 17, 1945, from AFHQ to SHAEF forward.

8. NA, RG 331, AFHQ, reel R-1 6-L, top secret AFHQ incoming message QX-32004, May 21, 1945.

9. NA, RG 331, AFHQ, reel R-1 6-L, FX-79904.

10. NA, RG 331, AFHQ microfilm R-152-H, "secret" memo CR/3491/4/G-1 (Br.) April 25, 1945, "Special Instructions for Officers i/c Liaison Groups for Soviet Citizens."

11. A4116, 5-23-45, from V Corps to 8th Army, secret, personal message for C of S.

12. NA, RG 331, AFHQ, reel R-16-L, message AG2/00866, November 25, 1946, from GHQ to AFHQ.

13. NA, RG 331, AFHQ, R-16-L, message A-4152, May 25, 1945.

14. NA, RG 331, entry 6, box 22, May 23, 1945, Reinhart document, p. 2.

15. N.N. Krasnov Jr., "The Hidden Russia" (New York, 1960), p. 47.

16. *Ibid.*

17. Reinhart document, p. 3.

18. NA, RG 84, Moscow Embassy, confidential file, box 78.

19. NA, AFHQ, reel R-16-F, message 95304, May 22, 1945, troopers to British Military Mission to Moscow.

20. Tolstoy, op. cit., p. 441.

21. Nikolai Tolstoy, "Secret Betrayal" (London, 1975).

22. Report X-38316, SHAEF, PWX Branch, G-1, "Repatriation of British, U.S. and Other United Nations Prisoners of War as of June 7, 1945."

23. *Ibid.*, p. 2, and RAMPs report, 1946.

*British intelligence had worked with the Ukrainian liberation movement prior to World War II, John Prados writes in "The President's Secret Wars," and "saw no reason to give up the relationship afterward." There were reportedly more than 100,000 anti-communist Ukrainians under arms behind Soviet lines at the end of World War II. It was the ideal opportunity for Churchill to destabilize Stalin using his own people behind Soviet lines. So in the form of this Ukrainian Waffen SS Division, the pre-World War II allies would once again join forces to fight communism.

The "Galizien" Division had been withdrawn from the front in July 1944 because of heavy casualties. As the Germans withdrew from the Ukraine, they no longer needed their Ukrainian police regiments, which were staffed with indigenous personnel. Eventually, some of these police regiments were integrated into the Ukrainian SS "Galizien" Division. Many of the police units had "assisted the SS in the extermination of Jews and Poles." Five regiments of the Ukrainian police "were incorporated into the SS division in the summer and fall of 1944 after the withdrawal of the Nazis from Poland." The regiments were: Galizisches SS Freiwilligen-Regiment 4 (Polizei) Galician SS Volunteers-Regiment 4., formed by the Orpo in 1943 and disbanded from June 1944, when its men went to the division; Galizisches SS Freiwilligen-Regiment 5 (Polizei), formed by the Orpo in the general government in July 1943 and absorbed; I. Btl. of Polizeischutzenregiment 32, saw action against partisans in Poland before being disbanded on June 9, 1944, when its men went into the division; Galizisches SS Freiwilligen-Regiment 6 (Polizei) formed by the Orpo on August 6, 1943, with its cadre coming from Polizeischutzen-regiment 32, disbanded in southern France on January 1, 1944, when 745 of its men went to the division at Heidelager; and Galizisches SS Freiwilligen-Regiment 8 (Polizei). It is not known whether this regiment was ever formed. It was to have been formed in November 1943 by Abwicklungsstelle PolizeiWaffenschule IV, Mastricht.

*To this day, the British government places the blame for the murder of more than 100 Cossacks on an overzealous military. The current disinformation line, propounded by Britain's most respected historians, is that once the government found out that its orders had been excessively enforced, they stepped in and stopped it. In fact, no officer was punished nor any career slowed by participating. The current disinformation also states that all relevant documents on forcible repatriation have been released to the Public Records Office. That is false. The British government stepped in and prevented the authors from obtaining hundreds of still-secret British documents related to this subject, located at the National Archives, Suitland, Md.

Chapter Eight

1. National Archives, RG 331, entry 6, Box 22, "Daily Evacuation Cables." A daily count indicates 4,165, not 5,241 as stated in RAMPs.
2. NA, RG 331, entry 6, box 24, May 17, 1945, memo entitled "United Nations Prisoners of War in Germany," p. 7; also, RG331, entry 7, box 78, "Strengths of Prisoner of War Camps in Germany as Known to PWX-GI Division, SHAEF" at 15 March 1945.
3. RAMPs, p. 31; also confirmed by "Daily Evacuation Cables."
4. NA, RG 331, SGS, G-2, 3, 4, 5, "secret urgent," #160007.
5. NA, SHAEF document FWD-23059, June 1, 1945, p. 1.
6. *Op. cit.*, daily evacuation cables.
7. *Ibid.*
8. NA, RG 407, entry 389, box 2611, The Adjutant General's Office, Statistical and Accounting Division, Strength Accounting Branch, September 6, 1946. These statistics cover all Army and Army Air Force personnel in the European, Mediterranean and Pacific theaters, from December 1941, through the end of the war. In order to arrive at the total number in Europe and the Mediterranean, it is necessary to subtract the 16,358 Pacific theater POWs from the total. This number is in *American Prisoners of War in WWI, WWII, Korea and Vietnam*, by Charles A. Stenger, P.D., "developed in cooperation with the Department of Defense, National Research Council, National Archives and other sources. As such it reflects consental agreement as to the accuracy and acceptability of the information presented," January 1, 1982, p. 2. All statistical totals arrived at after May 28th must be viewed skeptically, and independently verified with the raw data. Two additional sources exist to back-up the 1946 AG records which state that only 76,879 American POWs were actually returned, not the 92,922 currently accepted as the official figure. The "Daily Evacuation Cables," footnoted elswhere, indicate that 78,569 Americans were recovered in Europe and the Mediterranean theaters, after discounting the insertion of 9,671 and 4,682 on June 1 and 30th, respectively. Also, the number of liberated POWs shipped to the U.S. through May 28th was 40,190 (evacuation cable #15.) The number of former POWs waiting to be shipped at 2400 hours, May 28th, is 38,250, for a total of 78,440 former POWs that were

shipped back to the United States. The daily evacuation cables indicated that these cumulative totals were somewhat inflated due to double counting of hospitalized former POWs who were shipped by air transport.

Two documents located in RG 331, entry 6, box 25, also support a total of about 78-80,000. SHAEF, four page document entitled "Repatriation of British, US, and other United Nations Prisoners of War as of 7 June 1945," states that as of June 7th, 64,524 U.S. POWs "have been shipped back to the US." A letter in the same file, from Major General R.W. Barker, to Major General S.C. Henry, indicated that as of June 4th, there were 18,619 ex-POWs present at LeHarve, 410 on leave, 735 in hospitals and about 1,200 AWOL. The letter also stated that 17,000 were to be shipped between June 4th and 9th. The 20,964 documented in the letter must be reduced by whatever number were shipped between the 4th and 7th, when it is known that the cumulative total is 64,524. The daily shipping totals have not been located, so an approximation of the percentage of the 17,000 during first three of five days, 60% of 17,000, would suggest that as many as 10,200 were shipped, suggesting that only 75,000 POWs were liberated and returned to U.S. control. A more modest estimate closely supports the previously reported 78-80,000 figure.

Military Intelligence Service 6801 MIS-X Detachment, according to recently declassified documents obtained under the Freedom of Information Act, processed the following numbers, referenced in Headquarters, European Theater of Operations (Main.) United States Army, APO 887, Office of the Assistant Chief of Staff, G-2, June 21, 1945:

RAMP were processed by MIS-X in the following camps in these numbers:

Camp Lucky Strike	71,429
EX-PW Casual Det., UK Base	4,807
Ramp camp, Reims	1,826
Ramp camp, Namur	1,746
Ramp camp, Epinal	198
total	80,939

MIS-X teams of one officer and one enlisted man began activities 30 March in reception centers in Epinal, Sedan (later Reims) and Helmond (soon abandoned.) Nine officers and eight enlisted men began MIS processing in Lucky Strike 4 April. With establishment of the policy of sending to Lucky Strike all RAMP, whether or not processed in intermediate reception camps, MIS-X teams in Epinal, Namur and Reims were shifted May 13 to Lucky Strike.

(These documents will be placed in RG 332. Entry and box number not yet known. Other documents in the National Archives go as high as 98,000. The actual number liberated and repatriated appears to be between 78,000 and 84,000.)

On May 19, 1945, three days into the Leipzig neotiations, SHAEF advised the War Department that they expected a total of 105,000 American POWs in the European theater to eventually be repatriated. The message, S-88613, stated that 80,000 "US prisoners of war recovered from German custody now in US or British hands. . . ." The message concluded by stating the "numbers of US prisoners estimated in Russian control 25,000." (NA, RG 331, entry 1, box 87.) The 105,000 figure simply could not be covered by massaging statistics. It was ignored, and never repeated, justified, or explained away. SHAEF document FWD-23059 was issued on June 1, 1945, to historically cover the 25,000 American POWs held hostage by Stalin's army on the western front.

In 1947 the office of the Chief of Military history, U.S. Army, issued a historical manuscript, for internal consumption only, entitled "RAMPS: The Recovery and

Repatriation of Liberated Prisoners of War–Occupation Forces in Europe Series, 1945-46." It was the culmination of the historical myth revision of history.

RAMPS is divided into two sections, the first dealing with prisoners of war, and the second with forcible repatriation of Soviet citizens. At no point are the two connected, and forcible repatriation is treated as something that did not appear until September 1945, four months after the war in Europe ended, and long after the last American and British POWs returned home. There is no mention of hostage politics, POWs being shot while escaping, or the agreements reached at Yalta and Halle for the forcible repatriation of Soviet citizens as the price to be paid for the return of some of the American and British POWs.

RAMPS falsely concludes, on page 23, that "no special problems were encountered in the recovery and evacuation of ex-prisoners during the month of June, and that all United States ex-prisoners were recovered or accounted for during June. . . ." In fact, the exchange of personnel between the United States and the U.S.S.R. concluded on May 28th after only 4,165 of the 25,000 hostages were recovered.

The British had 199,592 confirmed POWs held by the Germans as of March 1945. In spite of this, RAMPs alleges on page 31 that only 175,000 were expected to return, but the 6,250 discrepancy is "attributed in part to unreported deaths occuring especially during the forced marches when the Germans attempted to prevent Allied prisoners from being evacuated." If 6,000 POWs had died while under German control during the last months of the war, the Allied propaganda machine would have investigated and exploited it. It didn't.

RAMPs suggests on page 61 that the Halle negotiations lasted only one day, and that "the principle of forced repatriation did not come into issue in the mass repatriation of Soviet citizens under the terms of the Halle Agreement." In fact, the Leipzig negotiations were deadlocked for six days over forced repatriation. The deadlock was broken when the issue of whom was to be forcibly returned was handed over to the diplomats that were attempting to decide those very issues.

RAMPs fraudulently declares on page 62 that the "Leipzig (Halle) Agreement was brought into operation on 20 May to recover promptly 2,200 United States and British liberated prisoners of war who had been assembled by the Soviet forces at Luckenwalde." These POWs had been held at Luckenwalde since April 22nd when the Red Army overran the camp. At least two had been shot and killed while trying to escape from Soviet control. Convoy after convoy had gone behind Soviet line in attempts to rescue these POW hostages. Thousands of the hostages escaped on foot or by truck prior to May 8th. Approximately 3,000 cannot be accounted for and were presumably shipped to the Soviet Union from where a few would be exchanged in 1946.

The most egregious historical myth contained in RAMPs is on page 64. In order to cover-up the 25,000 American POW hostages on the western front, it states: "the Leipzig Agreement for the mutual exchange of liberated citizens was brought into operation as repects liberated prisoners of war on May 20: by 23 May 23,421 liberated American prisoners were recovered from Soviet custody; and 5,241 were recovered by 28 May." The facts are considerably different. Only 180 Americans were exchanged between May 20th and 23rd, not 23,421, and only 4,165 were recovered by May 28th, not 5,241. Historians have consistently missed this most obvious of lies for the four decades this document has been available.

9. NA, RG 331, entry 3A box 18.

10. The *Times*, London., (May 30, 1945), p. 8.

Chapter Nine

1. "Information Received from Illegal Border Crossers," Aug. 20, 1946, IN-SCOM FOIA.

2. "American and Allied Soldiers Held by Soviets," Aug. 4, 1947, INSCOM FOIA.

3. Primo Levi, "If This is a Man" (New York, 1950), p. 221.

4. NA, RG 59, Department of State confidential memo, 611.61241/12-1655, December 16, 1955.

5. About one year later, Heinmiller was helping an aide to Senator Hugh Butler of Nebraska resettle Eastern European immigrants in the United States. The aide's wife was working to get anti-communist resistance members into the United States.

Four were sent to Alaska, and "one of the guys talked about the fact that he knew both his people and American soldiers had been taken away" by the Soviets to the gulag. A Lithuanian and a Latvian who had been German POWs and whom Heinmiller was helping to settle in Alaska, told him that the Russians had picked the younger, stronger and technically trained Americans for shipment to the Soviet Union. A Polish carpenter Heinmiller knew confirmed the story.

6. Reinhard Gehlen, *The Service* (New York, 1972), p. 41.

7. NA, RG 59, Department of State secret memo, from USPOLAD, Heidelberg, #100, to Department of State, 611.61241/11-1450, November 14, 1950, p. 6.

8. Volume 4, document 4-7, "Detention of American Personnel by Foreign Agency," obtained under the Freedom of Information Act, July 1990.

9. *Ibid.*, document 4-22.

10. *Ibid.*

11. NA, RG 59, 611.61251/2-1854, foreign dispatch #45, February 18, 1954.

12. NA, RG 59, 611.61241i11-1450, secret, Heidelberg, November 4, 1950.

13. NA, RG 59, Department of State incoming confidential telegram #11813, September 15, 1962.

14. *Op. cit.*, Detention of American Personnel.

15. Ilya Gerol, "Gorbachev Should Investigate the Disappearance of Allied Soldiers," *Star-Telegram* (Dallas., November 15, 1989, Commentary section.)

Chapter 10

1. Speech at AFL-CIO dinner Washington, D.C. June 30, 1975.

2. CIA economic intelligence report, "Forced Labor in the USSR: 1953-7," FOIA.

3. *Ibid.*

4. Alexander Solzhenitsyn, *The Gulag Archipelago* (New York, 1973), p. 60.

5. CA-10165, "Soviet Detention of United States Aircraft Incident Survivors."

6. NA, ASACSI, "US Prisoners of War in Korean Operation," Dec. 31, 1954.

7. INSCOM, "Americans Detained . . . ." FOIA

8. *Op. cit.*, USACSI.

9. *Op cit.*, Solzhenitsyn, p. 493.

10. Alexander Dolgun and Patrick Watson, *Alexander Dolgun's Story* (New York, 1975), p. 170.

11. Victor Herman, Coming out of the Ice (New York, 1980), pp. 266-7.

12. Dolgun p. 210.

13. *Ibid.*, pp. 210-211.

14. *Ibid.*, p. 265.
15. *Ibid.*, p. 210.
16. *Op. cit.*, Herman, p. 277.
17. *Op. cit.*, Dolgun, p. 125.
18. CIA economic intelligence report, "Forced Labor in the USSR: 1953-57," September 12, 1958, pp. 22-23, FOIA.
19. *Ibid.*
20. *Op. cit.*, Dolgun, pp. 249, 251.
21. Michael Solomon, *Magadan* (Montreal, 1971), p. 93.
22. *Op. cit.*, Solzhenitsyn, pp. 95-7.
23. *Ibid.*, pp. 93-4
24. *Ibid.*, p. 150.
25. *Ibid.*, p. 155
26. *Op. cit.*, Dolgun, p.155.
27. *Ibid.*, p. 176
28. *Op. cit.*, Solzhenitsyn, p. 418.
29. *Op. cit.*, Dolgun, p. 154.
30. *Ibid.*, p. 153.
31. *Ibid.*, p. 157.
32. *Op. cit.*, p. 252.
33. *Ibid.*, Dolgun, pp. 323-327.
34. Authors' interviews.

Chapter 11

1. NA, RG 59, 611.61241/11-53.
2. NA,RG 59, 611.61241/9-1252, letter from Mrs. Ida Mae Reitz-Stichnoth.
3. NA, RG 59, 611.61241/6-853.
4. *Ibid.*
5. NA, RG 59, 611.21241/11-1653, p. 6.
6. NA. RG 59, 611.61241/3-3054.
7. NA, RG 59, 611.61241/9-2254.
8. *Ibid.*
9.*Ibid.*
10. *Ibid.*
11. NA, RG 59, attachment to 611.61241/7-2255.
12. *Ibid.*
13. Don Keller, *Fullerton News Tribune,* June 18, 1956, p. 1.
14. *Ibid.*
15. *Ibid.*, p. 11.
16. NA, RG 59, 611.61241/7-356 HBS.
17. Ibid., p. 2.
18. Ibid.
19. Ibid.
20. NA, RG 59, 611.61241/5-857.
21. Ibid., p. 2.
22. NA, RG 59, 611.61241/7-1756,
23. NA, RG 59, 611.61241/8-156.
24. Ibid.
25. NA, RG 59, 611.61241/9-758; and undated AP story in the same file:
"Mom's 13-year Search For Son May Pay Off."

26. Ibid.

27. Ibid.

28. NA, RG 59, AP story dated 6-15-56, box 2524.

29. NA, RG 59, 611.61241/6-1556, October 15, 1956, letter from State Department to Mr. Goff.

30. NA, RG 59, 611.61241/7-3056.

31. NA, RG 59, 611.61241/508571.

Chapter 12

1. NA, RG 349, Entry 95C, Box 40, CCRAK 3M-101, February 24, 1953 no. 2.

2. NA, RG 153, entry 183, box 3, debriefing of Billie J. Lessman.

3. NA, RG 153, entry 183, box 2, Debriefing of Captain Robert A. Frederickson.

4. NA, RG 153, entry 183, box 4, debriefing of Captain Charles Martin.

5. Nov. 12, 1953 "Atrocities Speech–Preliminary Synopsis," Eisenhower Library.

6. Pentagon statements as reported by *U.S. News and World Report*, May 28, 1954, p. 74.

7. Evarest Buklemishev, *Sputnik* magazine 1991, "We Were the Invisible Men."

8. "Our Men Among Foreigners," NA STRAZHE, May 9, 1991, pp. 4-5 as quoted in "The Insider" Vol. II, No. 2, February, 1992. In June 1992, Russian President Boris Yeltsin admitted in a letter to the U.S. Senate that Soviet files contained the names of 510 Americans, along with 59 U.S. aviators interrogated by the Soviets. However, Yeltsin claimed that: "The documents contain no information about holding U.S. POWs on the USSR territory.

9. Joseph Goulden. *Korea: The Untold Story of the War* (N.Y., 1982), p. 591.

10. *Op. cit.* November 12, 1953 "Atrocities Speech–Preliminary Synopsis," Eisenhower Library.

11. There were other smaller facilities as well. After processing at a special Soviet interrogation center for American Airmen and other POWs, a group of seven "U.S. army spies, including Nisei," or Japanese Americans, were shipped directly to the USSR in 1952. [American Citizens detained in the USSR, FOIA.]

12. CIA report SO-91634, "Prisoner-of-War Camps in North Korea and China," July 17, 1952.

13. DoD statements as reported by *U.S. News and World Report*, May 15, 1954, p. 76.

14. *Op. cit.,* SO-91634.

15. NA, RG 153, entry 183, box 4, debriefing of Major David F. MacGhee.

16. NA, RG 319, 383.6, box 1693, debriefing of Sergeant Martin Watson.

17. NA, RG 153, entry 183, box 2. Debriefing of U.S.M.C. Maj. Gerald Fink.

18. Interview broadcast on CBN, September 14, 1990.

19. NA, RG 153, entry 183, box 1, debriefing of PFC Robert W. Bonetsky.

20. NA, RG 153, entry 183, box 4, debriefing of USMC CWO Felix McCool.

21. NA, RG 153, entry 183, box 1, debriefing of Master Sergeant John T. Cain.

22. Department of the Army, Office of the Quartermaster General, Board of Officers Review, January 16, 1956.

23. "Chinese Lieutenant who told seeing more than 1,000 UN prisoners– Americans, South Koreans and others–at the Harbin processing camp" *South China Morning Post* (Hong Kong, March 9, 1952), p.6.

24. INSCOM FOIA.

25. NA, RG 349, entry 95C, CCRAK, specific request number 66-53, August 10, 1953.

26. NA, RG 349, Entry 95C, Box 38, CCRAK-101, p. 2.

27. NA, RG 349, entry 95C, box 36, CCRAK-1 01, p. 1. Note: George Blake, an important Soviet mole in British intelligence, was recruited in a Korean War prison camp. "The MGB was . . . given unrestricted access to Western PoWs held by the Chinese and North Koreans," wrote Soviet defector Oleg Gordievsky, in *KGB: The Inside Story* (New York, 1990), p. 404.

28. NA, State Department, box 144, instruction CA-1030, August 26, 1953, "Information on UN Prisoners Retained under Communist Control."

29. Authors' sources.

30. State Department, RG 87, Foreign service dispatch #1716, "American POWs Reported en Route to Siberia" March 23, 1954.

31. 1954 State Department cable, various.

32. 1954 Soviet response, various.

33. Alexander Dolgun, *Alexander Dolgun's Story* (New York, 1975), p. 296.

34. *Esquire* magazine, 1953.

35. "Americans Detained . . ." It's interesting to note that when the US demanded an accounting for missing airmen in 1956, the Chinese and North Koreans–who at the same time were willing to give (often spurious) information on American Army, Navy and Marine personnel–said they had "no data" on Air Force POW/MIA's. Perhaps this was a hint that the airmen had been taken by the Soviets. March 2, 1956 Message from CICUNC to DEPTAR, FOIA for Army INSCOM]

36. *New York Times*, October 23, 1957.

37. Department of State Report, "Korean War Prisoners Reported in Soviet Union."

Chapter 13

1. Gen. Mark Clark, *From the Danube to the Yalu*, (NY), p. 298.

2. July 1992 statement from the Chinese Embassy in Washington, D.C.

3. NA, RG 153, entry 183, box 3, debriefing of Capt. John T. Hinman.

4. Army INSCOM, message from CICNUC to DEPTAR. FOIA.

5. Eighteen of the turncoats eventually left China. One Rufus E. Douglas, died in China during 1954. Two, Adams Howard and James Veneris, still lived there as of July 1992, according to the Chinese government.

6. "USAF Personnel Possibly Alive in Communist Captivity," 6004th Air Intelligence Service Squadron, August, 1955.

7. Undated TAG POW sheet, NA; 2 March 1956 Message from FOIA from Army INSCOM. One returned American claims that US Intelligence believed the man removed from the camp was not Glasser. According to US debriefers, "He (Glasser) as we knew him was not really Gerald Glasser." They claimed Glasser was killed when captured & a Russian agent took his identity to spy on us in the POW camp." [February 8 letter of former POW Tom Lyke.]

8. Air Force document AFM-200-25, January 16, 1961, obtained under FOIA.

9. Crash: Capt. Don Charles East, "The History of U.S. Navy Fleet Air Reconnaissance Squadrons One and Two (VQ-1 and VQ-2.) June 1986. FOIA from Office of the Chief of Naval Operations. "Swatow": 20 Aug. 1954 memo from the Judge Advocate General of the Navy to the DoD Director of Legislative Liason, subj: U.S. Servicement held by the Communists; "cages"; State Memo 9 Oct. 1953

611.95a241/10-953 SECRET; "captured"; *NYT*, March 10, 1953; "died"; "Replies to inquiries made regarding personnel purportedly held by the communists," August 11, 1954, Bureau of Naval Personnel, Department of the Navy.

10. RG 153, E 183, Box 5, debriefing of PFC Gildo C. Rodriguez.

11. RG 153, E 183, B 5 debriefing of Roy V. Ratliff.

12. RG 153 Entry 183 Box 5, debriefing of Homer Richardson.

13. RG 153, Ent. 183, Box 3, debriefing of Lt. William Lewis.

14. Various, including August 1955 Report, "USAF Personnel Possibly Alive in Communist Captivity," 6004th Air Intel. Service Squadron.

15. "Red Star": Air Force Manual No. 200-25A, FOIA; "criminals": August 1955 Report, "USAF Personnel Possibly Alive in Communist Captivity," 6004th Air Intel. Service Squadron.

16. *Ibid.*

17. Meeting transcript.

18. 17 June 1955, report by James Kelleher, Office of Special Operations, Office of the Secretary of Defense, Defense Advisory Committee on Prisoners of War "Recovery of Unrepatriated Prisoners of War" (DAC on POWs).

19. FOIA response from Naval Investigative Service.

20. *US News and World Report*, December 3, 1954, p. 26.

21. 17 August 1977 letter to KPA/CPV from UNC.

22. "Release of Americans Held as Prisoners of War in China," Far East Command J2, December 14, 1954.

23. *Op. cit.*, DAC on POWs.

24. *Ibid.*

25. Llewellyn and Kiba debriefings by 6004th Air Intelligence Service Squadron, August 1955; Authors' interviews with Kiba.

26. *Ibid.*

27.*New York Times*, November 28, 1954.

28. *Op. cit.*, DAC on POWs.

29. *Op. cit.*, East, p. 30.

30. Naval message from COMFEAF to HQ USAF, 9-6-56; Naval message from COMNAVFE to CNO, 10-20-56.

31. DoD "fact sheet," October 1987.

32. U. Alexis Johnson, *The Right Hand of Power* (New York), 1984.

33. U.S. intelligence and personnel agencies bungled the preparation of their own POW/MIA lists. The authors have discovered several internal reports showing that men believed to have been alive in communist hands were not on lists submitted for accounting, while other servicemen believed to be dead were sumitted on more than one occasion. The Pentagon has never gotten a firm handle on the identity, categorization or even the number of U.S. POW/MIAs from Korea. Take, for example, a December 28, 1955, cable from an Air Force Intelligence unit concerning POW/MIA lists then being used for negotiations with the communists. "Analysis indicates that 9 POWs, not shown on POW list of 23 Nov 55, or previously available lists, may be alive and that 5 POWs previously on POW list and recently declared dead under SEC9, PL 490, may be alive." The nine POWs not shown on any available list are: Captain Robert J. Bird, A0793217; Captain James B. Brown, USMC, 028801; 1st Lt. Melvin E. Clover, A01858509; 1st Lt. Robert M. Crosley, A02223682; 1st Lt. George B. Eichelberger, 20178A; 1st Lt. Robert L. Martin, A01912235; 1st Lt. Ralph A. Neis, A02090340; 1st Lt. George . Patton, A02222013; 1st Lt. Warren J. Sanderson, AO 2066184. The five POWs declared dead who may be alive are: 1st Lt. Lt. John H. Adams, AO 2061322;

A/1c Alvin D. Hart, Jr., AF16353684; 1st Lt. Waldemar W. Miller A01909506; 2nd Lt. Hugh K. Thompson, A01911888; 1st Lt. Paul E. Van Voorhis, AO2091867. "Additional evidence exists in this report that 27 POWs who are on current POW list of 23 Nov 55, may be alive." (December 28, 1955) from CINCUNC, Tokyo, Japan to DEPTAR Wash DC.

34. Army message to DA from CINUNC, Tokyo, re 69th meeting of MAC, Army INSCOM, 3-2-56, FOIA. In defending itself against charges of indifference, the Pentagon notes that a letter containing the list of American POWs continues to be presented to the North Koreans and Chinese every year at Panmunjom. A more realistic view of current efforts comes from a declassified 1979 State Department memo: "We are aware that UNC attempted in 1971 to terminate annual submission of letters but was instructed by Defense to continue with the ritual. Although there may be lingering bureaucratic reasons for perpetuating the submission of these letters, we think it is time to stop." June 20 1979 cable from American Embassy in Seoul to the Sec. of State.

35. 6004th Air Intelligence Service Squadron's semi-annual history, July 1-December 31, 1957. The Air Force now claims it has lost the files of Project American.

36. July 2, 1963 State Department letter to Sen. Philip Hart from Assistant Sec. Frederick G. Dutton.

37. Taiwan interview, November, 1989.

38. Vietnam case histories from POW Network/Project Homecoming II.

39. 1989 interview with Flynn.

40. "Preliminary Debriefing Site for Captured U.S. Pilots in Vihn Phu Province & Presence of Soviet & Communist Chinese Personnel at the Site," June 10, 1979..

41. Authors' interviews.

42. February 1, 1973.

43. John Barron, *The Secret Work of Soviet Secret Agents* (New York, 1974), pp. 239 and 242.

44. *Op. cit., London Evening News,* Feb. 1, 1973.

45. "Alleged Sightings of American POWs in North Korea from 1975 to 1982," March 9, 1988. FOIA.

46. AP report, *Pacific Stars and Stripes,* March 10, 1992.

47. *Ibid.*

48. Army INSCOM, information paper dated October 18, 1979, FOIA.

49. Asia Watch, "Human Rights in the Democratic People's Republic of Korea," Washington D.C., 1988.

50. DIA, "Sighting of Possible U.S. POW (Possibly Korean War Era) in North Korea."

51. KIRO-TV, Seattle, transcripts.

52. Interview with authors, November 15, 1989.

53. p. 70, "Years of Upheaval," Henry Kissinger, Little, Brown & Co., Boston, 1982.

54. Brig. Gen. Brent Scowcrot, Military Assistant to the President, replying for Mr. Kissinger, March 8, 1973 letter to Mrs. Ambraz, mother of Korean MIA Lt. Kenneth Nosk.

55. September 19, 1991 letter to Rep. John Miller from Carol W. Ford, Jr., the Pentagon.

Chapter 14

1. Interview with Roche. Also: John E. Roche, "Incident in the Sea of Japan," *Readers Digest,* September, 1957; see also Air Force FOIA, Monthly History of 15th Air Force, July, 1953.

2. NA, Telegram from State to Moscow Embassy, 711.5622/8-453, August 4, 1953.

3. *Op. cit.*

4. FOIA document, USAF Aerospace Studies Institute, "Some Significant Air Incidents Involving the United States and Communist Nations, 1945-1964," May 4, 1964.

5. Michael R. Beschloss, *Mayday* (New York, 1986), p. 78.

6. Joseph E. Goulden, *The Untold Story of the War* (New York, 1982).

7. "Sloppy record keeping" or intentional efforts to keep evidence from the historical record.

8. Anthony Cave Brown, *The Last Hero: Wild Bill Donovan* (New York 1982)., pp. 641-642.

9. *Ibid.*

10. *Ibid.*, p. 640.

11. NA, State Department memo from Walworth Barbour to Mr. H. Freman Matthews, 711.5622/11-452, November 4, 1952.

12. John Prados, *The Soviet Estimate: U.S. Intelligence Analysis and Russian Military Strength* (New York, 1982), p. 30.

13. INSCOM FOIA, "American Citizens Detained in the USSR."

14. *Ibid.*

15. *Op. cit., Prados,* p. 29.

16. John M. Carroll, *The Secrets of Electronic Espionage* (New York, 1966), p. 129.

17. Manual of the Judge Advocate General, investigation, April 11, 1951.

18. *Ibid.*

19. *Newsweek,* April 24, 1950.

20. CIA report SO-39921, May 17, 1950.

21. Memo for Chairman, Interagency Priorities Committee, January 25, 1954.

22. Memo for Chief of Naval Operations, June 22, 1973.

23. Memo from Department of the Navy to Head, Casualty Branch, to Director of Personal Affairs Division, August 11, 1954.

24. AF IR 3350-55, 6004th AISS, September 23, 1955. The Japanese prisoner later identified the American as Lieutenant Warren Sanderson from the RB-50 downed on July 29, 1953. However, Air Force intelligence officials apparently showed the former POW only a handful of pictures of missing Americans, and most likely, no pictures of the Privateer crew. Despite the identification of Sanderson, the background information of the flier leaves open the possibility that the American was from the Privateer.

25. Memo from CIA, Deputy Director Plans, to Director of Naval Intelligence, November, 1957.

26. *Op. cit.,* Carroll, p. 137.

27. July 18, 1955 Memorandum for the President from Sec. of State John Foster Dulles, Eisenhower Presidential Library.

28. State Department CA-10165, "Soviet Detention of United States Aircraft Incident Survivors," June 20, 1956.

29. Igor Yevgenyevich letter to the editor published in the *Express Chronicle,* Moscow.

30. *Op. cit.,* Carroll, p. 137.

31. Chip Bohlen, *Witness to History* (New York, 1973), p. 196.

32. Seymour Hersh, *The Target is Destroyed* (New York, 1986), p. 36.

33. NA, State Department, 711.5622/11-452.

34. State Department, 711.5622/12-1251, secret memo from Office of Eastern Affairs, Walworth Barbour, to Mr. Hickerson, UNA, and Mr. Johnson, FE, "Bomber Shot Down by Soviet Union."

35. NA, State Department, 711.5622/5-2252, "U.S. Bomber Shot Down by Soviets in 1951."

36. Nov. 5, 1952 Confidential State Memo from Samuel Klaus to Mr. Berg (IAD. Subject: US-USSR Dispute on B-29 Shooting in Far East–USAF Cooperation) 711.5622/11-522.

37. FOIA, *History of the 91st Strategic Reconnaissance Squadron,* June 1, 1952.

38. NA, State Department, 711.5622/6-1752, Acheson to Moscow Embassy, top secret, "Review of Missing Status, Case #546."

39. NA, State Department, American Embassy Moscow #699, to Vyshinski, June 18, 1952.

40. *Op. cit.,* INSCOM FOIA.

41. *Op. cit.,* CA-10165.

42. Letter from Koski.

43. *Op. cit.,* #546.

44. NA, State Department, 711.5622/7-3053.

45. August 1, 1953 secret telegram from Ray Thurston at State Amembassy Moscow 711.5622/8-153.

46. August 4, 1953 telegram from Moscow to state. 711.5622/8-453.

47. Dept. of State *Bulletin.* Dec. 6, 1954, pp. 857-862.

48. NA, State Department, 611.95A241/9-1655, Geneva Negotiations on Prisoners of War (OSD).

49. Secret Dec. 16, 1954. "Memorandum For the Secretary" from Henry Cabot Lodge, Jr. 611.61/12-1654.

50. UPI, in *New York Times,* September 12, 1956, p. 5.

51. UP, *NYT,* September 13, 1956, p. 5.

52. *Op. cit.,* FOIA AF Military Personnel.

53. *Op. cit,* Carroll.

54. FOIA to AF Military Personnel Center. Nov 9, 1961 Secret "Rereview of Missing status Case #546."

55. James Bamford, *The Puzzle Palace* (New York, 1983).

56. *Ibid.*

57. *Op. cit.,* #546.

58. *Ibid.*

59. *Op. cit.,* Bamford, p. 181-182.

60. May 4, 1959 Secret State Dept. telegram from Thompson, Moscow, to Secretary of State 761.5411/5-459.

61. NA, State Department, 761.5411/5-459.

62. NA, State Department, 761-5411/10-159.

63. *Op. cit.,* Carroll, p. 170.

64. William L. White, *The Little Toy Dog* (New York, 1962). p. 79.

65. *Ibid.*

66. Letter from Mrs. Elizabeth Woods to President Eisenhower (mother of July 29, 1953, crew member) found in State Department decimal files, 711.5620/7-2953.

Chapter 15

1. FOIA, account of Wilfred Cumish, Army INSCOM file.

2. William R. Corson an Robert T. Crowleh, The New *KGB-Engine of Soviet Power* (New York, 1985), p. 233.

3. Tom Bower, *The Paper Clip Conspiracy* (New York, 1987), pp. 182-183.

4. March 26, 1965 hearing before the Internal Security Act Subcommittee of the Senate Judiciary Committee.

5. FOIA, Army Intelligence, seven volume series, "Americans Detained by a Foreign Power."

6. Ian Sayer, *America's Secret Army*, (New York, 1989), p. 356.

7. *Ibid.*

8. *Ibid.*, p. 358-359.

9. *Op. cit.*, Americans Detained . . . .

10. *Ibid.*

11. *Ibid.*

12. *Ibid.*

13. *Ibid.*

14. *Ibid.*

15. *Ibid.*

16. *Ibid.*,

17. *Ibid.*

18. INSOM FOIA, June 9, 1953, Army memo for the record, "Procedure for Recovery of Army Personnel detained by Unfriendly Foreign Power."

19. Department of the Army, Office of the Assistant Chief of Staff For Intelligence, November 1, 1966, "Alphabetical List of Known, Reported, and Suspected US Army defectors to Communist Controlled Nations."

Chapter 16

1. Rod Colvin, First Heroes (New York, 1987), p. 204.

2. [p. 22 "The USSR in 3rd World Conflicts" Bruce D. Porter, Cambridge University Press, Cambridge, Eng., 1984; Soviet Union sent 3,000 troops to Vietnam, 13 were killed, according to Soviet articles reported in the September 9, 1991 *Ny Daily News*, p. 13]

3. 1989 and 1990 interviews with Jerry Mooney.

4. Australian *60 Minutes.*

5. *Krasnaya Zveda* (Moscow), April 13, 1989.

6. Minarcin-Sanders interview, September 4, 1991.

7. *Ibid.*

8. Larry Pistilli interview.

9. Ibid.

10. Ibid.

11. Ibid.

12. 1990 interview with Jerry Mooney.

13. "Soviet Officers Sait to Have Questioned U.S. Vietnam Prisoners," *Reuters*-Nov. 91.

14. p. 147, "The Bamboo Cage," Nigel Cawthorne, London, Leo Cooper, 1991.

15. "U.S. pilot captured in Vietnam reportedly taken to Soviet Union," *San Diego Union-Tribune*, Feb. 28, 1992.

16. *Ibid.*

17. Al Santoli, *To Bear Any Burden* (New York, 1985), p. 314.

18. *Ibid.*

19. *Ibid.*

20. *Ibid.*

21. *Ibid.*

22. *Ibid.*

23. *Ibid.*

24. Minarcin interview, September 4, 1991.

25. David H. Hendrix article in the *Press-Enterprise* (Riverside, CA), 3-13-86, p. 6.

26. Senate Select Committee on POW/MIA Affairs, hearing January 22, 1992, Minarcin statement, Appendix D.

27. "Amnesty: The American Puzzle", Edward F. Dolan Jr./ Franklin Watts (pub) NY 1976, p. 45.

28. Information from KGB defector Stanislav Levchenko, quoted from "Dezinformatsia–Active Measures in Soviet Strategy" Richard H. Shultz and Roy Godson, Pergamon-Brassey, WA, 1984.

29. January 30, 1992 *New York Times* p. A6, "Russian Offers Americans Access to KGB Files".

Chapter 17

1. George Orwell, *In Front of Your Nose 1945-50: The Collected Essays, Journalism and Letters of George Orwell* (NY, 1968), p. 62.

2. Alexander Solzhenitsyn, *The Gulag Archipelago* (NY, 1973), p. 85.

3. Truman Library, top secret records of the Psychological Strategy Board (PSB), December 28, 1951.

4. *Op. cit.,* Johnson, p. 13.

5. Aug. 8, 1952 State Dept Telegram Control #3581, Top Secret, from Truman Library.

6. August 31, 1953, Army copy of proposed speech by Sec/State to American Legion convention, St. Louis, Wednesday, September 2, 1953.

7. *Op. cit.,* PSB.

8. *Op. cit.,* Clark.

9. "Meeting of the POW Working Group," Operations Coordinating Board, Nov. 9, 1953.

10. Colonel M.A. Quinto memo, "Continuing State/Defense Efforts to Secure Accounting on Missing Prisoners of War," June 21, 1956.

11. Memorandum for the Record; "Meeting of the POW Working Group," Jan.uary 25, 1954

12. Memorandum for the Executive Office, "OCB Meeting Today," February 3, 1954.

13. Meeting of the POW Working Group," Operations Coordinating Board, February 5, 1954]

14. Feb. 1, 1954 Memorandum for the Operations Coordinating Board; "Supplement to Joint State-Defense Department Background on Efforts to Secure the Return of American Prisoners of War Who Might Still Be Held in Communist Captivity."

15. June 17, 1955 "Recovery of Unrepatriated Prisoners of War," Office of Special Operations, Office of the Secretary of Defense, p. 3.

16. *Ibid.*

17. Aug. 2, 1955 letter to Sen. George Bender.

18. Secret memo dated 16 Sept. 1955 from retired Marine General G.B. Erskine, Assistant to the Secretary of Defense (Special Operations) to Walter Robertson at the Department of State. Subject: Geneva Negotiations on Prisoners of War.

19. May 27, 1957 hearings by House Foreign Affairs Committee, Far East and Pacific Subcommittee, "Return of American Prisoners of War Who Have Not Been Accounted For by the Communists."

20. 6004th Air Intelligence Service Squadron's Semi-Annual History July 1-December 31, 1957.

21. Van Wees collection.

22. Sept. 8, 1960 dispatch from Brussels to Dept. of State, "Korean War Prisoners Reported in Soviet Union."

Chapter 18

1. Sanders received several phone calls from men who attended the convention that had talked to Colonel Hill, including Executive Director, Chuck Williams.

2. Richard Boylan and John Taylor, employees of the National Archives, separately and later together, told Sanders of the details of Hill's first visit.

3. Letters from Senator Jeff Bingaman (New Mexico), and Congressman Jeffords (Vermont).

4. The informant, who attended the meeting, telephoned Bill Paul at the Wall Street Journal shortly after it adjourned. The informant, who was not aware that Sandrs frequently shared research discoveries with Paul, advised him that "some guy named Sanders" was specifically targeted.

5. These files have been publicly available for ten years and completely declassified.

6. General E.B. Baker, Jr., letter to Forrest W. Howell, December 4, 1987, DoD number I-16759/87.

7. William Cunliffe to Terrence Gaugh, Army center fo Military History, July 8, 1988, obtained by Sanders under the FOIA.

8. Sanders January 31, 1989 letter to General Stofft.

9. William H. Cunliffe September 28, 1988 letter to Terrence Gaugh, Army Center of Military History.

10. Foreign Service despatch #1716.

11. Sauter interview with Colonel Millard Peck, January 28, 1991.

12. Letter from Janet G. Mullins, Assistant Secretary of State for Legislative Affairs, to Congressman John Miller, February 22, 1991.

13. Letter to Senator Bob Smith from Brent Scowcroft.

14. *Washington Times*, "Russia Querried on U.S. POWs," December 28, 1991.

* In July, 1992 Gorbachev angrily denied that Bush had ever asked him about U.S. POWs.

15. *New York Daily News*, "Moscow Gets U.S. MIA Unit," January 14, 1992, p. 10.

16. *Ibid.*

* As of June, 1992, Toon and his Russian counterpart had admitted that Russian security agencies were refusing to open their POW/MIA files. Russian intelligence may never admit its abduction of American POWs, since the men and/or their identities may still be in use by Russian agents and the medical experimentation conducted on the U.S. POWs could leave current and/or former Russian officials open to criminal prosecution.